LOST CITIES and FORGOTTEN TRIBES

Introduction by
ISAAC ASIMOV

Edited by
Richard F. Dempewolff

Produced by
The Editors of Science Digest

HEARST BOOKS
NEW YORK

Acknowledgements

The color photograph of the Mayan pyramid on the dust jacket of this book was provided by Dr. Francis Robicsek, M.D. who, besides being a recognized cardiovascular surgeon, is also a recognized authority on Mayan archaeology, a Research Associate of the Museum of the American Indian, and author of the book *COPAN*, published by the Museum of the American Indian and the Heye Foundation.

Photographs of the Coptic texts accompanying Chapter X are reprinted with permission from the UNESCO Courier.

Photographs of the broken Stela at the top of page 30, illustrating Chapter V, are from the National Geographic Society.

The stylized semitic heads, Bat Creek inscription and illustration of skeletons in Bat Creek Mound, accompanying Chapter X, are from the Book *Before Columbus* by Cyrus H. Gordon. Crown Publishers, Inc.

The rendering of the Poteau runestone in Chapter VI was originally painted by artist George Kelvin as a cover for *Science Digest*.

Chapter XXX, "Crackpots and Forgeries in Art and Science" is reprinted with permission from *Chicago Today*, a University of Chicago magazine. Copyright © 1968, the University of Chicago.

All other credits to commercial photographers, artists and agencies are carried with the individual illustrations. Acknowledgements to the authors of the various chapters in this volume are noted in the editor's Foreword.

 ISBN 0-910990-99-9. Library of Congress number 74-16419.

Table of Contents

PART I—SOUTH AMERICA

Secrets of the People of the Jaguar 3
Lost City of the Incas 11
Mystery of the Nazca Lines 17
Ancient Cities of the Dead 25
Mayan Astronomy—Science of a Super Civilization? 31
Were Semites First in America? 37

PART II—AFRICA

Physics and the Pyramids 47
Nefertiti, Egypt's Mystery Queen 55
Holy Cats and Sacred Cows 65
Coptic Voices From the Past 71
Secret of Zimbabwe—Search for King Solomon's Mines . . . 77
Was Swaziland a Birthplace of Modern Man? 85

PART III—EUROPE

Are These the Walls of Camelot? 93
Who Built Britain's 600 Stone Circles—and Why? 99
The Stones of Wiltshire 107
Is This Atlantis? 113
Enigma of the Lost Etruscans 117
St. Peter's Bones—Are They or Aren't They? 125

Table of Contents (continued)

PART IV—NORTH AMERICA

Riddle of the Viking Cryptograms 133
Mayan Secret of the Onima Caves 143
Digging Up Witch Lore in Salem 149
Mysterious Mounds at Poverty Point 157
Who Carved the Handprints on Prayer Rock? 163
Mystery Hill—Hoax or Archaeological Fact? 167

PART V—ASIA AND THE PACIFIC

Angkor—Jungle City of the Dead 177
A 2,000-Year-Old Chinese Lady Returns 183
City of the Sacred Turtle: Nan Matol 191
Isle of the Eyeless Watchers 197

PART VI—MISCELLANY

Archaeological Looters Even Murder for Money 209
Crackpots and Forgeries in Art and Science 215
Ancient Murders in the Digs 223

List of Illustrations

Olmec carved head 4
Machu Picchu 12
Nazca lines 19
Mayan numerals 30
Caracul 30
"Semitic" heads from Mexico 39
Bat Creek Stone and mounds 43
Khephren's Pyramid 49
Diagrams of the Pyramid at Giza 51
Nefertiti and the Aten 57
Ancient sculptures of the Aten 59
Coptic manuscript with wormeaten "bays and inlets" 72
Closeup of Coptic script 73
Zimbabwe ruins 79
Glastonbury Abbey with "Arthur's grave" 94
Glastonbury Abbey with foundations of "Camelot" 95
Ruined abbey at Tintagel—another "Camelot" 97
Stone circles, remnants of Britain's Stone Age man 101
Stonehenge 109
The "Heel Stone" 111
Thera, a possible Atlantis 114
Etruscan tombs and art 119
St. Peter's Tomb 126
The Poteau, Oklahoma, runestone 134
The Heavener, Oklahoma, runes 137
Inscriptions on the Kensington Stone, with translation 139
Runic alphabets 140
Prayer Rock 164
Mystery Hill "megaliths" 169
Angkor Wat 179
Remnants from a 2,000-year-old tomb 184
Han Dynasty artifacts in perfect condition 187
Aku 196
Carvings of the Easter Islanders 198
Unmortared walls on Easter Island 199
The Aku of the 19th Century on Easter Island 204
Etruscan warrior forgery 218

Introduction

THE PUZZLE OF MAN

by Isaac Asimov

The word "civilization" is derived from the Latin word "civis" meaning "citizen"; that is, "city-dweller." And, indeed, if we are told that a group of people have built a city we can assume they are civilized. The technological methods required to build a city and the necessary cooperation among many people that this involves, the community of views and aims, cannot be associated with the kind of cultures we think of as "barbaric."

The first cities we know of, tiny and primitive, dwelling-places huddled together on a hilltop within a protecting wall, were built in the Middle East about 8000 B.C. Civilization is that old at least.

What has taken place in the course of civilization is best determined by what men who were contemporary with the events have said about it. Speech is the only method of communication ever developed by human beings that is precise enough to give a connected story that is similarly perceived by all who listen. But speech dies as soon as it is spoken and lives on only in the memories of the hearers, sometimes only temporarily, and sometimes to be repeated once more in inevitably distorted fashion.

Writing is frozen speech and the contemporary tale can still be told without further distortion as long as it endures.—But writing is not coeval with civilization. It appears to have developed first in the Middle East, in the same general region where the first cities developed—but not until 3000 B.C.

In short, civilization in the Middle East existed for five thousand years before writing was invented and it became possible to tell its detailed story without further distortion over an indefinite period of time. Of the total stretch of ten thousand years of civilization in the Middle East, only the last five thousand years has a "history", the first five thousand years is "prehistoric."

This is true the world over. In other parts of the world, known civilization did not start till after it had started in the Middle East, often not till long after; in some places, not even till the present day, except where it is brought in from outside.

Wherever civilization began, however, the art of writing followed only a long time later, so that in every civilization a prehistoric period comes before the historic one.

Some civilizations, in fact, consist *only* of prehistoric periods, either because, as in the Inca civilization, writing was never invented; or because the writing, though it exists, cannot be interpreted, as in the Maya civilization and the Etruscan civilization.

Does it matter?

It certainly does. In every case, by the time history starts, the civilization is already flourishing and producing mighty works. In the first centuries of Egypt's history it produced the pyramids, and in the first centuries of China's history it produced the Great Wall. These are the most massive stone structures ever built by man and the techniques involved in building them must have had a very long and very interesting history.

If we are interested in the story of man, then, ordinary history doesn't tell us enough. It leaves out precisely the most important part. How did man learn enough to become so great; for what purpose did he labor over his huge structures, and how did they fulfill their function once they were built? Without knowing the beginning, we know so little, while if we *do* know the beginning, very much of what is puzzling in ordinary history might no longer be puzzling.

Well, then, in the absence of writing, how can we learn of what goes before?—From man's works themselves.

A mysterious mark in the ground, a circle of large standing stones, the traceries of a city in the mountain peaks, keep silence. They don't talk to us as writing does, but their silence is not entirely impenetrable either. What man has left behind him has shapes, orientations, relationships to other objects, and from that we can deduce something. Mounds, caves, crude paintings and carvings are all clues in the detective story called "archaeology."

Occasionally, there are enormous victories, especially where writing is involved. Less than two hundred years ago, the Egyptian hieroglyphics were deciphered and suddenly there was new knowledge of man's second oldest civilization. A lost library was located in the ruins of Nineveh, one century ago, and the history of Sumer, man's oldest known civilization, became a bit clearer.

Where no language exists to be deciphered, final answers may be impossible. Even so there are theories and sometimes the answers seem likely indeed.

Just a few years ago, the relics of an Aegean island that had been destroyed by a volcanic explosion in 1400 B.C. were uncovered. Fitting clue to clue, it began to seem very likely that that not-quite-forgotten event was the inspiration to Plato's story of Atlantis a thousand years later.

Some puzzles are more obscure still—the odd statues of Easter Island, for instance, or the odd ground markings in the Peruvian desert. They are there, but what are they, and why? A very popular book of recent years has given up on the whole problem by suggesting that extra-terrestrial explorers are the explanation of anything we don't understand. (But why the extra-terrestrial explorers? Why did they do what they did? Why did they leave? When will they return?—Like all silly explanations, they create far more mysterious problems than any they solve.)

Archaeologists prefer not to obscure the slow rise of man's civilization nor to insult his great accomplishments by any such fairy tales. They prefer to study the puzzles over and over again, with new techniques, new findings, new thoughts, and without ever despairing, until such time as the answers slowly come and slowly improve.

This is a book of a number of archaeological puzzles and mysteries from every part of the world, stretching back over the millennia. It will offer you no easy answers, but it will tell you what archaeologists are currently thinking—and may give you notions of your own.

Foreword

The machinery that resulted in the production of this book was assembled at a regular monthly editorial conference in the New York offices of *Science Digest* magazine, in 1967.

It had long been a conviction of mine, as a science writer and editor, that the world was acrawl with fascinating science mysteries—some that eventually would be solved; others that might never be answered—and that someone should gather together the best of them and wrap them between covers.

The writing and editing staff of the magazine at that time consisted of me; Daniel Cohen, managing editor; and two assistant editors: Bruce Frisch and Jeanne Reinert. All agreed that a science mystery book was an appealing idea. Out of the meeting came the decision to start immediately assigning a series of "science mysteries" that would be so labeled. They would not constitute a regular monthly feature, but whenever a good subject was assigned or submitted to us, we'd run it under the series label. One day, when enough material was in hand, the book would be proposed and, hopefully, published.

It didn't all come out that neatly. Things seldom do. While all the members of that first staff still contribute material to *Science Digest*, none are full time staff members any longer. Dan Cohen is a successful author of some 25 books; Bruce Frisch is managing editor of *Astronautics and Aeronautics*; Jeanne Reinert is a mother and part-time freelancer. But most of the editors who succeeded them fell in with the science mystery concept with equal enthusiasm. Barbara O'Connell Ford, who replaced Jeanne Reinert, wrote a number of mysteries herself while she was on the staff—and continues to produce them now that *she* has gone freelancing. Douglas Colligan, who replaced Ms Ford and is currently a staff writer, has produced several. David Coleman, who replaced Dan Cohen, edited many of the contributions and prepared them for publication originally. Richard Teresi, who replaced David Coleman, has been doing that job since David took off for greener pastures. When it came time to put the whole thing together, it was Bernice Pietracatella, my secretary, who spent hours at the Xerox machine copying manuscripts for the presentations, and pasting up the results.

What had happened, understandably, was that in seven years we wound up with more science mysteries than anyone needs. The day finally came when I sat down with Mr. James Fisher of the Hearst Books Division—the man who would help us get this volume off the ground—and outlined what we had in mind. He winced at the broad range of subjects and the endless list of random titles. "Which are the most interesting and intrigueing fields covered?" he wanted to know. There was little doubt in my mind—or his—that there was more fascination in the field adventures of archaeologists, anthropologists and paleontologists than in the more academic backgrounds of most other disciplines. The flavor of exotic locales was more pungent. The appeal that the history of man has for many people was stronger than, say, the cold, remote logistics of black holes or rare nuclear particles, significant though they may be.

And so, I selected 31 archaeological and anthropological mysteries and curiosities that seemed to provide a broad and interesting picture of those disciplines.

As the original concept had developed, when any of us had an idea for a story, it would be assigned to the author considered best to produce the sort of piece we were after. Consequently, a few authors produced a lot of chapters in this book, while some are represented by only one or two contributions, depending on their specialties. Here are the authors and the chapters they wrote:

Daniel Cohen, former managing editor of *Science Digest:*

Mystery of the Nazca Lines
Nefertiti—Egypt's Mystery Queen
The Baffling Stones of Wiltshire
Is This Atlantis?
Enigma of the Lost Etruscans
Ancient Murders in the Digs

Barbara O'Connell Ford, former assistant editor, *Science Digest:*

Were Semites First in America?
Holy Cats and Sacred Cows
Coptic Voices From the Past
St. Peter's Bones—Are They or Aren't They?
A 2000-Year-Old Lady Returns
Looters Even Kill for Pre-Columbian Treasures

L. Sprague de Camp, author of many well-known science fiction stories, and a student of archaeology:

Lost City of the Incas
Secrets of Zimbabwe, King Solomon's Mines
Angkor—Jungle City of the Dead
City of the Sacred Turtle: Nan Matol
Isle of the Eyeless Watchers

Jeanne Reinert, former assistant editor, *Science Digest:*

Secrets of the People of the Jaguar

Physics and the Pyramids

Janet Graham, British correspondent for *Science Digest;* a writer from a writing family, and an archaeology buff:

Are These the Walls of Camelot?

Who Built Britain's 600 Stone Circles—and Why?

Douglas Colligan, assistant editor of *Science Digest:*

Mystery Hill—Hoax or Archaeological Fact?

Mayan Astronomy—science of a super civilization?

Adrian K. Boshier, Field Officer, Museums of Science and Man, Johannesburg, South Africa:

Swaziland—a Birthplace of Modern Man?

Gerald Olson, Assoc. Professor of Soil Science, N.Y. State Colege of Agriculture and Life Sciences, Cornell University; with Anne Simon, writer, Cornell University:

Ancient Cities of the Dead

Ellen R. Hartley, Florida correspondent for *Science Digest:*

Mayan Secrets of the Onima Caves

Sharon S. McKern, science writer and anthropologist, University of British Columbia:

Digging Up Witch Lore in Salem

Katherine Bryn, former assistant editor, *Science Digest:*

The Sins of Salem

Mark A. Roberts, student of cryptography:

Riddle of the Viking Cryptograms

Franklin Folsom, author, student of archaeology:

Strange Mounds at Poverty Point

Reed C. Hildreth, freelance writer:

Who Carved the Handprints on Prayer Rock?

Our thanks to all of these people who contributed to a fascinating series of stories that we hope will interest archaeology-oriented people for a long time to come.

In the interests of cohesive narrative, the subjects covered have been grouped according to the part of the world in which they are located. An introductory page describes each geographic section in terms of the background, ancient and current, against which the events discussed unfolded.

Other than that, the book should need no explanations. It was meant to be enjoyed, and we hope it will serve that purpose.

Richard Dempewolff
N.Y., N.Y. June, 1974

PART I
south america

Hidden in tangled jungles from Mexico and Yucatan down through the countries of South America, archaeologists continue to find vine-ensnared ruins of spectacular civilizations. In many cases, glyphs indicate elaborate written languages, lost to posterity for want of a Western "Rosetta Stone" or some similar key to unlock the information they hold. Among the secrets will be clues to the origins of the Maya, the Olmecs, the Toltecs and latter day Aztecs, settling once and for all the controversies that rage in academic circles. Did all these people come across the land bridge from Asia, or did some, as Atlantic diffusionists insist, cross the Atlantic from the great civilizations of the Mediterranean in pre-Roman times, bringing their elaborate cultures with them? Or, as many anthropologists believe, are the cultural similarities merely a sign of coincidental simultaneous development in the normal growth of human cultures, isolated from each other though they may be?

Until the linguists and cryptologists are able to crack the codes of the Mayan-Olmec-Toltec glyph languages, archaeologists continue to dig up ancient cities and artifacts. Some of them already have provided startling intimations, if not proof, of answers. Many of the chapters in this section deal specifically with this subject. Others deal with mysteries equally intriguing.

CHAPTER I

Secrets of the people of the jaguar

In 1939 the first of the gigantic stone heads of the Olmecs was uncovered in Mexico. It was a hint of revelations to come about a strange people who had flourished and vanished, leaving a vague oral history, undecipherable glyphs and great art.

Late in the spring of 1967, in a tangled jungle of southeast Mexico, 17 men strained and sweated to lift up a life-sized stone statue, buried 3,000 years ago.

The find was a triumph of inductive reasoning. For Dr. Michael Coe of Yale University, the unearthing of the statue and many other finds was an archaeologist's dream-come-true. And he is that archaeologist. The process started with graphs and charts of the San Lorenzo plateau. Small crosses marked each artifact site from the first archaeological visitors of the then current, 1967, season. Workmen had just uncovered a stone stela (marker). Dr. Coe noted a north-south orientation to several finds. Could these statues have been buried systematically? He ordered the workmen to begin digging several feet to the north of the stone stela's location. The ground was unmarked, overgrown. Yet, after digging three or four feet, workmen began to uncover the life-sized figure, now headless. Dr. Coe, relating their astonishment, laughed, "They said I have eyes that can see through the ground." The statue had been made and buried by a forgotten people called the Olmecs.

Library shelves are lined with books on the past—Egypt, Greece, Rome. From the American continent come books on the Eskimo, Inca, Maya and Aztec. But there are relatively few references to the first known civilization in the Americas, the Olmecs. Yet, the Olmec world was the mother culture for all the fabled indian empires that rose and fell in Mexico and Mesoamerica. Little has been written about the Olmecs because archaeologists are just beginning to discover and to sort out the jumble of artifacts.

Dr. Coe is exuberant about the Olmecs. His eyes light up when he repeats, "It's luck, really luck." Spread about his third-floor, walkup

Giant basalt head from Mexico's jungles is a remnant of vanished Olmecs.

office in an old, converted house on the Yale campus are numerous mementoes from the excavations. He is a man of medium build, with dark, wavy hair and a love for his work. Nothing could make him happier than the fact that, "There are probably a thousand statues at San Lorenzo. I'll never have time to dig them all up."

His Olmec finds this year are spectacular. They include man-made mounds, stelae, a giant basalt head, a lifesized figure in a cape, a stone jaguar, an archaic Olmec statue with features scratched rather than fully formed, a "fantastic spider" the headless statue and yards of San Lorenzo waterworks. But key to his finds is in discerning a pattern.

The pattern for burying the monuments was determined long ago when dissident Olmecs overthrew their rulers. The rebels then set about destroying the art works of the old rulers. Why they did this is a mystery. As Dr. Coe points out, it is a difficult task to destroy a 10 or

20-ton basalt monument. The rebels apparently took the monuments to a special location (still unknown) deliberately to mutilate them. He thinks they used two methods: One was pockmarking the statues with a two-pronged instrument. The second method was to hoist one monument on a tripod, then drop it on another. This would at least knock off a head or mar the face. Thousands of stone monuments were so destroyed. Each was then moved to a ceremonial burial ground. There the Olmecs built a red gravel floor and placed the marred monuments on the north-south axis in straight rows. Then, basket by basket, they brought a massive fill to the burial grounds. Clay, earth, boulders, consolidated volcanic ash, bits of broken pottery were used for the burials. It took an enormous amount of organized labor to destroy and bury each monument. When the huge stone markers were covered, small mounds were built on top. These finger-like ridges still extend from the south of the San Lorenzo plateau, as much as 10 feet above the plateau. Until Dr. Coe realized the mounds were man-made, they were considered a natural part of the terrain. He thinks the mounds might have had houses or temples built on top of them.

Dr. Coe is confident that there was no invasion from neighbors or barbaric tribes because the pottery and other artifacts from the following periods are all Olmec. This is a new finding, as it was formerly believed the culture was overrun by other indians.

Who were these people, the Olmecs? Where did they come from? When did they flourish?

The name, Olmec, means "Rubber People". No one has any idea what the people called themselves or what language they spoke.

The first Olmec artifact to attract archaeologists turned up in a plowed field in 1902 not far from the Bay of Campeche in the Gulf of Mexico. Sculpted in pale green jadeite was a beautifully-carved fat, bald-headed Indian priest about eight inches high. Undecipherable glyphs were incised on its stomach. Also on its stomach was a Mayan date. The date corresponded to 98 B.C., well before any known Maya civilization and in the wrong area of Mexico for Maya.

The long-count calendar, attributed at that time to the Maya, is a more accurate calendar than the one we use today. It begins, for unknown reasons, in the year 3113 B.C. Closely correlated to astronomical observations, it can be read precisely for any day and year in the intermediate period and transcribed into a date in terms of our calendar. It is a masterpiece of mathematical and astronomical knowledge, and it was the Olmecs, not the Maya, who developed it.

The indian statuette was the first clue that some civilization predated the Maya and invented this calendar. Curious about this find, Mathew Stirling, an American archaeologist, led the first of nine expeditions into the Mexican Gulf coast. This area, later dubbed the "Olmec heartland", is 125 miles long and about 50 miles wide. At an island site, La Venta, Stirling found, in 1939, five gigantic basalt heads. Free-standing, these heads are five to nine feet high and weigh up to 20 and 30 tons each. All wore close-fitting caps that look much like today's football helmet. He also found great caches of jade, more prized than gold by the Olmecs. There were also altars and pyramids. La Venta, an island in a swampy and mysterious area, is perfect for a ceremonial site. Olmec people probably travelled to it to give offerings of jade and other treasures to the gods.

San Lorenzo, Dr. Coe's excavation site, may have flourished at the same time, between 1200 and 800 B.C. or possibly later. San Lorenzo, in the heart of an agricultural paradise, was probably the civil center and a population center. No caches of treasure have been uncovered, but the wealth of stone monuments suggests that there were probably thousands and thousands of wood carvings, textiles, maybe even painted language books, all since devoured by the sweltering climate that dumps 120 inches of rain annually on the area. That climate is perfect for growing corn, the staff of the Olmec diet

One of the pleasantries of life at San Lorenzo 3,000 years ago was an elaborate system of waterworks. Dr. Coe has uncovered several hundred yards and expects there will be miles of them. The Olmecs built six-sided artificial ponds or lagoons to supply water for the city. They then built irrigation networks from imported basalt blocks. The basalt was brought from at least 80 miles away, probably on rafts. They chopped out troughs and made tightly-fitted basalt covers. Even today, when the lagoons are filled during the rainy season, water runs in the network although it has been unused for 2,600 years.

San Lorenzo was deserted about 400 B.C. Then about 1,800 years later, other people settled there, leaving pottery fragments that can be dated by carbon-14 methods.

The legends of the later Aztecs give the only hint of the vast Olmec culture in a group of legends of a golden land of long ago. The legendary land was called "Tamoanchan." This name, however, is not Aztec, but is now known to be an archaic Maya word. There are two translations. One is the "Land of Rain and Mist", a perfect description of the Olmec heartland along the Mexican Gulf coast. The other meaning is "Bird-Serpent", a symbol that recurs in Olmec art. The myth says this was the land where everything began.

Dr. Coe believes that the Olmecs were the earliest Maya and then died out, persisting only in this legend which contained the memory of a rainy and misty land. The whole Olmec world was in ruins by the time of the Aztecs.

The Olmecs were gifted both as artists and artisans. Their sculpture is unsurpassed. They worked not only in the imported basalt, but also in jade. Without metal tools, they designed massive, three-dimensional, free-standing figures of many types. "We can say they were the inventors of sculpture and their monuments represent the first appearance of this art. We consider them among the most extraordinary sculptors that Mesoamerica ever produced," judged Ignacio Bernal, a Mexican archaeologist and authority.

Consider the great basalt heads, now numbering about 20. They all have similarities such as the flat, rather infantile noses. All are plump. Archaeologists have speculated that they may represent war lords. The one head that still has the original finish was smoothed to a satin luster, the stone looks like skin texture. And apparently the heads were painted as one still shows a white lip painted purple.

There also are figurines, plates, bowls, cooking utensils, beads, ear plugs and axes made of clay, jade, magnetite and loadstone.

The most common motif of the spectacular art works is the jaguar. This powerful cat is unusual in that it loves water, is often found near rivers and, swims well. It was no doubt worshipped as a god by the Olmecs. The evidence suggests that the Olmecs probably believed the rain-gods descended from a union of a jaguar and a woman. This is the subject of one Olmec monument. Further impressive evidence for this theory is the abundance of figures with part human, part feline features. Olmec art runs a gamut from pure jaguar features to statues with barely perceptible jaguar mouths. A common motif is the stout, sexless, nude figure, frequently shown in postures identical to those of a young baby. Mouths droop down at the corners, reminiscent of a snarling jaguar. Many of the figures have a slight cleft centered above their foreheads. Often maize or other grain plants are depicted sprouting from the cleft, probably symbols of agricultural fertility.

Most Olmec jaguar figures have a curious look suggesting Mongoloidism or cretinism. Perhaps from time to time a congenital defect showed up in an abnormal baby. This, says Dr. Coe, may have reinforced the Olmec belief that there could be gods that were part jaguar, part human child. There are deformities in which the soft spot in the skull never closes. The Olmecs may have believed this was a sign from the gods.

Perhaps the Olmecs worshipped such a child and carried it about reverently. They may have believed it a sign from the rain gods. In later indian cultures, and possibly originating in the Olmec culture, infants were sacrificed to the rain gods. The people believed that the more the baby cried and tears streamed down its face, the more rain would be sure to fall.

Trade was well-integrated into the Olmec life. There were probably extensive water routes between Olmecs and surrounding peoples. The Olmecs may have set the pattern for the later spread of culture throughout Mesoamerica.

Some archaeologists think the Olmecs arose in Guerrero, now famous for its resort city of Acapulco. There are ceremonial sites in this state and probably jade sources. Two unique Olmec finds have been found in Guerrero. One is a wooden mask, encrusted with jade, miraculously preserved in excellent condition. The other find was reported this spring by Dr. Carlo T. E. Gay, an amateur pre-Columbian expert. It consists of three paintings and three drawings, found in a cave, all in the distinctive Olmec style. The best painting is a life-sized figure of a bearded man, dressed in a yellow and red striped shift and carrying a pelt. Another figure possibly is a spirit of the earth. The paintings and drawings are in good condition with only a few areas obscured by calcite. Although they are the oldest paintings ever found in the New World. The colors are vivid reds, yellows and black.

The Olmecs loved color. They decorated their bodies with stripes and designs. Among the artifacts are dozens and dozens of rollers to spread the colors evenly over the large portions of their bodies.

Temple walls, floors and sacred grounds were splashed with color. For example, one abstract design of a jaguar mask was found 25 feet below the topsoil of La Venta. The ancient Olmecs laid green polished paving blocks in a yellow clay border, then inserted blue clay for the eyes, nose and mouth.

Nothing remains of the houses or structures such as temples. There is a single bottle from Tlatilco which is shaped like a house or temple. The structure is probably of thatch with pole sides and covered with adobe, much like Mexican construction of today. This bottle is the only glimpse of how Olmec structures may have appeared.

Nothing is known of the family makeup or political complexion of the Olmecs. There are some undeciphered glyphs (picture, language symbols) that may some day provide a bit of history. Or perhaps still unexcavated ruins will answer the many questions surrounding these mysterious and little-understood Olmecs who created the first great civilization in North or South America.

CHAPTER II

The lost cities of the Incas

Overhanging a 3,000-foot precipice on a saddle between twin 10,000-foot peaks, the remnants of an Inca Citadel, Machu Picchu—along with its origins and history—are likely to remain forever hidden in mists that swirl about the towering Andes.

On the morning of July 24, 1911, three men emerged from a trail on the banks of the Urubamba River in Peru.

The three men were a guide, a Peruvian soldier, and a young professor from Yale named Hiram Bingham. Nervously they inched their way across the flimsy bridge of poles lashed together with vines, which spanned the gaps between the boulders. These boulders protruded from rapids, where the Urubamba roared past on its long journey to join the Amazon. Safely across the chasm, they attacked the steep slope. Sweating, slipping, creeping on all fours, and scaling tree trunks placed against the slope, they climbed until they reached a long flight of ancient terraces. Above these they found themselves in a maze of ruined houses made of ponderous granite blocks.

Half hidden by brush, the ruin stood in a saddle between two enormous peaks, both rising over 9,000 feet above sea level: Huayna Picchu to the north and the even higher Machu Picchu (10,300 feet) to the south. Four thousand feet below, the Urubamba, looking like a mere brook, curled snakelike about the foot of Huayna Picchu. Outlying works occupied the slopes of the two peaks; some of these, on Machu Picchu, overhung a 3,000-foot vertical precipice.

This extraordinary citadel had no known name. None of the Spanish chroniclers mentioned it. It was locally known as Machu Picchu, after the taller of the two peaks.

Next year, Bingham was back with a larger expedition, which cleared the site and explored the old Inca roads.

Bingham led further expeditions there in 1914 and 1915, before going on to a distinguished career in aviation, politics, and business up to his death in 1956. The fact that Machu Picchu was so long unknown, the appalling site on which it stood, and the silence of the

chronicles about it all wrapped it in mystery. Today, however, one can visit it much more easily than could Bingham sixty-odd years ago. One takes a train along the Urubamba Valley and transfers to a bus, which snakes up a terrifying switchback road to a tourist hotel amid the crags. From there it's but a short walk to the ruins. Still, much mystery remains.

The city of Machu Picchu—whatever its dwellers called it— straggles for 700 yards along the saddle between the two peaks. The southern end, towards the peak for which it has been named, consists of more than fifty argicultural terraces and a few stone buildings. A single, massive stone wall bounds the terraced area on the southeast.

The northern end of the settlement, separated from the southern by a long, straight ditch and a pair of walls athwart the saddle, consists of stone houses, with only a few terraces. The houses are divided into groups, as if they were meant for separate clans. Most of the lower walls are of massive cyclopean masonry, fitted and keyed with meticulous care, while the upper parts are made of smaller stones.

The houses were crowded together, but the many narrow streets and rock-hewn stairways made it easy to get about the town. Where possible, houses had little garden plots. Machu Picchu was furnished with over a hundred stairways, some having as many as 150 steps. In some cases, an entire flight of six to ten steps was laboriously pecked out from a single ledge or boulder.

Was Machu Picchu a fortress, a walled city in the usual sense? That depends upon what we mean by "wall." Machu Picchu had plenty of walls bounding agricultural terraces; but it possessed no single, continuous defensive wall encircling the entire structure. There is some fortification where the trail up the mountain enters the main gate. Otherwise it is hard to tell whether any of the massive stonework was meant as a defense rather than as a house or terrace wall. But then, a city surrounded by such hair-raising precipices hardly needed defensive walls of the usual kind. The terraces furnished platforms whence to drop rocks on attackers' heads.

Bingham insisted to the end of his days that Machu Picchu was the "Tampu Tocco" of Fernando Montesinos, a seventeenth-century priest and historian. According to Father Montesinos, long before the

Photo Trends
Peru's lost city of the Incas, Machu Picchu, was discovered in 1911; stonework, sacrificial chambers and private baths can still be seen.

Incas, a mighty dynasty called the Amautas ruled the Andean region. In the reign of the sixty-second Amauta, about A.D. 800, barbarian hordes overran the empire and slew the emperor in battle. Some of the Amauta's men took his body to a refuge called Tampu Tocco, buried it, and chose a new king.

The little kingdom flourished until population pressure made its rulers look abroad. About the twelfth or thirteenth century, King Manco Capac (Manku Ohapag) seized Cuzco, and founded the Inca Empire.

Bingham matched details of this story with things he had seen in his Peruvian travels. These resemblances led him to identify Tampu Tocco with Machu Picchu. Thus, Montesinos said that Manco Capac built a wall with three windows at Tampu Tocco, and Bingham found such a wall at Machu Picchu.

Most modern students of Andean history, however, disagree. They do not think Montesinos trustworthy for ancient events. Nor do they admit that Manco Capac was real; more likely he was a culture hero—one of those mythical demigods whom many peoples have credited with founding their nation and discovering the useful arts. Or he represented, not a single real ruler, but a whole pre-Inca dynasty.

Even if he were real, the legends say he came to Cuzco from the south—perhaps from Tiahuanaco, another ruined city with a mysterious prehistoric past. But Tiahuanaco lies several hundred miles southeast of Cuzco, while Machu Picchu is northwest of Cuzco, in the opposite direction.

If Bingham was wrong, the likeliest explanation of Machu Picchu is this: The Incas did not fortify whole cities. Instead, near each city, they built a hilltop fortress—like those of Troy and Zimbabwe in the Old World—which they called a *pucará* and to which the citizens could flee. The immense fortress of Sacsahuamán, surrounded by sixty-foot walls made of stones weighing up to 200 tons, was the pucara for the Inca capital of Cuzco. And Machu Picchu could have been a pucara for villages on the Urubamba. Some think it was built in the early fifteenth century, against the raids of the Chunchos from the Amazonian jungles to the east.

This prosaic solution does not, however, clear up all the enigmas of the Andes, for it leaves unsolved the far greater mystery of the vanished Tiahuanaco Empire, which preceded the Inca hegemony.

In 1532, Francisco Pizarro, by seizing the person of the Inca Atahualpa in the midst of his tens of thousands of well-trained warriors at Cajamarca, gained control of an empire that compared in wealth, power, population, and territory with that of the early Pharaohs. Within a year, the Spaniards completed the astounding conquest of Tahuantinsuyu, as the Incas called their empire. During the following decades, a number of Spaniards—priests, soldiers, and Garcilaso de la Vega who was half Inca himself—wrote down such historical traditions of the Inca Empire as they could gather. Since the Andean nations had no writing, historians had to depend upon oral traditions; but these were fairly voluminous.

According to these traditions, the dynasty started with the probably mythical Manco Capac in the twelfth or thirteenth century. Other Incas followed, becoming more historical until Inca Viracocha, who reigned 1347-1400, is a fully historical figure. Under Viracocha, the realm began its expansion, which continued until it embraced all of Peru, much of Ecuador and Bolivia, and the northern half of Chile.

The original Incas were a leading clan of the Quechua (or Keshwa) tribe. This clan ruled the tribe, and the tribe ruled the empire. The head of the clan, who became the emperor, was called Sapa Inca, "the only Inca;" but all his fellow clansmen were Incas, too. As the empire grew, the Sapa Inca found that he did not have enough kinsmen to occupy all the posts in the empire, so he promoted promising men to be honorary Incas.

The Inca Empire may have been the world's most successful benevolent despotism. Every peasant family, clan and tribe had lands assigned to it. The assignments were revised from time to time to make sure each family could support itself. Along with their own plots, the Andeans had to farm those of the church and the state. Church lands supported the priesthood of the state religion. This was sun worship; but, in addition, the gods of the conquered peoples were welcomed into the pantheon.

The state lands supported, not only the Inca and his officials and soldiers, but also aged and crippled subjects and those who had lost their own crops through misfortune. Since the empire had no money, taxes were in the form of labor. Every year, each able-bodied man had to put in so many days at such labor, constructing roads, public buildings, and so forth. Men in their fifties were given only light work or retired on pensions.

Still, Inca rule had its drawbacks. Even if he never starved, the ordinary Andean peasant dwelt (as many still do) in frightful squalor. He lived a very restricted life, unable to move, to change his occupation, or to travel on the excellent roads without special leave. He was so severely regimented that, when the Spaniards overthrew the Incas, he obeyed his new masters as meekly as he had the old. At least, he obeyed them until the oppression of the Spaniards—who exploited the peasants more harshly than the god-kings ever had—drove him to frantic but futile revolts.

Under the Incas, the Andean indians reached a level of civilization much like that of the Egyptians of the first two or three dynasties. As far as anyone knows for sure, they did this on their own, without influence from the Old World.

The most striking of the pre-Inca cultures was that of Tiahuanaco, whose remains lie at the southeast end of the 12,644-feet-high Lake Titicaca, the highest navigable lake in the world. To judge from the spread of its artistic styles, Tiahuanaco was once the center of an empire comparable to that of the Incas. The ruins, scattered over a sixth of a square mile, include truncated pyramids or artificial hills, a terraced pyramid fifty feet high, rows of monoliths, platforms and underground chambers.

There are also monolithic gateways, in which the two upright supports and the lintel are carved out of one solid piece of stone. The largest of these, the "Gateway of the Sun," was chiseled from a single block of hard andesite. It is ten feet high, 12.5 feet wide, and weighs nearly ten tons.

What little we know about Tiahuanaco is the following: An earlier, simpler culture, Tiahuanaco I, appeared before the Christian Era. A later, imperial Tiahuanaco II arose between A.D. 500 and 1000, spread its rule far and wide, and fell before the Incas rose. When the Incas conquered the bleak *altiplano* around Lake Titicaca, they found Tiahuanaco deserted; at least, that is what they said. The people of the region were the Aymaras, a dour, silent folk who still grow potatoes and herd llamas in the thin air of the frosty plateau with its glaring suns and frigid nights.

Legends contain a few hints of the Tiahuanaco Empire, but nothing whence we could reconstruct its history. Since the Tiahuanacans had no writing, there is no way to restore the lost story of Tiahuanaco. Without it, both the history of the Inca stronghold at Machu Picchu and the enigma of the Tiahuanaco Empire are likely to remain forever hidden in the mists that swirl about the towering peaks of the Andes.

CHAPTER III

Mystery of the Nazca lines

Prehistoric people made gigantic rock drawings visible only from the air above the Peruvian desert that have survived 1500 years. How were these 1500-year-old glyphs produced—and what do they mean?

One of the world's most fascinating archaeological mysteries sits right in the middle of one of the world's most inhospitable places. Some 250 miles south of Lima, the capital of Peru, in the unbelievably barren coastal desert between the Ica and Nazca valleys, there is an intricate 60-mile network of strange tracings in the earth.

From the ground the tracings look like nothing more than obscure lines, for in this position one can see only a tiny portion of them at a time. But from the air these lines present a very different picture. Some are straight and look like roads. Others form geometric figures like rectangles and squares. Still others trace the outlines of gigantic birds, spiders, monkeys, whales or a host of bizarre creatures of fantasy that are impossible to identify.

The lines and figures were etched into the desert gravel at least 1,500 years ago by a prehistoric people who lived in the desert. That is the first part of the puzzle—how was anyone able to live in such a place?

The desert runs for some 2,000 miles along the coast of Peru. It is quite narrow, varying in width from one to 25 miles, and is made up of high plains and low hills which roll back from the coast of the Pacific Ocean. The great Andes mountains rise steeply from its eastern edge.

For most of the year the coastal desert is cloudless and extremely hot. Between May and November the desert is shrouded in a dense, almost constant fog, but it never rains.

It is the entirely rainless nature of the landscape that accounts for the survival of the Nazca lines and figures, for they are very fragile. Their construction was simplicity itself. The floor of the desert is covered by a layer of dark rocks and pebbles. These surface pebbles were removed to expose the lighter soil beneath them. The surface material was then piled in a uniform way on both sides of the line. From the air the figures and lines seem drawn by a light colored line, which is itself outlined by two darker filaments. In most places in the world such a simple construction would have been washed away by the first spring rains, but in the Peruvian desert the lines have endured for centuries.

It is impossible to determine exactly how old these lines and figures are. The only date we have for them is A.D. 500. That date was obtained from radio-carbon dating a tree stump that was found at the end of one of the lines. The stump had probably been placed there by the builders as some sort of sighting marker. The stump, since it was abandoned, must have been brought to the desert during the last phase of construction. How long they had been under construction before the stump was set up we do not know.

The rocks and pebbles on the surface of the desert are dark because they contain iron and iron oxidizes on contact with the air. When desert stones are exposed to the air for a long time they are said to have received a coat of "desert varnish." The oxidation must take place at a regular rate, so someday we should be able to determine the age of the lines by their color. The older they are, the longer the artificially exposed stones would have had to oxidize and the darker they would be. One day oxidation will cause the lines to fade entirely. But since we do not know the rate at which oxidation takes place in the desert the color of the lines is of no help in dating them.

The lines and figures in the desert were once a part of the great Inca empire. But the Incas were latecomers to Peru and the lines and figures of the Nazca predated them, probably by many centuries. The people who made the lines and figures or their descendants must have been conquered by the Incas. The Incas had no written language so they could not have left any record of the peoples they conquered. The Incas seemed quite indifferent to the Nazca tracings and an Inca "highway" runs right through them.

The conquistadors under Francisco Pizarro, who conquered the Inca realm in 1533, also showed scant interest in the figures. The early Spanish chronicles contain no mention of them. The people of the Nazca region, who might have retained some knowledge about the history of the figures, were ultimately wiped out in the bloody civil wars which ripped Pizarro's Peru.

Recently a number of imaginative writers have proposed that the

Nazca lines were made by "little green men" from outer space who used them as markers or signs that could be fully observed only from high above—presumably from their space ships. While an intriguing, if whimsical, theory it is far more likely that the figures were meant to be viewed by the gods. Sun worship was the religion of most South American cultures. But there are even more practical explanations for them.

Despite our lack of information about the people of the Nazca region we can, in a general way, determine who made the lines and figures in the desert. To the modern visitor this desert seems an impossible place to live and indeed very few live there now. But 2,000 years ago a large number of people were able to wrest a living from this hostile environment.

The eastern flank of the long desert is cut by some 40 valleys. The valleys have been formed by rivers and streams carrying water down

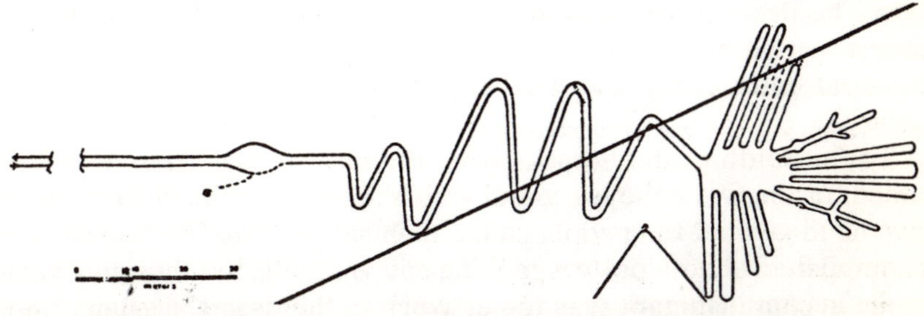

Bird figure above, with snakelike neck, is 600 feet long. Road cuts across it. Spider, below left, and smaller bird are hard to distinguish due to low profile. Small bird is 400 feet long.

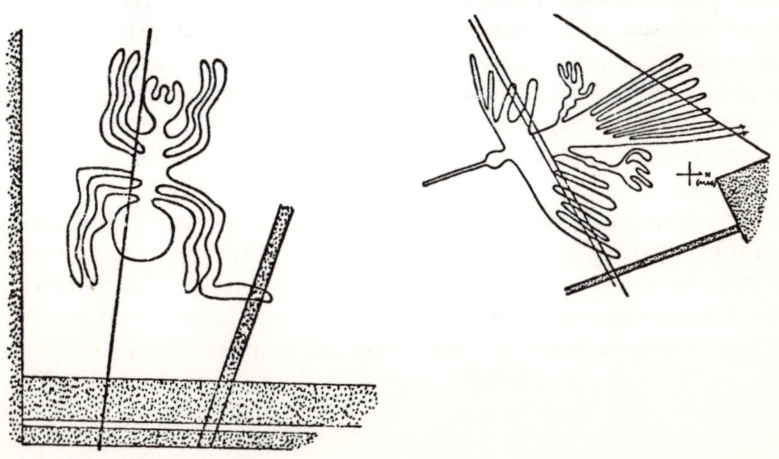

to the sea from the torrential storms that drench the rain forests of the Andes. The water deposits fertile silt in the valleys. By employing painstakingly careful methods of irrigation, crops can be grown there. We don't know when man first moved into these desert valleys, but long before the Incas arrived, high cultures were flourishing there.

Racially and culturally all the people of the desert came from the same basic stock. But the valleys were separated from one another by long stretches of burning desert so each of the cultures developed in a highly individualistic way.

In the northern portion of the desert was a tribe known as the Mochicas. Mochica pottery, made in the form of realistic representations of men and animals, is among the finest pottery ever produced.

In the center of the desert were the Paracas. These people buried their dead in deep underground caverns. In the dry and almost sterile air of these caverns the Paraca mummies remained in a remarkable state of preservation. Over 400 of them have been found by archaeologists. The Paracas wrapped their dead in magnificently embroidered fabrics, which have also been wonderfully preserved. They were as skilled at embroidery and weaving as the Mochicas were at making pottery.

To the south of the Paracas were the Ica-Nazcas. They have been named for the two valleys around which the culture flourished, but we have no idea what the people called themselves. The Ica-Nazcas were accomplished at both pottery making and weaving, but their most celebrated accomplishment was the artwork in the desert. Designs found in some Ica-Nazca pottery and weaving have been repeated on a grand scale in the desert figures.

As we said, the lines and figures themselves were fairly easy to etch into the surface of the desert. But still, moving and piling all those rocks and stones, not to mention the time that it took to lay out the figures in the first place, must have entailed thousands of man hours of work in the broiling sun. These figures are not just gigantic doodles. They must have had some use or some meaning to the people who made them.

In modern times, when people again became aware of these strange lines they were referred to as "Inca roads." The lines were not Inca and they were not roads. Some of the lines are only a few yards long, while others run for miles, but begin nowhere and end nowhere. Modern travelers regarded the lines as interesting curiosities and nothing more.

The first scholar to really take an interest in the lines and figures was Paul Kosok, a professor of history at Long Island University. In 1941 Dr. Kosok was in Peru studying pre-Inca culture. He became interested in the lines after examing aerial photos of the Nazca region which had been taken during the previous ten years.

Dr. Kosok and his wife visited the desert on June 22, 1941. They followed the lines up a small mesa, puzzling over their significance. In the Southern Hemisphere June 22 is the winter solstice, the shortest day of the year. As Dr. Kosok and his wife pondered the strange lines, the sun began to set, and to their amazement it touched the horizon right over one of the lines at whose base they stood. Quite suddenly Dr. Kosok had the inspiration that these lines were part of a gigantic system of astronomical calculations. Later he wrote, "The largest astronomy book in the world seemed spread out before us."

Dr. Kosok could not continue his study of the lines because he had other commitments. But while in Lima he discussed his theories with Dr. Maria Reiche, a German-born mathematician and astronomer who was living in Peru. Since that time Dr. Reiche has become a passionate, almost fanatical student of the Nazca lines and figures. She lives in a simple adobe hut near the desert and spends her days charting and measuring the lines and comparing them with the positions of the stars and planets at different times of the year.

Dr. Reiche has undergone hardship and danger in studying the Nazca lines. She has photographed them while strapped to the outside of the low flying airplane, so that she could get just the right angle. She has fought off road builders and land developers who would have destroyed the figures in the desert.

In spite of such devotion to her work, she is regarded by some scientists as a woman obsessed with a theory, rather than a careful scientist. Dr. Reiche has produced all sorts of correlations between the lines and the positions of the sun, moon and stars. She postulates a gigantic "desert calendar" with which the ancient Peruvians could mark the passing of the years. Her opponents argue that with so many lines and so many astronomical bodies with which to make alignments, it is possible to work up many correlations but that they are meaningless.

Dr. Kosok returned to the Nazca region to continue his investigation about a decade after his first inspiration. However he died in 1959, long before his projected work on the Nazca lines and figures was completed. Since that time Dr. Reiche has carried out her studies alone.

Some of the things that we know about the civilizations of ancient Peru make the calendar idea seem plausible. First the Nazca people were farmers, so an exact knowledge of the change of seasons would have been very useful to them. Like most of the ancient Peruvian societies the Ica-Nazca people were probably a theocracy, ruled by priests whose main duty it was to study the stars.

The people of ancient South and Central America were fascinated by the calendar. The Indians of Central America had developed a calendar that was better than any developed by the more advanced civilizations of Europe and Asia.

But even Dr. Reiche's diligent calculations cannot account for all of the lines and figures of the Nazca with astronomical correlations. Some of these lines may really have been roads or more accurately, ceremonial avenues along which passed religious processions. The rectangles and some of the other geometric figures could have been sacred enclosures in which were performed the rituals of this theocratic society.

Most puzzling of all are the drawings of spiders, whales, birds, monkeys and other figures. What could their significance have been? It has been theorized that the gigantic figures were not meant for the eyes of men, but only for the Ica-Nazca gods who lived in the sky.

And how were these figures planned and executed so precisely, by people who could never see them? Again we have only theories, but the most reasonable is that the figures were first drawn as scale models, then calibrated and laid out in their enormous size on the desert floor.

The Nazca figures are the largest and most exuberant, but by no means the only prehistoric figures constructed to be seen only from the sky. Somewhat similar figures dot the other valleys of Peru and Chile. Gigantic figures made by prehistoric Indians have been found etched into the soil of the Southwestern United States, notably Southern California.

There is also a striking similarity between the figures of the Nazca region and the great Indian mounds throughout the Mississippi valley. Most of these mounds, constructed in the shape of fantastic animals, are also so large that their true shape can be appreciated only from an airplane. While the Nazca figures were etched into the gravel of the desert, the mounds were heaped up out of the soil.

The story of the Nazca drawings remains unfinished. We are plagued by a host of unanswered, and perhaps unanswerable questions. So much of the evidence has been lost that the Nazca drawings will probably always remain something of a mystery. But their similarity to the Indian mounds of the Mississippi valley and to the Indian drawings in the Southwest adds a bit more weight to the theory that the pre-Columbian civilizations of South and Central America were more closely connected with the Indian cultures of North America than anyone had previously suspected.

CHAPTER IV

Ancient cities of the dead—victims of ecological suicide

Two creative cultures a world apart appear to have eroded to death mysteriously. But there's a reason why Tikal and Sardis stand as warnings to modern man. It is explained here by Professor Gerald Olson, a soil specialist from Cornell University, who visited both places to find out.

When civilizations vanish, and leave behind only the vine-tangled ruins of their great cities, historians most often look for clues of social turmoil, military campaigns and conquests. Usually, scant attention is paid to the possibility of environmental catastrophes.

As a soil scientist, I've always wondered if the growth and demise of many lost civilizations might be traced, at least in part, to the relation of man to his environment, and especially to soils.

Soil not only contains the nutrients which support food and fiber production, but it also sustains natural vegetation and animal life. Buildings are constructed over and with soils. Trails and paths, the basis of primitive transportation and communication, have to go over and around soils of different types. The nature of soils also determines the quality and quantity of local water supplies to a considerable extent.

Although the final fall of a civilization can sometimes be attributed to a critical war, it has always seemed more logical to me that a society may already have weakened itself with ecological practices that forced landslides, droughts, floods and famines, all soil-related phenomena, on its inhabitants, thus making them more vulnerable to invaders. If the land were tenable, why wouldn't a conqueror stay on and exploit his winnings?

Recently, I had an opportunity to check my theories at the University of Pennsylvania excavation site at Tikal, deep in the lowland jungles of northern Guatemala. It was a fascinating and rewarding experience.

Tikal's known history goes back some 2,500 years when a group of peoples settled on a rise of land in this rain forest area. Their descendants were to create one of the most astonishing civilizations the world has ever seen. Tikal became the primary city of the Yucatan Mayas. During the years A.D. 600-900 the civilization matured and crystallized, and the site grew spatially and architecturally to its final magnificence.

Even today, the magnificence of Tikal is in the ruined roof structures of huge, white, terraced temples, rising above the thick vegetation that ends many miles to the east, at the Caribbean Sea.

These high, remote structures probably served for intricate religious ceremonies. Signs of ritual burning and incense are found within rooms in the temples or on the stairs. Burials of important individuals have been found in their chambers. The temples dominated the great Maya public plazas where, it is assumed, the populace assembled to witness priestly processions up the stairs to the chambers hidden from the public eye. (If you accept the theory that the ancient Mayas practiced ritual drunkenness, these stairways must have caused some spectacular tumbles.)

By all archaeological accounts these buildings appear to have been the centers of the Maya civilization, the religious precincts within which their religious leaders communicated with the gods of rain, sun, wind and corn through the use of incense, incantation and calculation.

Yet around A.D. 900 the building of temples and plazas and the elaborate religious ceremonies that made Tikal the center of a great civilization came to an abrupt halt. Unfinished structures at some places within the city suggest some sudden catastrophe.

The actual causes of this sudden rapid decay are still not completely answered by traditional archaeological studies.

The purpose of my trip to Tikal in June of 1968 was to seek a better grasp of what went on in ancient times, especially how people organized themselves in relation to their environment and, possibly, reasons for the Maya collapse.

A variety of theories have been proposed to explain the mysterious Maya decline. One of the foremost explanations has concerned the simple inability of the land to support a population expanding to well over 10,000 inhabitants and a possible critical uprising of starving peasants against their luxuriating rulers.

Our investigations have supported the idea of rapidly decreasing land fertility. But the factors contributing to diminishing soil quality are very complex.

To raise their crops of maize, beans, squash, sweet potatoes and cacao beans, the Mayas had to clear the forest with stone age tools. Some of the large trees could be killed by girdling with fire, but most of the forest had to be cut with stone axes, a very difficult job. When the Mayas had wrested the necessary land from the forest they usually found a very fertile but thin and quickly weed-infested soil.

It has been suggested that the Maya method of slash-and-burn agriculture was so wasteful of soil fertility resources that in time an increase in population would have accelerated Tikal's decline.

Our studies have confirmed this. When jungle forests were cleared, burned and made suitable for cultivation there was a dramatic decline in organic matter, nitrates and soluble salts, all essential nutrients for plant growth. The losses can be attributed to a combination of erosion, leaching and oxidation.

However, the Maya style of constructing tightly paved ceremonial centers, often covering many acres, strongly accentuated their erosion problems.

When it rained (in a tropical rain forest there is often as much as 80 inches of rain annually) great floodwaters would rush off these elevated plazas and pour downhill, over the agricultural land, stripping it of fertile topsoil.

In areas which accumulated drainage from the ceremonial centers of Tikal, large flats with more than 19 inches of sediment over the original soil were found. Our observations that some upland soils, bared of natural vegetation during the Maya occupation, were lighter in color with less organic matter further confirms the Maya erosion problem.

We also observed that the temperatures of the uncovered soils reach higher levels than those under forest cover. Great temperature fluctuations often have adverse effects on soil fertility and vegetative growth.

Additional evidence documenting Tikal's serious erosion problem is found in Maya reservoirs where sediments many feet thick have been found. These deposits in the domestic water supplies had great detrimental effects on the water quality.

That was 2,500 years ago. But Tikal's erosion situation is analogous to the problems created by the construction of many of today's large shopping plazas. When inadequate drainage facilities are built for these centers, heavy rainwaters often strip the surrounding area of fertile soil, move great quantities of earth and may even destroy building foundations.

Modern man should also remember that some of the Maya soils, stripped more than a thousand years ago, still haven't recovered their original high content of organic matter.

Even if poor land management practices accelerated the Maya collapse, one of the greatest mysteries to me is how the Maya culture reached its peak in a region with such adverse climatic conditions. Unlike most other "cradles of civilization," which are found on fertile floodplains near the rivers and easily cultivatable land, the Maya, armed only with stone tools and fire, struggled in steaming heat and humidity with overpowering jungle for land to sow their crops.

To see if a different civilization, richer in natural resources and with more advanced technical knowledge, made better use of its resources, I joined the Cornell-Harvard archaeological expedition at Sardis, Turkey during the summer of 1970.

The history of Sardis goes back beyond 1300 B.C. Successively conquered by the Lydians, Persians, Greeks, Romans, Byzantines and Ottomans, a gold strike in its fertile valleys brought untold riches to this city during the middle of the 7th century.

Not only did artists, architects and sculptors patronize Sardis, but philosophers and kings came to admire the city that was the first to issue gold and silver coins, and among the first to create a permanent shopping center complex. During the reign of the Lydian king Croesus, reputed to be the world's richest monarch, Sardis became a capital of fashion in the eyes of its mideastern neighbors.

However, it was not only Sardis' eminence in ancient affairs that lured me to the excavation site about 70 miles inland from the Aegean coast, but also its long history of people working with a soils environment.

On arriving at Sardis we could see that over the centuries earthquakes and erosion had toppled fortifications, buildings and city walls. This glimpse into history hinted that Sardis was the victim of an extraordinary series of natural disasters.

As at Tikal, my work focused on analyzing soils and relating their properties to soil-related phenomena such as droughts, earthquakes, land slides and floods. Because the land formations at Sardis are more exaggerated than those at Tikal, with contrasting infertile and virgin forest soils together with obvious landslides and flood deposits, we worked to relate land misuse to historical events.

Our investigations forced us to label the Lydians as the first major documented ecological offenders at Sardis. By overlooking the hazards of building on floodplains, these people doomed later generations to disastrous floodings.

The walls of one building, built of mudbrick around 650 B.C., clearly show marks where torrents of floodwater emptied out of the windows after rushing through the house. The wall was excavated from beneath many feet of sand and gravel, where it had been buried for several thousand years before being discovered.

The Greeks, who followed the Lydian occupation, proved to be equally guilty of poor land management. Because of overgrazing, the steep slopes south of Sardis became nearly bare, capable of supporting only a small number of goats.

Soil studies indicate that these slopes probably once provided pasture for the famed Lydian cavalry horses that were the terror of the world. Today the slopes, covered with prickly weeds and close-cropped grass, cannot even support many goats.

Besides the cutting of agricultural production, the bare slopes yielded to erosion and landslides. Once these scar the land with massive earth movements it takes more than 50 years to regain even minimal fertility.

One could hypothesize that the short-term farming failures during these intervals could have triggered famine and long-term social turmoil.

Our studies showed, however, that the worst exploiters were the Romans. By chopping down entire forests to provide fuel for their baths, social centers during Roman times, they ignored the need for continued productivity of the forest.

As this stripping practice continued, erosion and landslides increased, only to cover their own structures. As the elaborate Roman buildings degenerated with each flood-deposited layer they became lower class dwellings, and eventually the sediment forced their abandonment.

The examples of Tikal and Sardis clearly show that we can learn ecological lessons from the past. Technology may permit modern man to make better use of his soil resources, but he must be warned that the varying soil properties that the ancients encountered resemble those of today.

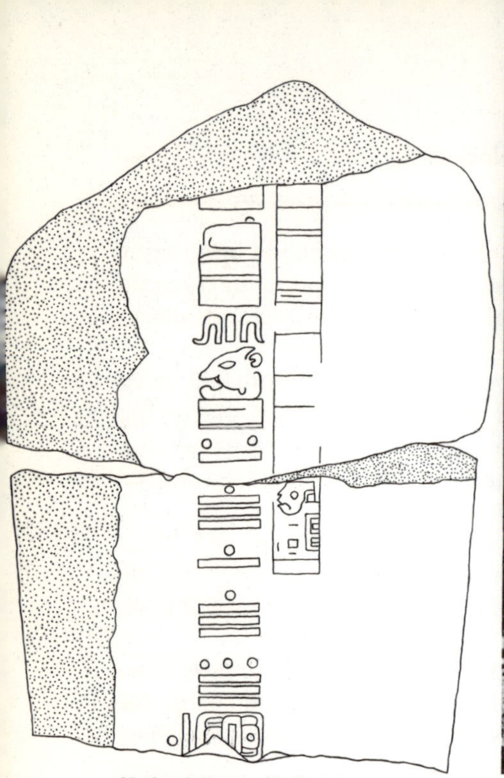

National Geographic Society

The ancient Olmec Stela, above left has the dot-bar system of mathematical numerals that the Mayans later borrowed. The stone, when dug out, right, was missing its top. This was found later. Below is the Mayan Caracol in Chichen Itza, which some believe was used as an observatory.

CHAPTER V

Mayan astronomy—science of a super civilization?

Centuries before the invention of the telescope, the priest-astronomers of the Mayan civilization could plot the movement of planets and predict solar eclipses with the kind of accuracy that still amazes astronomers today.

Joined together for the most hallowed of all rituals, the scientific convention, the 16 astronomers represented the finest minds the science of their era had to offer. They met to discuss the problems of making accurate predictions of solar eclipses, to study lunar phases and to adjust their calendar to conform to current astronomical observations.

This scientific convention was not held recently, however, but 1400 years ago in the ancient Mayan city of Copan, which is located deep in the jungles of what is now Honduras. The only evidence we have that this meeting took place is an elaborately carved altarpiece which has the 16 scientists represented on the side of it. The convention was probably the first of its kind in North America.

The culture that produced these astronomers, archaeologists believe, began somewhere around 2500 B.C. and settled in the jungles of middle America in an area made up of what is now Guatemala, Honduras and the Yucatan peninsula. Between 250 A.D. and 900 A.D. huge cities had been built in the jungles with mammoth stone pyramids, sweeping courtyards, elaborate temples and ceremonial centers. Cities with names like Tikal, Palenque, Piedras Negras and Copan, the astronomical center of the culture, grew and flourished during this classical period.

The Mayans met by the Spanish explorers under Cortez in the 16th century were just the decadent remnants of a people past its prime. Archaeologists and scholars have found that in its heyday that the Mayans were a people of tremendous accomplishments in a variety of fields, especially astronomy.

This grew out of the Mayans' obsession with time and what they could learn from it. It was their belief that history would literally repeat itself and by dating and studying past events they could anticipate what the future would bring.

The people's concern over the future could take on a practical nature such as when was the best time for planting and harvesting crops; or it could be purely religious, such as picking the best day to name a child or make a sacrifice to a particular god. For answers to problems like these the people looked to the priests. And the priests looked to the stars.

These priest-astronomers realized soon enough that the steady movement of the planets was probably the most dependable timepiece they could find. So they began a careful systematic study of the sky taking note of the rhythms and motions of the sun and planets. Special schools were set up where they passed on their knowledge to priest-novices and a select few of the aristocracy, and soon the science of astronomy began to flower, like the Mayan civilization, in the fourth century A.D.

"I suspect," observes Dr. Charles Smiley, chairman of the department of astronomy, Brown University, Director of the Ladd Observatory there, and the leading expert on Mayan astronomy, "that part of their studies were caught up in what we call astrology today—trying to predict the future on the basis of what's happened in the past."

For the Mayans this was complicated business and the priests knew for the sake of their own power that they had to be right, or at least appear to be right A much oversimplified look at their calendar system will give some ideas of the problems they faced.

They had two ways of marking off time, a Short Count and a Long Count. Each day in the Short Count had a four-part name. The first two parts were a day number and a day name of a certain god. A complete series of these day name and numbers was a 260-day cycle known as a Sacred Round, or *tzolkin* which had some religious, ceremonial significance.

The second two parts of a date's name was a month-number and a month-name, also a god's. When the cycle of these was completed they resulted in a 365-day Solar Round, or *haab* year Every 18,980 days, or 52 years, the two rounds would fall into step and complete a Calendar Round.

To eliminate date ambiguity the Mayans also kept a continuous count of the days elapsed since the beginning of the Mayan civilization (somewhere between 3645 B.C. and 2593 B.C.). This was a four-part number called the Long Count and ticked off the time in centuries, decades, years, months and days. Of particular interest to the Mayan priests were the units of measurements called *katuns*, each approximately 20 years long.

There were certain gods, some well disposed to men, some not, that ruled over individual days, months, years, and even *katuns* and it was the job of the priest-astronomer to be able to predict which gods would be in control on a given day and which ones would dominate. To further complicate matters, other deities or disasters could spring up.

Each lunar month and each revolution of Venus had its own divine patron. The day the 52-year Calendar Round ended was a potentially dangerous day as was the day of a solar eclipse when horrible creatures were thought to descend to earth.

Mayan scholar J. Eric S. Thompson describes the problem in his *Rise and Fall of Maya Civilization:* "The Maya wished to know which gods would be marching together on any given day because with that information they could gauge the combined influences of all the marchers, offsetting the bad ones with the good in an involved computation of the fates and astrological factors. On a successful solution depended the fate of mankind."

To cover themselves the priests sometimes resorted to a little showmanship to account for apparent lapses

"Some people have insisted that the Mayans would predict solar eclipses and then make 'white magic' to prevent them," Dr. Smiley observed. "If they did, they were extraordinarily clever because if you predict an eclipse, make white magic and the eclipse fails to appear, you've been successful as a magician. If you predict an eclipse, make white magic and it happens, you've been a failure as a magician, but a success as a predictor." In other words, Mayan astronomers had it made no matter what the results.

There was still a lot of science behind their showmanship. They made careful note of phases of the moon, changes in the apparent motions of the sun, the movement and periodic appearance of Venus, and the periodic nature of a solar eclipse. Much of this information was preserved for future reference as carvings on stelae, stone monoliths erected to honor some Mayan god or local ruler and at the same time record some important dates.

After 889 A.D. the Mayans used a more portable system of record keeping with books called codices. Most of these were destroyed by jungle moisture or overzealous Spanish missionaries. At least three are known to have survived and of these one called the Dresden Codex, named after the museum where it is kept, contains an elaborate series of tables attempting to relate solar eclipses to the periodic reappearance of Venus and the new moon.

Making these kinds of records and the calculations that often went with them required a thorough knowledge of a system of mathematics. The one the Mayans used was a dot and bar system adapted from the Olmecs in which each dot represented a single unit and each bar stood for five.

They could not multiply or divide with their system and they worked only with whole numbers.

"They multiplied by adding and they did something similar to division by subtracting," Dr. Smiley explains. "Their method of dividing is very close to a modern system called continued fractions."

Being able to use only whole numbers could have been a problem, especially in astronomy where exact measurements are often computed to the nearest decimal place. For example, the period from one new moon to the next is 29.53 days; the synodic period, or the time it takes Venus to reappear, is 583.92 days; the length of a tropical year is 365.2422 days.

This did not keep the Mayans from arriving at exact, or near exact figures of the more important astronomical figures. They would figure things out to the nearest whole number, writing, for example, that 405 lunar months add up to 11,960 days. Modern computations for the same period give a figure of 11,959.1 days.

There was nothing like a telescope or any elaborate astronomical equipment available. They depended on what they could see with their unaided eyes and what they could compute. "I would say the reason they built their pyramids," Dr. Smiley remarks, "is because the blasted trees kept getting in the way of the horizon. They wanted to get up higher so they could look over the tops of the trees and see where the sun was rising, where the moon was rising. I'm almost certain that the pyramids with distant markers provided their astronomical basis."

One construction that has caused some debate in this area is a building named the Caracol, meaning *snail* in Spanish, because its spiral staircases reminded the Spaniards of a snail's shell. The remains of the building were found in the post-classic era city of Chichen Itza where some scholars think it may have served as an ancient observatory.

Because of the renowned Mayan preoccupation with astronomy, the building's resemblance to an observatory, and the fact that certain astronomical observations can be made from the three windows that remain, some archaeologists are convinced that it was used by astronomers.

Dr. Smiley is a little more skeptical because he claims there were no angle-measuring devices of the kind attributed to the Caracol found at other Mayan astronomical centers. In addition, the Caracol was constructed in a city built long after the peak period of astronomical studies and no other structures like it can be found in any other cities where astronomy was studied intensively.

About 500 years before the Caracol was constructed the Mayans had already made tremendous strides in their knowledge of the heavens. They had figured out the length of a month according to the phases of the moon; they were able to anticipate seasonal changes in the context of their calendar system; and they had careful records of the movement of Mars, Jupiter, Saturn and especially Venus.

Although the synodic period of Venus, the time it takes for the planet to make two successive passes by the earth, fluctuates between 580 and 588 days, the Mayans were able to compute the average period as 584 days. The modern figure for this is 583.9, an error difference for the Mayans of one day every 6000 years.

"I can picture some nice old gentleman whose job it was to check off the days, add them up and say all right Venus is back, Venus is here, Venus is there," Smiley continues. "They'd get the 584 day period easily and by sheer routine. But the guy who did the work on the eclipse, he was top drawer."

And it was working with eclipses that the Mayan astronomers really demonstrated their skills in sky-watching and mathematics. The Mayans devised two tables which are recorded in the Dresden Codex, each of which was an attempt to successfully predict a solar eclipse.

This is not an easy task because as Dr. Smiley points out, both the moon and earth have a non-uniform orbit of an eclipse, and it is an extremely long period of time before the same eclipse returns to an area.

One table, called the Venus Table, attempted to date future eclipses using the regular movements of Venus as a time reference, for example, predicting an eclipse so many days before or after a conjunction with Venus

"They were very smart in choosing Venus," Smiley says, "because its motion is beautifully regular." Still, this table, which Smiley labels a solar eclipse prediction table, did not give them the accuracy they wanted. Sometimes an eclipse would appear two days after a predicted day, or worse, two days before.

This apparently was one topic of discussion at their astronomical conference in Copan. The result was a changeover to a Lunar Table, which Smiley calls a solar eclipse warning table. Unlike the Venus Table it did not attempt to predict the specific day of an eclipse but used the phases of the moon to predict the new moon preceding two new moons when at least one or possibly two solar eclipses might occur.

"They couldn't possibly have had any idea how good this was," Smiley remarks. "It's a marvelous system. It not only warns of eclipses visible in Central America but all over the world."

The warning table was the work of a real genius. The table he devised warned of every eclipse that occurred on earth in one 33-year period without missing once. This same technique, Smiley says, works just as accurately in the 20th century and will remain accurate through the 25th century, as far into the future as astronomers have plotted eclipses.

Today astronomers do not need to rely on Mayan techniques to predict future eclipses.

Yet the Maya have something to offer the 20th-century astronomer. Referring to their habit of keeping meticulous records of celestial events, Dr. Smiley says, "We are in the interesting position that if only we know a little more about the Mayan language we can improve our astronomical tables"

What else could have been learned will most likely remain a mystery. For reasons still unknown, in the 10th century A.D. the Mayans abandoned their cities and their astronomical inscriptions to the jungle they had beaten back centuries before. Yet even the little evidence we have of their accomplishments is more than enough to support Dr. Smiley's remark that "the people who start assuming they were ignorant savages are really in trouble."

CHAPTER VI

Were semites first in America?

Unmistakably African Negro and Semitic figures from Mexico and Yucatan imply that waves of immigrants may have arrived in the Americas long before Columbus.

Scene: An elementary school classroom in the U.S.A. in the year 2000 A.D.

Teacher: "John, who discovered America?"

John: "America was discovered by many waves of voyagers from across the Atlantic long before Christopher Columbus arrived here in 1492. For example, over two thousand years ago, a party of Jews reached the U.S. mainland and traveled to what is now the state of Tennessee before they died."

Unbelievable? Perhaps. But if a theory put forward by Dr. Cyrus Gordon, chairman of the Department of Mediterranean Studies at Brandeis University, is accepted, John's answer will be the correct one. Dr. Gordon, a noted expert on ancient scripts, believes that successive waves of immigrants from the Near East sailed across the Atlantic to the New World, beginning in preliterate times. Although they were eventually absorbed by the original inhabitants who had immigrated across the Bearing Straits long before, the newcomers left traces of their origins in the customs, art and literature of our hemisphere.

The theory, which enlists a few scholarly adherents other than Dr. Gordon, is known as "Atlantic diffusion." A similar theory, "Pacific diffusion," which holds that voyagers came from across the Pacific instead, is somewhat more widely accepted. Dr. Gordon is among those who believe that diffusion took place for millenia across *both* oceans. Most scholars, however, still believe that parallel developments among New and Old World cultures account for any similarities.

In a book called *Before Columbus* that he published recently, Dr. Gordon builds up an interesting case for Atlantic diffusion based on similarities he notes between Old and New World cultures. One of the key links in his case is a small, dark stone about the size of a 10-cent Hershey bar that was found some 80 years ago in a grave at Bat Creek in Loudon County, Tenn. Carved on the stone are a number of signs. According to Dr. Gordon, they are ancient Hebrew letters. Five of the letters written side by side he reads as "for the land of Judah" or, possibly, "for the Judeans."

A sign below the five-letter phrase he translates as "the year 1". The whole text, then, could be read as "the Golden Age of the Jews, year 1".

What is a 2000-year-old Hebrew inscription doing in a Tennessee grave? During this period, Dr. Gordon explains, the Roman persecution of the Jews was at its height. He believes that the skeletons found in the Tennessee grave with the stones are those of a party of Jews who took to the seas to escape the long arm of the Roman Empire. Like voyagers before them, of whose sailing feats they had probably heard, they traversed the Atlantic and landed in the New World. Then the party journeyed through the wilderness to Tennessee where they were either killed or, possibly, committed suicide.

Before they died, however, they inscribed the small, chocolate-colored stone with the evidence of their origins. The incident, Dr. Gordon notes, recalls the suicide of the Jews at Massada in A.D. 73 when defeat at the hands of the Romans was inevitable.

If Dr. Gordon is right, the Bat Creek stone is obviously of extreme importance to the diffusionists' case. But the Tennessee grave excited little interest back in the late 1880's when Smithsonian archaeologist Cyrus Thomas, a well-known scientist in his day, discovered the site. Thomas was looking for American indian remains and he thought the mound-like grave was Cherokee, a not unreasonable assumption in that area. The script of course, he surmised was Cherokee, too. Thomas advanced this theory in the *Twelfth Annual Report of the Bureau of Ethnology to the Secretary of the Smithsonian Institution, 1890-91.*

He accompanied his report with a photograph of the stone that Dr. Gordon now maintains was published upside down.

In his report, Thomas describes the grave where the stone was found in some detail. It contained nine skeletons lying side by side in two neat rows, seven in one row and two in the other. The stone was partly underneath a skull in the two-skeleton row. The grave also yielded two metal bracelets, a small fossil with a drill hole in it, a

From *Before Columbus* by Cyrus H. Gordon; Crown Publishers

Mayan artifacts with semitic features resemble Mediterranean types.

copper bead, a bone implement, and a few pieces of polished wood with traces of copper sheathing. Thomas gathered up all the artifacts and some of the bones and shipped them to the Smithsonian. The area in which the finds were made, meanwhile, has been farmed over, the mound under which the grave lies having been leveled in the process.

Meanwhile, the artifacts and bones collected by Thomas repose in the Smithsonian archives, where he deposited them some 80 years ago. The pieces of polished wood, unfortunately, were coated with shellac in the best tradition of the archaeology of that day, which makes it impossible to subject them to carbon 14 dating techniques. The bones weren't coated, but carbon 14 dating of bones, as a Smithsonian staff member explains, requires a special technique that is not reliable enough to date them with any certainty. Dr. Gordon thinks the artifacts belong to the Adena culture, the latest date for which is 500 A.D.

That leaves the inscription on the stone as the chief indicator of the grave's age, a situation that is satisfactory as far as an expert on ancient scripts like Dr. Gordon is concerned. His argument is persuasive.

"Any student who has had two lessons in old scripts should be able to read three of the five letters I've translated. The other two do take more finesse." The remaining two letters on the stone, he says, are still "open to discussion. Even the style of the inscription can be nailed down to the Hebrew coins of the Roman period." He leaps up from his desk and jots down the letters "L-Y-H-W-D" on a piece of paper. Underneath he writes the numeral one. "This is the perfect spelling for Judea and this is the regular way to indicate the year. This style is actually used on Hebrew coins. It isn't something I made up."

He adds: "Now there's one letter cut off at the left here—it could be an M and in that case, the inscription reads 'for the Jews.' Otherwise, it's for 'Judea'. It's all perfectly clear."

But it wasn't all perfectly clear to Dr. Gordon a few years ago when he saw a photograph of the Bat Creek stone in a book published and sent to him by an amateur archaeologist, Joseph Corey Ayoob. Ayoob is Lebanese, a member of a group considered to be the descendents of the ancient Phoenecians. His book is not a particularly scholarly defense of his theory that the Phoenecians discovered America. The theory is at least partly based on the work of another amateur U.S. archaeologist, the late Dr. W. W. Strong, a reputable physicist in his day. Strong, too, was convinced that the Phoenecians had discovered America.

Looking for evidence to back up his theory, Dr. Strong had come across the paper published by his contemporary, Dr. Thomas. Strong's unpublished research came to the attention of Ayoob, who published a copy of the mysterious chocolate-colored stone—right-side up—in 1950. Ayoob read three letters, L-Y-H, correctly on the stone in his book published in 1964.

When Dr. Gordon received the Ayoob book, however, he put it aside, fearing involvement in an "amateur" controversy. The matter rested there until a colleague of Dr. Gordon's, Dr. Joseph Mahan of the Columbus, Ga., Museum of Arts and Crafts, came across the Thomas report himself. Dr. Mahan was searching for evidence of early contact between American indians and eastern Mediterranean cultures, a search stepped up by the discovery, in 1966, of what is now called the "Metcalf stone." The stone, found on the grounds of Fort Benning in Georgia, seems to bear writing resembling Minoan more than any other known script, in Dr. Mahan's opinion. Other authorities, including Dr. Gordon, agree with this opinion.

Dr. Mahan secured a good print of the Bat Creek stone from the Smithsonian and sent it off to Dr. Gordon with Thomas' paper. When the Brandeis professor saw the clear photograph all the pieces suddenly fit together. He had little trouble reading off five Hebrew letters and the numeral. He had already completed *Before Columbus* but the new find fit in so neatly with his theory that he added a postscript to the book on the Bat Creek grave.

Dr. Gordon thinks the case for the origin of the Bat Creek inscription now rests on firm ground. He makes these points:

1. The stone was found in an undisturbed grave, as indicated by the roots of a dead tree growing down through it and the arrangement of the skeletons in two neat rows.

2. The stone was found and the report of its discovery published by archaeologists of impeccable reputation.

3. The stone actually contains what looks like five Hebrew letters and a numeral written in a script which was not even deciphered until the nineteenth century, and in a variety of the script not analyzed until 1862. The letters are *not* Cherokee.

4. The style of the script is typical of that of Hebrew coins of the period, which have been found at three widely separated sites in Kentucky.

One of the archaeologists who takes issue with Dr. Gordon's interpretation of the Bat Creek stone is the Smithsonian's Dr. Gus van Beek, curator of Near Eastern Archaeology. He told *The Sciences*, the publication of the New York Academy of Sciences, that the stone has additional scratches on it received since its picture was first published. "These may indicate that it was not cut in ancient times because both the letters and the scratches have the same patina," he says. "The stone might go back to Roman times, but it might also be as late as the 19th century, inscribed by someone who copied down the Jewish letters of the Roman period."

Dr. Gordon repudiates this suggestion. The undisturbed condition of the grave, he says, indicates that it was dug before the 19th century. The scratchings are due to damage by the excavators who, as Cyrus Thomas noted, struck the stone with a sharp tool. If the letters were modern, it would mean that the American indian who dug the grave would have had to make an inscription for himself in a script not even deciphered until after his death.

The scholarly controversy that swirls about the stone seems to invigorate the Brandeis professor, who has published some 15 books and a host of articles in his field during his long career. "I've thought through this and there is no doubt about it," he says confidently. "The only trouble with this stone, as another archaeologist said recently, is that it was discovered in the wrong place. If it had turned up in the Mediterranean, it would make a little footnote to some paper. But it's the spread of the Mediterranean culture to this continent that interests me. If this was found in Palestine, I wouldn't be interested in it."

But the Bat Creek stone is only the most recent piece of evidence that supports his case for Atlantic diffusion, as Dr. Gordon points out. In *Before Columbus*, he describes a number of similar links between New and Old World cultures, particularly the culture of the ancient Mediterranean, his area of interest. One is the Metcalf stone, which Dr. Mahan sent to him in 1966 after it was picked up at Fort Benning by Manfred Metcalf, a civilian employee of the fort. Then there are the Bar Kokhba coins (132-135 A.D.) dug up at three sites in Kentucky between 1932 and 1967. A century earlier, in 1823, Chief Justice John Haywood of the Supreme Court of Tennessee found Roman coins in Tennessee inscribed with the names of three second century emperors: Antoninus Pius, Marcus Aurelius, and Commodus.

The most startling evidence is an eight-line inscription said to be copied from a stone found in Brazil in 1872 that can be read as an ancient Canaanite text. Dr. Gordon's translation indicates that the writer was a subject of King Hiram III of Phoenecia who reigned from 553 to 533 B.C.

The trouble with the Metcalf stone, the Roman coins and the Phoenecian inscription is that they were all found by amateurs, a fact that makes professional archaeologists dubious about the circumstances of their discovery. What, they ask, is to stop a publicity hungry amateur from planting ancient coins or a stone inscribed with Phoenecian characters? The same doubts, obviously, do not apply to the Bat Creek stone. Cyrus Thomas, whatever his shortcomings as a modern archaeologist ("I've got to admit," says a Smithsonian staff member, "that Cyrus Thomas wasn't the best digger"), was a scientist of unimpeachable reputation in his day.

But Dr. Gordon brings out other evidence for Atlantic diffusion in his book: Pre-Columbian human figures and heads from Middle America with strikingly oriental, Semitic, and Negroid features; references to a land west of the Atlantic in the writings of the ancient Greek authors; the Aztec belief that Quetzalcoatl, the famous bearded white god who appeared as a plumed serpent, came from the East; bearded

The inscription above, found at Bat Creek, Tennessee, has been translated to read: "For the Land of Judah, the Year I."

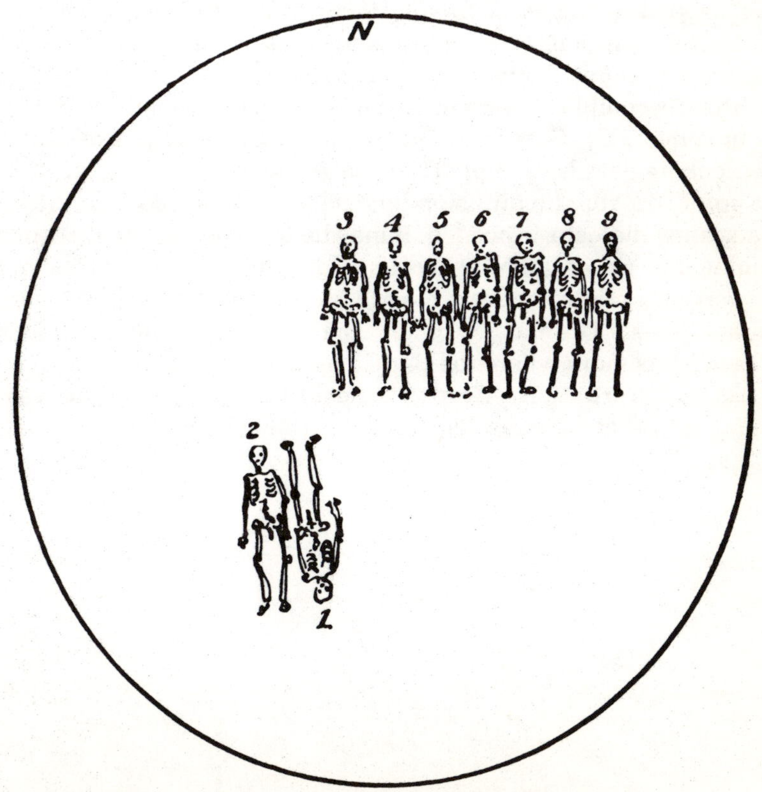

Arrangement of skeletons as found with the stone above.

white men's heads with the bodies of plumed serpents appearing on the pediment of a temple on the Athenian Acropolis; the fact that American cotton is a hybrid produced by crossing native American plants with old World plants such as those grown in Egypt; the marked similarities between an American indian agricultural festival and the ancient Hebrew harvest festival of Tabernacles.

The most striking literary evidence of the existence of a pre-Columbian link between Old and New Worlds described by Dr. Gordon is in the *Popul Vuh,* the sacred book of the ancient Quiche Mayas. In this volume, the Quiche described their ancestors as "coming from the other side of the sea, where the sun rises"—or, in other words, from the East. Quiche history has some interesting parallels with Biblical history: a similar parting of the waters miracle, a deluge, a Garden of Eden episode complete with a maiden tempted to pluck a fruit endowed with wondrous powers. For both the Quiche and the Biblical maiden, the plucking of the fruit was the prelude to human procreation.

"Isolated details may prove little or nothing in any specific case," Dr. Gordon cautions, "though cumulatively a thousand such details might prove much. However, the evidence for diffusion grows when an intricate complex, with numerous interlocking details, is involved."

In spite of Dr. Gordon's ingenious weaving together of numerous interlocking details to support his case, most archaeologists still find the proof for Atlantic diffusion inconclusive. Much corroborative evidence, they indicate, is needed. It may be forthcoming. In Dr. Gordon's opinion, the soil of the New World holds other evidence of the numerous waves of migration from the Mediterranean area beginning in preliterate times. "The earth is full of what was lost in the past," he says. "There's lots more where the Bat Creek stone came from."

As for his critics, Dr. Gordon believes they have only one way out: denial. And that, he considers, is their problem, not his.

PART II
africa

There's little argument with the view of most anthropologists that the clues to man's beginnings lie hidden in primeval layers of sediments on the Dark Continent. Remains of ancient man dug up by the Leakeys in Olduvai Gorge, and by Raymond Dart in Southern Africa, indicate that things were stirring there before they stirred elsewhere. But following the development of early humans in Africa isn't easy.

Except for the elaborate civilization of Egyptian and Sumerian people, whose glyphs and written language recorded the history and fables of their tribes for posterity, most records of interior peoples consist of oral histories. These, passed down from generation to generation via specially designated members of the witch-doctor cult, could and often did change with the telling. And in tribal warfare when entire settlements were wiped out, the oral histories were wiped out with them. So answers come hard. What is a ruined city of stone buildings doing in the jungles of Rhodesia, for instance? How much can the stones tell? Quite a bit, but not enough.

Even where ancient historians recorded the development of their people and their cities, much has been left unexplained. That is the fascination of archaeology. The chapters in the section that follows, deal with some of Africa's most baffling mysteries, and what's being done to solve them today.

CHAPTER VII

Physics and the pyramids

Is Egypt's Second Pyramid of Giza really solid stone, or do secret chambers exist? Archaeologists may at last find the answer—without damaging the pyramid—through new methods in physics.

An alabaster coffin, gold-plated thrones and sylvan fittings for slave-borne platforms, necklaces and bracelets of hammered gold and precious jewels, jars filled with food for an afterlife banquet, perhaps even a few remaining royal bones, swathed in dignity from 4,500 years ago—unusual results from a physics experiment. Yet these finds are the maximum possible from an eight-year-old experiment in Egypt. The minimum find will also be hard news—that the Second Pyramid of Giza, also know as the Pyramid of Chephren, is a solid structure without unexplored chambers of any size—the conclusion so far.

The exploration is taking place without disrupting the pyramid in any way. That's a far cry from earlier attempts which called for forcing tunnels through the pyramids, as grave robbers sometimes did, to an 1837 attempt to blast into chambers with gunpowder. This new technique is possible because of new methods in physics, available only in the past few years.

The recent exploration used cosmic rays, computers and spark chambers. It took a physicist, Dr. Luis Alvarez of Lawrence Radiation Laboratory, to concoct a method that would produce a three-dimensional look at the interior of the Second Pyramid, complete with chambers and a rough indication of their size. The project is a joint venture of the University of California and Ein Shams University in Cairo.

The three pyramids at Giza have fascinated travellers since they were built between 2,600 and 2,500 B.C. Majestic monuments towering over the desert sands, these three are the most impressive in Egypt. They were built by three early rulers. The most famous is the Great Pyramid of Cheops or Khufu. Chephren's is second in size. The third Giza pyramid is that of Mycerinus, the smallest and latest of the three.

For hundreds of years before the pyramids were built, Egyptian pharoahs had been preoccupied with providing themselves with elaborate burial chambers. Traditionally, these chambers were within the ground and furnished with numerous rooms that contained all the needs for the pharoahs' life after death.

Pyramids were a technological breakthrough for their time. Just as we are designing and building the first spaceships, the Egyptians were designing and building the first free standing structures in stone. At first, they used stone to imitate the old mud-brick structures. But mud-brick buildings crumble and cannot be very large. Stone offered a whole new dimension and a flurry of pyramid construction followed the discovery.

The very first pyramid evidently began as a flat box of solid stone masonry about 200 feet square and 25 feet high. It topped a tomb shaft 90 feet below the ground surface. It then occurred to an Egyptian architect to place a similar flat box, somewhat smaller, on top of the first box. Soon five boxes of solid stone were built, stepwise, on top of one another. There was no thought of interior rooms.

Later, pyramids were constructed the same way, but steps were filled with rubble to support a facing of limestone that sloped smoothly from top to bottom. Architects learned how to increase structural strength. They used larger stone blocks, and packing blocks were placed in slightly concave layers so courses tip up at the corners of the structure. Blocks were more accurately squared. These design improvements made it possible to build chambers within the pyramid itself. The Great Pyramid contains two chambers and two passageways to them within the pyramid, as well as an underground chamber.

To archaeologists and treasure-hunters alike, it seems odd that the Second Pyramid is solid. As Dr. Alvarez puts it, "Why would Chephren, after a boyhood spent watching his father's slaves erecting a beautiful and complex series of chambers and passages in the Great Pyramid, be content to erect a solid and uninteresting pile of limestone blocks as his own pyramid?"

The standard reply to a question of this type is that Chephren probably knew that his father's pyramid was robbed soon after the burial ceremony. Concluding that a pyramid could not be secured against grave-robbers, he abandoned any attempt to misguide would-be robbers. Instead he simply had himself buried in the central ground-floor chamber. The pyramid was just a monumental gravestone, erected to his memory.

The other possibility is that the upper chambers were so well hidden they have not yet been found. Or at least have been unknown for the past 3,000 years. No two pyramids have exactly the same floor plan. Dr. Alvarez points out that the subterranean chamber of the Great Pyramid was known to the Greek historian Herodotus in the fifth century B.C., but the upper two chambers were not discovered until the ninth century A.D. They were found by accident when a large slab fell from the passageway, shaken loose by tunnellers as they forced another passage. The sound of the falling slab led them to the original passage and thence to hidden chambers.

Is it possible that Chephren's architects were so wily they managed to hide the upper chambers until now? If so, Dr. Alvarez's experiment was designed to find them.

Although the art of putting rooms in the pyramid was known by Chephren's reign, it was a difficult feat. The pressure of the stone resting on the rooms was severe, requiring forethought and engineering skill to keep the roof of any chamber from collapsing.

The known burial chambers in the large pyramids are all small—18 feet high by 17 feet wide and from 18 to 46 feet long. The smaller the room is, the less difficult are the problems of weight. Dr. Alvarez's experiment depended on any hidden rooms being roughly the same size as the known chambers. If a room was unusually small, it might be missed by this experiment.

A formidable amount of gadgetry and equipment is needed to explore the pyramids via physics. Alvarez' gear weighed about 70 tons.

Khephren's pyramid at Giza (the one at left) should have secret burial chambers like Cheops', but no one has been able to find any. Even cosmic rays have detected no voids, so now physicists will try radar.

Photo Trends

Half of it was hauled into the underground burial chamber of the Second Pyramid. The rest went in a repeater lab outside.

The closest comparison between the pyramid study and another familiar process is that of X-ray photography. At the end of the pyramid study, the physicists achieved an outline of the pyramid's internal structure. This picture, like an X-ray photograph, was the result of sending high-speed radiation through a body that is not ordinarily translucent.

The pyramid study, however, differs in many important ways from a doctor's X-ray. For one thing, the rays employed are naturally occurring whereas X-rays are emitted from machinery built to focus them on a target. Because the pyramid study depended on rays that come from all directions, the angle of approach had to be known.

The equipment inspected the pyramid by measuring the rate of decay of that part of cosmic radiation called muons. These tiny, subatomic particles bombard the earth from all sides. The speed with which muons travel has been analyzed and measured since they were discovered in the 1940s. In their travels through atmosphere and objects, muons strike other particles which cause them to split into smaller fragments or to deflect from their original path.

Muons' speed and density depend on the substance they are travelling through. Thus, they speed through cotton candy and snow drifts, but plow more slowly through car doors, elephants and bar bells. In fact, the density of the material determines the muon's speed and quantity as it exits. The density of the material can therefore be gauged from the muon's path after it leaves a given material.

To measure the speed and angle of a muon's path requires a spark chamber. The simplest spark chamber is made of two flat metal plates, spaced about two-fifths of an inch (one centimeter) apart. When a muon travels through the two plates, an electronic circuit suddenly applies a high voltage between the two plates. This causes a spark to jump between the plates, very nearly along the path of the muon. Anyone watching a spark chamber can see the spark with the unaided eye. In many spark chambers, the spark's path is recorded by two cameras so both the north-south and the east-west direction of the spark's jump can be noted. However, other methods of recording the muon's path have been developed without having to resort to photography and analysis of photographs. One of these puts two spark chambers a foot apart. Both are horizontal. Instead of sensing energy from the spark as light, the same energy is sensed as a flow of electric current. This signal can be recorded directly on magnetic tape for a computer.

The next problem the physicists faced, explains Dr. Alvarez, is

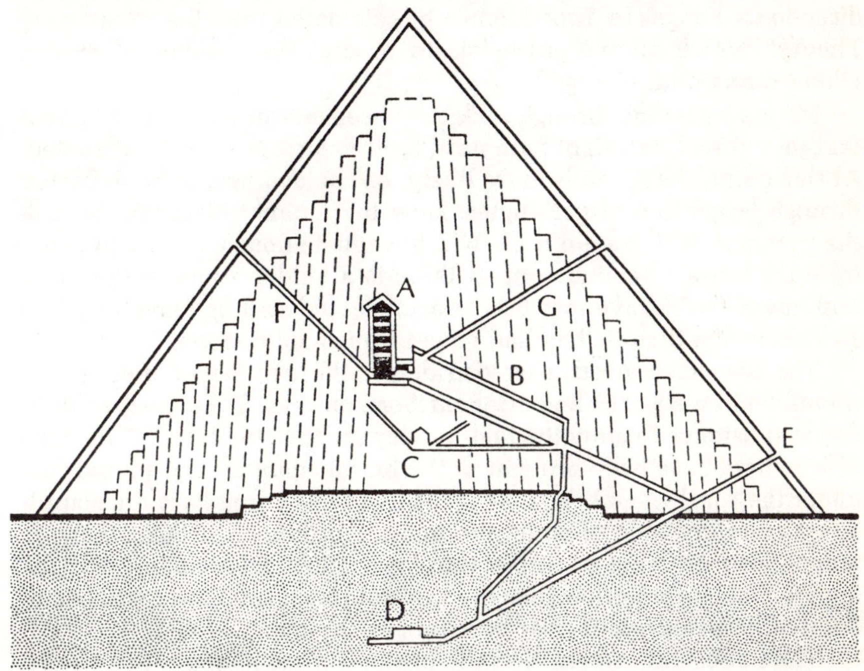

Sectional view through the Great pyramid of Khufu shows the Grand Gallery leading up to the king's chamber in the center of the pyramid, with the queen's chamber below it. Shafts lead down to king's chamber from sloping sides. Main entry was closer to the base. The structure dates from 2700 B.C. and was 480 feet from base to apex. At right is closeup of king's chamber.

"How nearly true is it that the muon we record in our spark chambers is still moving along the same straight line that defined its trajectory as it passed through the burial chamber?" As particles move through objects, they collide and have normally small changes in direction. Changes in direction can be calculated from the "Scattering Theory" which allows physicists to predict the number of muons whose direction is changed.

Muons travelling through rock have been measured and it is known that they travel a straight path until their energy is almost exhausted. At this point, the muon is more likely, on the average, to be deflected through larger and larger angles. Now the muons travelling through the pyramid, if it is solid rock, will have just enough energy to penetrate the burial chamber roof. If there is a hidden room in the pyramid, muons will have met less resistance and will be travelling in a straighter line than if they had gone through solid stone.

The physicists need a way to detect the number of muons still travelling in a straight line after further journeys. They need another dense substance to slow the fast-moving muons still more. Thus, tons of iron bars have been brought in the burial chamber and placed just under the spark chambers. Under the five feet of iron bars are scintillation counters, able to count the number of muons striking them. If muons also are able to strike this layer, then their energy will be known. This information, plus the angle of travel from the spark chamber, will indicate whether or not there are hidden chambers.

The important information the physicists are looking for is a difference in the rate of muons coming in from one area. It doesn't matter that the initial counts were higher than the physicists anticipated. The picture they expect to create with the muon information depends on a difference in rate caused by muons travelling through a void, or room, in the pyramid.

Paths of muons were recorded on magnetic tape daily for a period of many months. It only takes one operator to check the equipment daily to be sure it is working and to put a new tape on the recorder. Tapes filled with data are sent to Ein Shams, U. in Cairo for processing.

There was a delay of several months in the project because of the Middle East War. But the tapes finally were ready for analysis by a computer in Cairo. There are several ways of doing this.

The matrix of numbers can be analyzed for small regions in which each sample is studied. Analysts would search for several neighboring regions which have statistically significant differences from the pyramid as a whole. If such a region showed up, the numbers could be converted into a picture comparable to an X-ray photograph. The numbers would be projected as lines on a cathode ray oscilloscope, a common practice, and this could be photographed by a camera. It is then possible to locate the region of a hidden chamber, if there is one.

Dr. Alvarez states, "There were no technical reasons why the proposed experiment would not detect the chambers it was designed to find." The cosmic rays now know and the equipment available are exactly suited to exploring pyramids. If muons moved 10 times slower, the experiment would be impossible. If they moved 10 times faster, it would be impossible.

If the pyramids were 20 feet higher, the muons could not penetrate as far as the underground chamber. If there were no underground chamber and one had to be blasted out in order to put the spark chambers inside the pyramid, the experiment would not be practical financially. Actually, the study cost about a half-million dollars.

What did it reveal? No chambers. But that's not the end. If there was a chamber and it had sufficient gold in it, the gold might absorb as many cosmic rays as solid limestone, according to Dr. Alvarez. So now a radar probe will be conducted by the Stanford Research Institute. It will do a more complete scan using shortwave radio emissions to probe under the pyramid as well as right to the top. If there is a hidden chamber crammed with gold, it will reflect a strong radar signal.

The joint pyramid project is an exciting one. It will be even more exciting if the physicists do reveal a network of chambers or even a single unplundered chamber that would give the 20th century a look at an ancient pharoah's funerary pomp and pageantry.

CHAPTER VIII

Nefertiti—Egypt's mystery queen

Next to the Sphynx, the most familiar symbol of ancient Egypt is the famous bust of Queen Nefertiti. But statuary and glyphs make her a part of one of the most intriguing puzzles of antiquity.

Next to the pyramids and the sphynx, probably the most familiar symbol of ancient Egypt is the bust of Queen Nefertiti. Thousands, perhaps millions, of reproductions have been sold and pictures of it appear on postcards, pendants, earrings and a host of other novelty items that can be purchased from Cairo to Los Angeles.

Nefertiti, with her classically delicate features and long graceful neck, is thought of as the symbol of beauty in ancient Egypt. In fact, the bust is not typical of Egyptian art, and the queen was not typical of Egyptian royalty. She is part of one of the most intriguing sets of puzzles of antiquity. These might be called the mysteries of the Amarna period, and they have fascinated scholars and laymen for over a century. They are being investigated today as actively as they ever were.

The Amarna period came at the end of ancient Egypt's golden age, the eighteenth dynasty, which began in 1580 B.C. when the princes of Thebes drove invaders out of Egypt and established an empire which stretched from the middle of the Sudan to Syria. For two centuries the prestige and wealth of the pharaoh rose and his power was unchallenged. The dynasty culminated in the reign of Amenhotep III, rightly called "the magnificent." Though his artists show him in all the traditional poses of leading his armies into battle and crushing his enemies, he was no warrior as his ancestors had been. He preferred to spend his days among the palaces and gardens of Thebes.

Amenhotep III died around the year 1375 B.C., after a long and tranquil reign. He was succeeded by his son, Amenhotep IV. It was with this strange young man that the mysteries of the Amarna period begin.

What we know of the period comes from inscriptions in tombs and temples, from a few surviving official documents, and from the art—above all from the art—for the art of the Amarna period is unique, and a startling departure for the rigidly traditional Egyptians.

While the bust of Nefertiti shows her as a beauty, the new pharaoh is depicted as a monstrosity, a man with a long narrow face, thick lips, hatchet chin, thin neck, vestigial breast development, wide hips, thick thighs and spindly legs. These characteristics are so pronounced that many Egyptologists have speculated that the pharaoh suffered from a serious illness, perhaps a hereditary glandular disorder.

There had doubtless been other ill or ugly pharaohs, but one would never guess it from the art, which displays them as an endless and almost indistinguishable line of great stone faces with bodies frozen into poses of traditional dignity. It's strange that the Amarna artists were allowed to depict the new pharaoh as grotesque.

Nefertiti (whose name means, "the beautiful one has come") may have been a close relative, even a sister or half-sister, of her deformed husband. Marriages between brother and sister were common in the Egyptian royal family. Some art shows Nefertiti as possessing some of the same general physical characteristics as her husband. This, however, may have been an artistic convention, for the art of the period tends to show that everybody resembled the pharaoh.

The pharaoh is most famous for the religious reforms he attempted. He has been called the heretic pharaoh and the world's first monotheist, though the latter title may be misleading. The ancient Egyptians were not strict polytheists, any more than all of the ancient Hebrews were strict monotheists. Early in the history of the Hebrews Yahweh was little more than the chief god; strict monotheism developed slowly. The Egyptians, on the other hand, did not worship all of their multitude of gods with equal vigor. They too had a chief god. He was Amen, once city god of Thebes. With the rise of Thebes to political power Amen became chief, and very nearly exclusive god of Egypt. There were political as well as religious reasons for this. The priests of Amen were favored by 18th dynasty pharaohs at the expense of the priesthoods of other gods, from other regions.

The new pharaoh tried to insert a new god in place of Amen, and perhaps in place of all the gods of Egypt. This new god was called Aten, or more properly *the* Aten, for unlike other gods this one was not represented by a man or animal, or human-animal hybrid. The Aten was shown as the physical disc of the sun, usually with rays extending

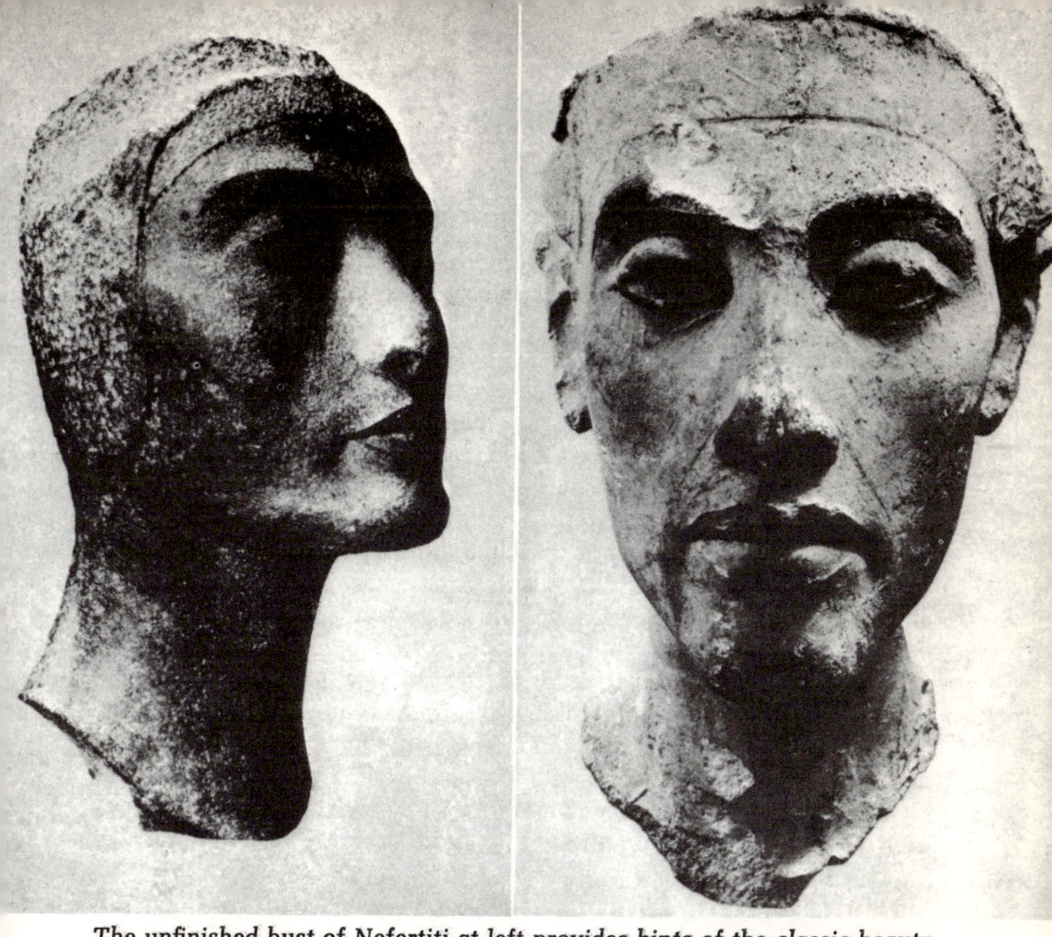

The unfinished bust of Nefertiti at left provides hints of the classic beauty for which she is famous. Amenhotep, her husband (right) was ugly.

from it ending in tiny hands which held the ankh or hieroglyph for life.

At first the new pharaoh seemed content to move slowly in his religious reforms. While he built temples to his new god, he continued to restore and enlarge the temples of Amen. The religious revolution began in earnest during the sixth year of his reign. At that point he changed his name frome Amenhotep IV to Akhenaten (or Ikhnaten).

After casting Amen out of his own name, Akhenaten began a campaign to destroy the old gods, and most particularly the once favored Amen. He had the names of the gods chiseled out of all the inscriptions in which they appeared. He even defaced the tombs of his ancestors when their names contained the name of Amen.

Akhenaten also moved his royal residence from Thebes, "the city of Amen," to a new city he had been building over 200 miles to the north. He called his capital Akhetaten, "The horizon of Aten." Today the spot is known as Tell-el-Amarna, a name drawn from the Bedouin tribes that have occasionally lived there. It is from this modern name that the name Amarna, often used to describe this entire period, has come.

Akhetaten ran along the eastern bank of the Nile (another departure from tradition, for royal cities were usually built on the western bank) for five miles and backward toward the hills, utilizing the fertile strip bordering the river. Expeditions from many countries have today cleared almost all of the remains of Akhetaten. It is the only fully excavated ancient city in Egypt. The unique history of the city made excavation there relatively easy. Akhetaten was built on virgin land; it flourished and was abandoned within 20 years. Since the time it was abandoned, over 3000 years ago, only a few nomadic encampments have occupied the site.

For the modern tourist there is little to see. The stumps of mud brick walls and some empty tombs cut into the cliffs are all that remain. Yet the story of Akhenaten and Nefertiti has been a magnet for archaeologists. Today we have a fairly complete picture of how the city looked during the glory. One fact stands out; Akhetaten was primarily a religious city dominated by the temple of the Aten and the palaces of the king.

In 1912 a German expedition led by Ludwig Borchadt was uncovering the workshop of a sculptor named Thutmose at Tell-el-Amarna when they found the famous limestone bust of Nefertiti. Miraculously this limestone statue had remained in almost perfect condition after being buried for nearly 3300 years. No tedious piecing together of scattered fragments or painstaking reconstruction was necessary. Only the headdress and the ears were damaged. The left eye of the statue was also missing, but it seems the sculptor left that part of his work unfinished.

Under the agreement that allowed Borchadt to dig in Egypt, he would have had to turn the bust over to the government. This he would not do, and the statue "disappeared," only to "reappear" two years later in the Berlin museum. The Egyptian government was neither fooled nor amused by what had happened. They had lost the most valuable single piece of artwork ever found in Egypt. They retaliated by banning all German archaeologists from the country. During World War II the bust of Nefertiti disappeared again. In 1946 a U.S. Army team recovered it from a salt mine where it had been placed for safekeeping during Berlin's bombardment.

The second important find at Tell-el-Amarna were letters to the king from vassal princes in the Middle East. Unlike most Egyptian documents which were written on fragile papyrus rolls these were written on clay tablets in Akkadian cuneiform, the diplomatic language of the ancient Middle East. In the dry climate of Egypt such tablets will last practically forever. They outlasted the archive building which housed them and the royal city itself.

In 1887 an Egyptian peasant woman came upon the tablets accidentally. She didn't know what they were, but she did know that they were very old and that she could probably sell them. They were dumped into a sack and carried to the dealers at Luxor. By the time they reached the hands of scholars who could read them, more than half had been destroyed. Only 350 were salvaged, but enough to document dramatically the chaotic conditions that existed on the frontiers of Egypt during the reign of Akhenaten.

Many of the documents are pleas from rulers loyal to Egypt for help from the pharaoh. We do not know if Akhenaten answered these letters or even saw them, but he sent no help. We have learned that most

The traditional god, Amen, below right, was replaced by a new one named Aten by Amenhotep II, left, worshipping Aten, who is symbolized by the sun.

of the cities mentioned in the Tell-el-Amarna letters either expelled their pro-Egyptian rulers or were overrun by the Hittite empire expanding from the north. We can guess that the pharaoh and his court were so involved in religious reforms that they totally ignored foreign policy.

By the 15th year of Akhenaten's reign there appears to have been a sharp and unexplained change at Tell-el-Amarna. The idyllic family life of Akhenaten and Nefertiti was suddenly shattered. The queen moved or was exiled to a palace at the north end of the city. Archaeologists have deduced from the names on objects dug up at the site that she took with her the pharaoh's probable half-brother Tutankhaten and his wife, Ankhsenpaaten, the third of the royal couple's six daughters. Nefertiti called her place of exile "The House of the Aten".

After Nefertiti left, Akhenaten appointed one of his brothers or half-brothers, Smenkhara, as coregent. The new coregent married the pharaoh's eldest daughter Meritaton and was accorded many public honors once reserved for Nefertiti.

There is a single official act traceable directly to Smenkhara, but it is a highly significant one. He went to Thebes and made offerings to Amen. When Akhenaten first built a city for his new god he inscribed a vow on all the boundary stones that he would never leave the city. There is nothing to indicate that he ever broke this vow. Perhaps the new coregent served as an emissary from the royal family to the hostile outside world, for by now it must have been clear that the new religion was not winning general acceptance.

Within three years of the break between Akhenaten and his queen, all the major figures of the Amarna revolution had disappeared from history. We find the boy Tutankhaten had come to the throne. The discovery of "King Tut's" unplundered tomb in 1922 gave this pharaoh a fame that his short and inglorious reign did not justify. The new king ruled for a brief time at Tell-el-Amarna, then moved the capital back to Thebes and changed his name to Tutankhamen to rid himself of identification with the unpopular god. Life at the city of the Aten continued at a feeble pace after the departure of the king, and soon the city was abandoned. The temples of Amen and the other gods which Akhenaten had tried to destroy were restored.

The objects in Tutankhamen's celebrated tomb were not really his. Many are designed in the Amarna style and were originally meant for the tomb of Smenkhara. Tutankhamen usurped them after Smenkhara disappeared.

Tutankhamen died after a reign of nine years and the throne was taken by Ay, who had been chief counselor to Akhenaten and Tutankhamen. Ay ruled for about two years and was replaced by Horemhab, an army commander who had never been intimately associated with the group of Aten worshipers.

Now the last traces of the religious revolution were destroyed. During Horemhab's time all members of the Amarna family were officially branded as heretics and Horemhab was recognized as the first legitimate ruler since the death of Amenhotep III. All references to the Aten, and Akhenaten and his followers were systematically hacked out of the monuments, just as Akhenaten had tried to erase the name of Amen. Many Aten monuments were completely torn down and the stone used to build temples to the traditional gods.

Thus archaeologists have been able to piece together the outlines of this ancient royal drama. But many mysteries remain. For example, what were the fates of Akhenaten, Nefertiti and Smenkhara? There is no clue as to how and when they died. The tomb Akhenaten had constructed for himself and his queen at Tell-el-Amarna was excavated in the 1880s. It had never been finished and had been brutally defaced, probably by the king's enemies after his death. Nothing indicates that the king or queen was ever buried there.

In 1907 a strange coffin was found in an improvised tomb in Thebes. It had been made for a woman, and probably was intended for one of Akhenaten's daughters, but it contained the mummy of a young man. This had been carelessly prepared, indicating a hasty burial. But among the meager adornments were a few which hinted that the body belonged to one of the Amarna kings. Which one—Akhenaten or the shadowy Smenkhara? It had the long skull and broad pelvis so familiar in pictures of Akhenaten. On the other hand, Smenkhara had been depicted as having a similar physique. Experts who examined the body suggested that it belonged to a man who died in his late 20s. Smenkhara would have been about that age when he disappeared from the records. Akhenaten would have been a good 10 years older. Still, determining the age of death from poorly preserved remains is difficult, and if Akhenaten had suffered from a disfiguring glandular disease, that might throw off all of the calculations. Opinions vary on the identification of the mysterious Theban mummy.

From time to time *ushabiti*, or funeral statues of Akhenaten, have turned up in shops of dealers in Egyptian antiquities. The source of these *ushabiti* is unknown. Akhenaten's true tomb has not been located.

An even more intriguing riddle concerns Nefertiti. Was she really the force behind the Aten revolution? It has long been suspected that she wielded great power for a queen, because in most of the existing art of the Amarna period the queen is accorded a place almost equal to that of her husband. This view is supported by the results of an extremely complex reconstruction job recently completed by the University of Pennsylvania.

The project involved a temple to the Aten built early in Akhenaten's reign at Karnak, a traditional place of worship in Egypt. After the collapse of the Aten revolution, Horemhab had the temple torn down and its stones used in the construction of a monument to other gods. He made sure that blocks from the Aten temple were used so their decorations could not be seen. But over the centuries Horemhab's temple fell into ruins.

In 1926 the French archaeologist Henri Chevrier was put in charge of reconstructions at Karnak, and it was he who first discovered the blocks from the Aten temple. All recognizable Aten blocks were separated from the blocks of the later temple. Some Aten blocks found their way into museums and the hands of private collectors. Most of the estimated 35,000 found by Chevrier were stacked in warehouses or in the open at Karnak. There they sat until 1956, when the site was visited by Ray Winfield Smith, a University of Pennsylvania archaeologist. Said Smith, "I was dumbfounded that such a mine of beauty and historical lore should lie neglected.

Smith conceived a plan to piece together this massive jigsaw puzzle. All the stones were photographed. Then the characteristics of the drawings and carvings on each stone were fed to a computer, which attempted to match it with the characteristics on other stones. The results yield a much better picture of the Aten temple than had previously seemed possible.

The pictoral reconstruction of the temple provided a major surprise. Images of the queen, not the king, dominated the structure. Never before had an Egyptian temple so emphasized a woman. A century earlier Egypt actually had been ruled by a woman, Queen Hatshepsut, but she was referred to as "king" and was often shown wearing a false beard. Nefertiti never disguised her sex.

The Karnak reconstruction seems to support the theory that it was Nefertiti, not Akhenaten, who was the real mover and shaker in the royal family: Smith believes that Akhenaten was not only physically deformed, but may have been weak-minded as well. Moreover he believes that the pharaoh may have been sterile and that the six princesses were not his daughters. He notes that the princesses are usually shown with their mother, not their father.

What is the true story? Was the beautiful Nefertiti also one of the most revolutionary religious reformers in history? We probably shall never know exactly.

CHAPTER IX

Holy cats and sacred cows

Cats, crocodiles, hippos, baboons, hawks, beetles and a host of other animals were held so sacred in ancient Egypt that a Roman soldier who killed a cat was stoned to death. People shaved their heads on the passing of a pet. The reasons were not just sorrow.

University of Michigan dentists engaged in an X ray survey of the teeth of Egyptian pharoahs turned up a unique oddity a few summers ago. An X ray photograph of a 16-inch bundle removed from the coffin of Queen Makeri, who died around 1000 B.C., showed the embalmed body, not of the queen's baby, as the dentists expected, but of a hamadryas baboon. The young female baboon, which had been beside the queen in the royal sarcophagus, is identified on the outside of the coffin as Princess Moutemhit, the queen's infant daughter. The university says the animal is the first ever found inside a royal sarcophagus.

Egyptologists are still puzzling over the misidentification, but the presence of an ape in a queen's coffin probably wouldn't have raised an eyebrow in ancient Egypt. By the time Queen Makeri, the wife of Painetchem I, reigned, most animals in Egypt were regarded as sacred—including the hamadryas baboon, the cat, the crocodile, the hippopotamus, the hawk, the beetle and a whole host of other creatures, big and small. A man who harmed a sacred beast, even accidentally, was lucky if he was let off with a fine; he might be executed. A Roman soldier who killed a cat at Alexandria was stoned to death by the enraged populace.

Egyptians kept dogs, cats, apes and other animals as pets, too. When a pet died, it was mourned almost as much as a member of the family, according to the Greek historian Herodotus. "If a cat dies in a private house by a natural death, all the inmates of the house shave their eyebrows," writes Herodotus, who visited Egypt in the fifth century B.C., when animal veneration was at its height. "On the death of a dog, they shave their head and whole body."

These favored beasts were embalmed and buried, sometimes in or near their owner's tomb and sometimes, apparently, in their own special burying ground. Cats, who were associated with the cat-goddess Bast, were entombed at her shrine at Bustabis. Hawks and mice went to Buto, the ibis to Hermopolis. Piebald Apis bulls, a particularly sacred animal, had their own individual stone sarcophagii at Saqqara.

No one knows exactly how the Egyptians developed this high regard for animals, but each of their gods has been associated with an animal since an early point in their history. The hamadryas baboon, for example, represents Thoth, the Sun God. An obelisk set up by Shalmaneser II (860-825 B.C.) shows several of the sacred baboons being led on leashes, probably as gifts of tribute to the king. Sometimes the animal chosen to embody an important deity seems ridiculously inappropriate to the western mind. Thus the creator god, Kephra, is a beetle; the goddess Heket, a frog; Nekhbet, protector of the king, a vulture. Several powerful gods are geese. Towards the close of their civilization, the Egyptians adopted a belief in the transmigration of souls that seems to have reinforced their veneration of animals. Immediately after death, they thought, the human soul entered an animal and then migrated through all the creatures of land, water and air until, thousands of years later, it returned to human form.

Similar ideas about animal representations of gods and transmigration of souls pop up all over the East. In India, a civilization that rivals ancient Egypt in its veneration of animals, the Hindu gods sometimes appear with animal parts, or as entire animals. Ganesa, the god who helps overcome obstacles, has an elephant's head. Monkey effigies of Hanuman, the god of dexterity and intelligence, hang in many Hindu homes while outside, monkeys regarded as sacred because of veneration of Hanuman, romp through the streets without restraint. Newspapers regularly print reports of their pranks. One troupe of monkeys hopped aboard a train and squirted toothpaste on sleeping passengers. Another band of simians invaded a bank and stole 10,000 rupees.

Hindus think an animal existence is definitely lower than that of a man, but because an animal is simply an evolutionary stage, as it were, they are treated with touching solicitude. The solicitude is particularly strong in the case of the cow. The present indian constitution specifically preserves the inviolability of the cow, and some 3,000 organizations exist solely to care for its welfare. The number of indian cattle is estimated at about 200 million, the greatest cattle population of any country in the world. About half of them are superfluous since the cows yield little milk, many bullocks do not work and Hindus, of course, will not touch beef as food. Even the non-working cattle provide one product in abundance, however—dung, India's main cooking fuel.

Cattle are regarded with special favor throughout the East. In ancient Egypt, a representative of the Apis bull, the embodiment of the god Ptah, led a life even a Pharoah might envy. The chosen bull had to have a white triangle on its brow, a white crescent on its right side, a light spot shaped like an eagle on its back and two kinds of hair in its tail. Once such a bull was found, it lived in a suite if rooms in Ptah's temple in Memphis where it rested on carpets, roamed a large yard and had its pick of a harem of cows. It functioned as an oracle, the interpretation depending on which room it entered after a question had been put to it or whether it accepted or rejected food.

Another much-venerated beast in the Eastern tradition is the elephant, which is sacred to both Hindus and Buddhists. To Buddhists, a white elephant is the embodiment of The Enlightened One, and in a Buddhist country like Thailand, a white elephant is—or was—so revered that even the king can't ride on its sacred back. Anna Leonowens, the 19th century English governess who is the original Anna of *Anna and the King of Siam*, describes the life of a white elephant in a floating palace that bears him to his permanent home within the royal enclosure:

> "The floor is . . . laid with gilt matting curiously woven, in the center of which his four-footed lordship is installed in state, surrounded by an obsequious and enraptured crowd of mere bipeds, who bathe him, fan him, feed him, sing and play to him, flatter him. His food consists of the finest herbs, the tenderest grass, the sweetest sugar-cane, the mellowest plantains, the brownest cakes of wheat, served on huge trays of gold and silver; and his drink is perfumed with the flower of the dok mallee, the large native jessamine."

In the royal place, the lucky elephant had his own court, attendants and slaves and was decked out in a crown, gold chains and a purple velvet cloak. Every day, the king spent some time in religious contemplation of this splendid object.

Like the Apis bull of Egypt, the white elephant of Siam functioned as an oracle. Priests scrutinized and recorded every detail of its behavior for omens by which they would advise on the future actions of the king or ministers. A single unusual grunt from the animal was enough to alter the highest policies of state.

A sacred elephant or bull is a large and powerful mammal worthy to represent divinity, but some of the sacred animals strike us as a little ludicrous. A favorite of the Romans was the sacred chicken, which was always consulted about the outcome of battles. A priest drew a circle on the ground, wrote the letters of the alphabet around it and put a grain of wheat on each letter. Then he put the fowl in the middle of the circle and noted which letters it picked. Clodius, a Roman admiral during the First Punic War, carried some holy pullets aboard his ship so he could ask them about forthcoming naval engagements. On one occasion, the chickens got seasick and refused to eat. Clodius, angry, shouted, "If they won't eat, let them drink," and tossed them overboard. The chickens must have known something; Cicero reports that Clodius' fleet was defeated in its next battle.

The Greeks had their own lowly oracle, the crow, which was killed so that the priests at Delphi could prophesy from their entrails. The lobes of the liver were supposed to be particularly significant.

The sacred animals of the classical tradition are the most familiar to us but a whole menagerie of animals have been venerated by peoples living all over the world. The Mayas of Central America buried sacred bats beneath their altars. In Peru, the Incas fashioned hollow clay statues of llamas which they set in niches and fed grains of maize. Tribes in Nigeria hold the python sacred. Each priest has his own python and any python is welcomed in people's homes because it's thought to bring luck. In the western Pacific, there was a cult of the sacred turtle that centered on remote Nan Matol island. Some Moslem peoples believe in a mysterious creature called the jinn that takes the form of reptiles; reptiles are carefully spared since any one of them might be a jinn. Supernatural rabbits, dogs and mice figure in American plains indians beliefs.

Among the animals regarded as sacred by hunting and fishing peoples are the very ceatures on which they depend for food and clothing, which presents them with an unpleasant quandary. They must kill the sacred animal but, being sacred, it may take its revenge on them. To propitiate the revered creature, they perform elaborate ceremonies. The indians who lived along the northwest coast of North America, who depended on the salmon for food, thought that the salmon were a race of supernatural beings who lived in a huge house under the sea. There they went about in human form, feasting and dancing like people. When the time came for the annual salmon run, the salmon people assumed the form of fish to sacrifice themselves for the indians. After death, the spirit of each fish returned to his house beneath the sea, resumed his human shape and repeated the salmon run the following year. The first salmon caught in the annual run was treated by the indians like a visiting chief. They addressed lengthy speeches to it and presented it with offerings. Then they cooked it and ate it in a formal feast. After eating a salmon, all bones had to be thrown back in the water, so the salmon people could resume their full human form.

In the space age, many of these animal-revering cultures have vanished, but a few persist. In modern Thailand, there's still a good deal of reverence for all white animals, including the white elephant. Some African tribes today retain their spiritual identification with animals, a tradition that may well have come down to them from their ancient neighbor to the north, Dynastic Egypt. The Australian aborigines still participate in rainbow serpent cults, believing the rainbow to be a huge serpent linking heaven and earth. And in India, even the rat is sacred, worshipped at the temple of the goddess Durga. Treated with a hands-off policy, he eats, it's been estimated, some eight million tons of grain a year.

CHAPTER X

Coptic voices from the past

Scholars spent four years fitting together jumbled fragments of Coptic texts found in 1945. Worms had eaten "inlets" and "bays" into 200 pages of the papyrus volumes, but some historic surprises emerged.

Shortly after the end of World War II, a party of Arab workmen accidentally unearthed a large jar in an ancient cemetery near the town of Nag Hammadi in Egypt. Inside were 13 papyrus books bound in soft leather covers and secured with thongs. Eleven books were in fairly good condition, their pages intact. What happened next to the little library isn't clear but a few years later the books had surfaced on the Cairo antiquities market. The Egyptian government purchased them in 1951.

Scholars who examined the books in the Coptic Museum of Cairo reported that they contained approximately 1,000 pages, 800 of them intact, that were written in Coptic. Coptic is a language derived from ancient Egyptian but written in Greek characters. Feather bookmarks still marked some of the pages. The experts were in general agreement that although the books were in Coptic, they had probably been translated from Greek. The circumstances of the find suggested that the library belonged to a Gnostic community that lived in caves in the cliffs above the Nag Hammadi cemetery in the fourth century A.D.

The 13 volumes contained some 50 essays by a number of authors which had apparently been translated into Coptic by another group and copied into books by still a third. But the most interesting aspect of the ancient library is its date. The books were written not in the fourth century A.D., when the Gnostic monks actually occupied the Nag Hammadi caves, but earlier. The earliest book has been dated in the first century B.C. or A.D., the latest at around 200 A.D. In other words, the books span a very familiar era: that of the New Testament.

Many of the figures described in the approximately one-third of the essays that have been translated to date are the same as those who play leading roles in the New Testament—Christ, the Apostles, Mary, and others. But the words of these familiar figures often have a peculiar ring to Christians.

Here, for example, is a typical passage translated from "The Gospel According to St. Thomas":

> Simon Peter said to them, 'Let Mary go out from among us, because women are not worthy of the Life.' Jesus said, 'See I shall lead her so that I will make her male, that she too may become a living spirit, resembling you males. For every woman who makes herself male will enter the Kingdom of Heaven.'

The "Gospel According to St. Thomas" begins with these words: "These are the sayings of the Living Christ which were written down by Didymus Jude Thomas." It contains over 100 sayings attributed to Christ, many of which do not appear in the New Testament.

Actually, this particular book is not entirely new to scholars, as the other Nag Hammadi texts that have been translated are. It sounds very much like the Oxyrhynchus papyrus, published at the beginning of this century. Both texts are probably versions, with variations, of the same original.

Scholars spent four years fitting together jumbled fragments of Coptic texts, in which worms had eaten "inlets and bays" through 200 pages.

Photos from the UNESCO Courier

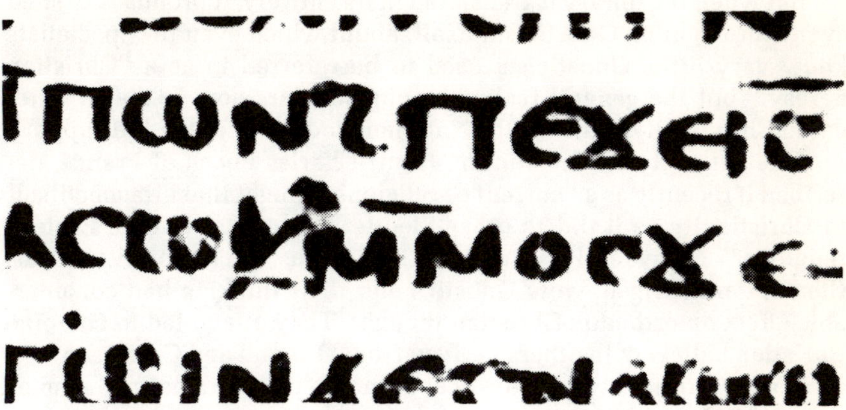

Nag Hammadi texts describe religious views of the Gnostics in various dialects of the Coptic language, but the characters used are Greek.

With about one-third of the books translated, scholars say that the Nag Hammadi library rivals the Dead Sea Scrolls in importance. In fact, as one authority, Dr. James Robinson of the Claremont Graduate School in California puts it, the Nag Hammadi books "pick up where the Dead Sea Scrolls left off." The latest Dead Sea Scroll, points out Dr. Robinson, who is head of Claremont's Institute of Antiquity and Christianity and serves on a Unesco committee dealing with Nag Hammadi library, dates from about 70 A.D., the earliest from the first century B.C. or A.D.

"The shift from 'scroll'—a book in the form of a long roll—to 'codex'—a book in the form of pages as we use today—is typical of the transition from the 'Dead Sea Scrolls' to the Nag Hammadi 'Codices'," he says in the Unesco [United Nations Educational, Scientific and Cultural Organization] *Courier*.

Both the Dead Sea Scrolls and the Nag Hammadi codices, he points out, deal with off-beat religious sects. In the Dead Sea Scrolls, the sect is the Jewish Essenes; in the Nag Hammadi codices, it is the Gnostics, who may be a mixture of Christian, Jewish and perhaps other religions. The Gnostics were a sect oriented toward an other-worldly, speculative view of religion that swept the ancient world in early Christian times. In spite of the exaggerated version of Christianity that the Gnostic texts seem to describe, scholars think they will shed light on some early Christian practices that lingered on among the Gnostics.

But when the library is translated in its entirety, it promises to shed even more light on Gnosticism itself, about which even the specialists know very little. Gnosticism used to be referred to as a "Christian heresy," but the general feeling among scholars now is that it antedated Christianity, a theory the Nag Hammadi codices tend to support.

One authority on Gnosticism, Henri-Charles Puech of France, described it recently as a "current of religious thought that attached itself to Christianity as it did to other Mediterranean and Middle Eastern religions." Many early Christian theologians, including Valentius, Clement and Origen, were Gnostics and their thinking had considerable effect on orthodox Christian thought. They attempted to combine Christian beliefs with others derived from Oriental and Greek sources, especially those that were mystical or metaphysical in nature, such as those of Plato and Pythagoras.

A few puzzling bits of lore that the Nag Hammadi codices may help explain have come down to us from the Gnostics. One is the word "abracadabra," which now refers to an incantation. The Gnostics used it as a magic formula to ward off disease and misfortune. If written in a certain way and hung around the neck, the word was claimed to be a charm against fevers by no less an authority than the Gnostic physician Quintus Serenus Samonicus. The word may be derived from the word some Gnostics used for the Supreme Being, "Abraxas".

To the Gnostics, the purpose of life was personal salvation and much of their literature consisted of apocalyptic, or revelational, writing. The name of the sect, in fact, comes from the Greek word "gnosis," which means revelation. The Nag Hammadi codices contain at least three revelational books, including the "Apocryphon," or "Secret Book of John," which takes the form of a visionary account of the revelation made by Christ after his Passion to the apostle John. Henri-Charles Puech thinks it may be the most important book found at Nag Hammadi. It supposedly explains many religious mysteries, including the creation of the world.

We know even less about the particular group of Gnostics that buried the Nag Hammadi library than we do about Gnostics in general. Shortly after the circumstances of the Nag Hammadi discovery became known, Jean Doresse, a French historian, tracked down the remote site of the burials. He reported that the cemetery, which dates from Roman times, is located in a narrow strip of desert between the Nile River and a vertical cliff. In the cliff are a number of artificial caves that that had been cut in the rock as tombs during the Sixth Egyptian Dynasty. By the fourth century A.D., however, the tomb-caves were looted and empty. The fact that Christian monks inhabited the caves is attested to by large crosses and the opening lines of some Old Testament psalms painted on the walls.

From inside the caves, Doresse noted, the monks could look out over the cemetery in the sand below where they would probably be buried someday. At the foot of the cliff are masses of fallen stones that form an irregular inclined plane up which one can scramble from the desert floor to the face of the cliff some 11 yards above. Late in the fourth century, the monks apparently descended to the cemetery and buried their treasured library in a jar, an accepted way of preserving materials in that day.

The reason why the library, which the feather bookmarks indicate was well used by the monks, was buried can only be conjectured. Dr. Robinson thinks the monks may have done so for reasons of safekeeping. In the late fourth century A.D., the Roman Empire was officially Christian and persecution may well have descended on an offbeat sect like the Gnostics. Bishops of that day often commanded that condemnations of "heretical" views be read in public. The efficient Roman provincial government could put teeth in such denunciations.

As for why the Nag Hammadi Gnostics were in that remote area, Dr. Robinson thinks they may well have retreated there to seek a more other-worldly atmosphere than could be found in the established monasteries in Egyptian cities. Nothing could be more natural, he points out, than that these "heretical" monks would take along their "heretical" library.

To make the entire Nag Hammadi library available to translators all over the world, an eight-volume facsimile edition of the 13 books was prepared for publication in 1973 by a United Arab Republic-Unesco committee. It is based on photographs of the 800 intact pages, plus photographs of the fragments of the remaining 200 pages. Assembling the fragments has been a herculean task. Institutes in the U.S.A., the U.A.R., Switzerland, Germany, France and several other countries painstakingly sifted through the fragments, identifying a large number of them.

It was not simply a matter of fitting together the pieces like a jigsaw puzzle, as Dr. Robinson explains. "The worms ate 'inlets' and 'bays' into the papyrus, so that it was a matter of placing 'peninsulas' and 'islands' in the correct relation to each other." Complicating the task was the fact that the original fragments were locked up for safekeeping, forcing the scholars to rely on photographs and translations.

In addition to the facsimile edition, a five-volume English edition of the Nag Hammadi codices is being prepared under Dr. Robinson's direction.

It would be almost impossible to overestimate the importance of the Nag Hammadi texts that the new editions will make available, scholars tell us. Henri-Charles Puech says: "Before these texts became available, our knowledge, at least of early Christian Gnosticism, was based on indirect evidence and writings about heresies which were often oversimplified and hostile. We now have at our disposal an abundance of authentically Gnostic texts which in number, scope and quality far surpass the few later Gnostic texts in the Coptic language previously available to us."

CHAPTER XI

Secret of Zimbabwe—search for King Solomon's mines

In the Rhodesian jungle stands the ruin of an ancient stone city. Some say it was Ophir, site of Solomon's mines; others think it's the fabled Land of Punt. Actually, no one knows who built it, lived in it or why it was deserted.

The 1850s and '60s were a time of mighty stir in Africa, as the explorers Burton, Speke, Stanley, Baikey, Livingstone and others plunged deep into the hitherto unknown interior. Although Europeans had long been settled along the palmy shores, most of the African hinterland was still almost as mysterious as the Martian surface or the other side of the moon.

The interior of sub-Saharan Africa, however, had remained inviolate, because nature had hedged it with formidable barriers. The Sahara Desert guarded it on the north, save where the narrow corridor of the White Nile snaked across the desert. But the ascent of the Nile was blocked by enormous swamps—the *sadd* of the southern Sudan.

South of the Sahara, the coasts were mostly flat tidewater plains, swampy and heavily forested. The uplands beyond were delightful, but to hack one's way through these insect-swarming, disease-ridden jungles was a task to daunt the stoutest adventurer.

The problem was aggravated by the tsetse fly, whose bite was fatal to all beasts of burden. Because of the fly, man had to do all the carrying. And man makes an inefficient beast of burden. An average man can carry only 60 or 70 pounds for long distances, compared with 200-300 pounds for a horse and 400-500 pounds for a strong camel.

So these coasts presented an almost insuperable logistic problem. Even if the explorer did not succumb to disease, accident, desertion or hostile spears, the amount of supplies and trade goods he could carry limited his range to a few score miles inland.

These barriers isolated black Africa from the main cultural currents of the Old World almost as completely as the oceans isolated the Australian aborigines, the Pacific islanders and the American indians. This isolation explains the cultural backwardness of the tribal Africans, just as it explains that of the Polynesians and the Amerinds.

In the extreme south, climate and topography were easy, and the native Bushmen and Hottentots offered no serious resistance to invaders. Here the main barrier to European penetration was simple distance. As the ocean-going ship was perfected in the 16th and 17th centuries, this factor no longer mattered, and in the 18th and 19th centuries, Europeans overran and settled South Africa from the south, just as the blacks invaded it from the north.

Between the Bushman-Hottentot area of South Africa and the Sahara dwelt various black peoples: the tall, lean, cattle-raising Nilotes of the southern Sudan; the slender, sharp-featured, curly-haired Erythriotes of the Sudan and Ethiopia; the Pygmies of the northeastern Congo; and the burly Forest tribes elsewhere. Archaeology indicates that, during the last few thousand years, the larger sub-races of the black race have vastly expanded at the expense of the primitive hunters—the Bushmanoids and the Pygmies. Before the 19th century, some black peoples had achieved a state of civilization, comparable to that of the Egyptians and the Sumerians several thousand years ago. They had farming, cattle, weaving, pottery, metals, stone buildings, large towns and large-scale government. Some were even beginning to experiment with their own systems of writing.

In South Africa a century ago, rumors of great, glittering inland cities, living or dead, ran riot among the encroaching whites. Back in the 16th century, the Portuguese had published reports of a vast empire between the Zambesi and Limpopo rivers, ruled by a sovereign called Monomotapa, who reigned from a capital called Symbaoe or Zimbaoche. In the 17th century the Portuguese reduced the Monomotapa to a powerless puppet, although a family still claimed the empty title down into the 19th century. But, in the uncritical minds of hunters and miners, all these tales swirled together to form a vision of a golden metropolis of gleaming towers and palaces, where an enterprising man would find a fortune ripe for picking.

In 1871 an unusual man appeared in Mashonaland, in southern Rhodesia. He was Karl Gottlieb Mauch, a 34-year-old Swabian geologist who had worked his passage to Africa to make his mark as an explorer.

After hiking widely over South Africa, usually by himself, Mauch in 1871 found himself at the end of his tether. Half starved, he was threatened with captivity by a chief named Dumbo, who had poisoned

The ruined fortress city of Zimbabwe in Rhodesia is still a mystery.

his beer in order to rob him. Just in time, another big, strong white man turned up to ransom Mauch. The newcomer was Adam Renders, a German-American trader and ivory hunter.

Mauch, delighted to find another German-speaker, confided that he hoped to crown his work by exploring the ruins of the ancient seat of the Monomotapa. He had heard about it from a German missionary named Merensky, who had heard about it from a native chief. Easy, said Renders. He had not only heard Merensky's tale, but had actually camped at the ruins during his elephant hunts.

Learning that an old acquaintance, another ivory hunter named Philips, was nearby, Mauch sent a message to fetch him. Then Renders, Mauch and Philips went to the site and spent several days there.

Mauch returned to Germany and published a book about his discoveries. He concluded that the rites of a local native cult were of Semitic origin. He fancied that the ruins were the Ophir of the Bible, whence (according to I Kings 9:26) the ships of King Hiram of Tyre fetched over 12 tons of gold to King Solomon. In fact, said Mauch, the building on the hill was an imitation of King Solomon's temple on Mount Moriah, while the large elliptical building in the valley was a copy of the palace in which the Queen of Sheba had stayed when she visited Solomon. He even asserted that the ruins had been the residence of Queen Bilqis herself, who had brought Phoenician workmen thither to erect the buildings.

Everywhere the name "Ophir" conjured up a picture of hidden wealth. No matter how leaky Mauch's theory, the word "treasure" touched off another gold rush. A stream of soldiers, explorers, adventurers and archaeologists headed for the site, whose name, after passing through many guises, received its modern form "Zimbabwe" from the hunter Frederick C. Selous.

In 1889, Cecil Rhodes organized a British company to settle the lands north of the Dutch-settled Transvaal and named the new country Rhodesia after himself. Armed settlers and company police poured in, at first peacefully. When the Africans saw they were losing their country, they fought. But all—war-like MaTabele and peaceful MaShona alike—were crushed.

At the height of the gold fever, a group of treasure hunters got a franchise from Dr. Leander Jameson, the adventurer associate of Rhodes, for an Ancient Ruins Company, with the exclusive right to prospect all the ruins in Rhodesia for gold. In the next few years, these scoundrels devastated forty-odd sites, especially Zimbabwe. They got a few thousand dollars' worth of gold, but they also removed ancient relics, confused the stratigraphy and contaminated the sites with modern objects like liquor bottles and broken umbrellas. The sites were not legally protected until 1902, when R. N. Hall was appointed curator of Zimbabwe.

Zimbabwe lies in the valley of the Mapudzi River. This is a broad, rolling valley broken by granite hillocks of many shapes. The countryside is typical African parkland, with loosely scattered groves and single trees. It has a moderate rainfall with dry winters (June to August) and wet summers. Animal life is much sparser now than it was in the days of Renders and Hall.

The ruins are on top of a steep-sided knoll, Zimbabwe Hill, and spread out over a quarter of a square mile south of this hill. The ruins consist of the so-called Acropolis atop the hill; an oval structure, the Temple or Elliptical Building, 600 yards south of the Acropolis; and about a dozen smaller structures, the Valley Ruins, north and east of the Elliptical Building.

The Elliptical Building consists of a massive, roughly elliptical wall, about 220 by 280 feet in diameter and 830 feet around. A few small walls lie outside the ellipse, and within it a number of smaller walls run hither and yon among platforms and towers. All these walls are of dry-wall masonry, made by piling up small blocks of granite laid in courses. The blocks were obtained with a minimum of shaping from nearby hillsides, where the granite had cracked off from boulders and ledges in layers like those of an onion. The builders used no mortar but plastered the lower parts of the walls with a sand-lime cement.

The walls have a pronounced batter—that is, a taper from bottom to top. They are neatly rounded at the ends, and drains at the base of the main wall let water out of the enclosure. All the walls have suffered from the ravages of time.

The outer wall is still in fairly good condition. Having lost a foot or two of the topmost courses, it is still 20 to 33 feet high. At its thickest, it is 15 feet wide at the bottom and 10 feet wide at the top. It has three main entrances. The wall is rounded off on each side of these entrances, and a kind of stile of stone steps passes through the entrance. Flanking each portal is a pair of cylindrical structures, often with ax grooves that once held some sort of gate.

The interior walls form several enclosures and long, labyrinthine passages. At the southeast side of the main enclosure stand (or stood) two conical stone towers. The larger is 30 feet high; it was five feet higher until Mauch, thinking there might be a crypt inside, climbed to the top and began throwing off stones until he convinced himself otherwise. The smaller cone, less than half as high, was pushed over by a tree growing beside it, so that only its stump remains.

The Acropolis is atop a 90-foot precipice on the south side of Zimbabwe Hill. It is a congeries of curving walls, which incorporate the many outcrops and boulders occurring naturally on top of the hill. Access is by several narrow, winding, easily defended passages. A cave below the walls of the Acropolis has strange acoustics. A man speaking naturally in the cave can clearly be heard in the Elliptical Building, a quarter-mile away, but nowhere else in the valley. Doubtless the native priests put this phenomenon to nefarious use.

The remaining Valley Ruins reproduce on a smaller scale the features of the two main buildings. Other smaller but similar ruins lie scattered about Rhodesia, Mozambique and Botswana.

The MaShona of the Zimbabwe area are rather slender, athletic people speaking one of the many Bantu tongues. Most of the early explorers found them polite, good workers and reasonably honest, but timid, having lost their courage from being raided and massacred by more warlike neighboring tribes.

If the unmarked stones of Zimbabwe could speak, they could tell us who piled them up and when and why; but they cannot. In the absence of written records, the history of black Africa is inevitably vague and sketchy before the coming of the whites.

Between 1000 B.C. and 1000 A.D., the Africans learned the arts of agriculture, cattle raising and iron working. These advances enabled them to spread out over a vast area at the expense of the Bushmanoid and Pygmy hunters. The Bantu—a linguistic subdivision of the Forest Negroes—are believed to have reached Rhodesia from the north some time after 500 A.D. By the time of this Bantu movement, the Arabs had already set up trading posts along the east coast of Africa as far south as Zanzibar. Some of these posts grew into thriving city-states, which fought viciously among themselves and could not even unite to resist the conquering Portuguese of the Age of Exploration. A mixed Arab-Negroid race grew up along the coast, speaking a kind of Basic Bantu with many Arabic words, which we know as Kiswahili or (less correctly) Swahili.

When the Portuguese reached Rhodesia around 1570, marching inland from the Arab cities they had conquered, they found Bantu miners mining gold, silver, copper, iron and tin. They also found the Monomotapa ruling a large and fairly orderly empire, with its capital at Zimbabwe, and trading gold, slaves and other exports with the Arabs.

In 1629, the Portuguese forced the Monomotapa to accept their "protection." His empire crumbled because the intensification of the slave trade disrupted mining and other normal activities, and more barbarous tribes then invaded the land.

Mauch's speculations about King Solomons' mines loosed a flood of theory about Zimbabwe. Dr. Carl Peters, the German explorer, thought Zimbabwe was the land of Punt, with which Egyptian monarchs traded.

J. T. Bent, who dug at Zimbabwe in 1891, thought the ruins had been built by Arabs, Phoenicians or some such Semitic people. R. N. Hall also thought the ruins were Arab. Others proposed the Dravidians of southern India or the Malays as the builders of Zimbabwe.

Zimbabwe had the bad luck to get involved in the 20th-century dispute over the differences among the races of man. Those who wanted to prove the Caucasoid or white race superior to the Negroid were eager to show that Zimbabwe had been built by whites—or at least not by blacks.

Later and more scientific excavations at Zimbabwe—those of David Randall-MacIver in 1905 and of Gertrude Caton-Thompson in 1929—showed that Zimbabwe was much more recent than the more romantic theories had assumed. They also indicated that the naked Bantu had built the structures after all. From the fragments of Chinese and Persian trade goods he found, Randall-MacIver thought that Zimbabwe had been built about the 15th century of the Christian Era. Miss Caton-Thompson put the date earlier, in the 9th or 10th century. She pointed out, moreover, that the ruins were not near any known gold deposit and so could hardly have been built as a gold-mining center.

Finally, a log used as a lintel over a drain in the Elliptical Building was tested in 1950 by the radio-carbon method and was found to have been put in place about the 7th century of the Christian Era. So, while Randall-MacIver gave the ruins much too late a date, they cannot possibly have had anything to do with King Solomon, because they were built at least 1,500 years after his time.

As the picture looks now, an early wave of the great black expansion reached Rhodesia from the north about the 6th or 7th century of the Christian Era. The invaders mixed with the native Bushmanoids and taught them their own early iron-age peasant culture (or vice versa, depending on whom you ask about it). Their descendants built Zimbabwe and similar centers. The Elliptical Building was probably a royal compound, divided into compartments for the king's cattle, women and servants, or a combination of compound and temple. The Valley Ruins were the compounds of subchiefs, and the Acropolis was a fortress.

Meanwhile, Asian traders—Arabs, Persians and perhaps Indians—were extending trading posts down the coasts. In time the Zimbabweans learned to mine gold to buy trade goods from these posts. Later waves of tribal migration submerged the original builders; Zimbabwe was probably abandoned, reoccupied and rebuilt several times. The last rebuilding may have been as late as the 18th century. In the 19th century it was abandoned for good, although the local tribes tried for a while to keep up the religious cult that had centered there.

Much more we cannot say. Although archaeology will probably

settle many doubtful points of African prehistory, the detailed history of Zimbabwe, lacking written records, is probably lost forever. As Miss Caton-Thompson wrote: "Zimbabwe is a mystery which lies in the still pulsating heart of native Africa."

CHAPTER XII

Was Swaziland a birthplace for modern man?

Recent discoveries in this remote South African region have revealed some surprising facts about its early inhabitants. Implements and bone fragments provide evidence of a history reaching back to the dawn of man. Adrian Boshier, of S. Africa's Museums of Science and Man, tells the story.

Bomvu Ridge is not the sort of place many anthropologists are willing to accept readily as a cradle of mankind. The mountain of red stone lies in the North Central highlands of Swaziland in Southern Africa. Swaziland is mysterious, remote, and the smallest (6,700 square miles) of African countries, in a part of the world not popularly associated with the image of a seed bed of *Homo Sapiens Sapiens*.

Even Professor Raymond Dart's discovery, in 1942, of a Swaziland child's grave, recently carbon dated to 46,000 B.C.—5,000 years earlier than prior evidence indicated the existence of modern man in more popular regions of Asia and East Africa—became a bone of anthropological controversy (the skeleton was "immature" and could be anything, detractors said). No less stormy was Dr. Dart's Australopithecus Africanus skull—a hominid between apes and man—extracted from South African digs in 1924. The fracas over that one, which became known as "The Missing Link," echoed through academic and theological halls until 1936 when Dr. Robert Broom found additional African Australopithecine remains, followed by the Leakeys' discoveries in East Africa, including a 2.6 million-year-old hominid skull.

In any case, it was not with any great expectation, beyond my own love for the challenge of field work, that I agreed to pay my first official visit to Swaziland in March, 1964. I'd been invited by the Anglo American Corporation of South Africa to take a look at some unusual artifacts turned up by their dozers on Bomvu Ridge. The mining concern had found that the red mountain contained some 48 million tons of high grade iron ore (haematite). My job was to make an archaeological survey before the mountain literally was leveled by giant earth movers.

From the Swaziland capital, Mbabane, I pounded 12 miles westward, over barely discernible tracks, in a borrowed lorry. Bomvu stood stark and barren on the highlands. Climbing the face of the ridge on foot, that first day, I was amazed to find the ridgetop covered with tens of thousands of stone implements. Many were typical tools of African Middle and later Stone Ages. There were many large crude rocks that didn't belong to the locality—dolorite stones that had been carried thousands of feet up the mountainside where they had been battered, flaked and then abandoned. I was amazed. What were they doing here?

On the second day the significance of these rocks became evident. Following a bulldozer cutting a new road, I noticed progress occasionally was faster because of irregular soft patches in the otherwise solid haematite. In the patches were thousands of crude artifacts. Examination of the spongy areas revealed they were diggings from which a bright red variety of haematite had been extracted. The workings had been refilled with soil, rubble and stone mining implements.

After plotting the locations of 10 of these ancient quarries, I visited two "caves" on the western side of the ridge. In small trenches were more thousands of stone mining tools, plus ochre-covered grindstones, pottery and polished stone bracelets—a bonanza of artifacts. Mine geologists determined that pockets of specularite, a sparkling black form of haematite, had existed in these places before removal during some ancient mining enterprise.

Then one of those weird things that seem to happen only in the African bush occurred. African miners suddenly dropped their tools and walked off the site. My investigation was halted. I reported this to the mining company and learned it was not an isolated case, but part of a mass walkout by the Swazis. Some sort of traditional belief was the cause. The mine manager suggested I investigate.

This led to two days of meetings with Chief Mpethambalo Shongwe of Motsane. He told me the history of the mine and the reasons his people were reluctant to work it. The mountain originally was called Emabomvini, or "where the red ochres are," and here the Swazis had always mined haematite, used as a cosmetic and an ore from which iron was smelted. Also, specularite was dug from the workings and used in rituals by chiefs and witchdoctors. This sparkling ore was known to them as Ludumane, or "the thunder four times."

The chief said the ridge was sacred to the Swazis, though it had been mined previously by the Basutos (People of the West) and even by others before that.

An old counsellor, a seasoned witchdoctor, described problems of mining on Bomvu Ridge. Inside the mountain lived one of the Swazi's greatest deities, a huge horned snake called Inyoka makhanda khanda or Ikanyamba. Without offerings to the reptile no work could be done. Even worse, no rain would fall, as only Ikanyamba—who lived in the mountain—could rise from the earth, lay atop the clouds and force them to release their water. Thus, the old man explained the tribe's quandary. They appreciated the economic benefits that Swaziland would gain from the mining, but couldn't reconcile this with the effects the enterprise would have on their gods.

By now the railway was almost completed, huge earth-moving machines were being erected and a great conveyor belt stretched from the base to the summit of Bomvu Ridge. The old man said, "Our mountain will be taken away and with it will go our spirits; no more rain will fall and the land will die."

I finally persuaded the miners to return to work by promising that a portion of the Red Ridge would be undisturbed so the gods would have a home. Today it is pledged to the people as a shrine and a national monument.

At this time I was assistant to Prof. Raymond Dart, who ordered me to drop other work and concentrate on the ancient mines. A full-time archaeologist, Peter Beaumont, was hired and with a team of Swazis he spent two years excavating in and around the early mines.

The results called for a complete reassessment of Southern Africa pre-history. Evidence of recent Bantu mining was found, with radio carbon dates of iron production going back 1,500 years. Also, the remains of many Stone Age fireplaces were discovered. Charcoal from various levels, using the Carbon 14 method, revealed ages of 9,000 to 43,250 years, the latter seven times older than the date previously ascribed to the start of mining anywhere.

These readings had been associated with Stone Age cultures when men mined the Bomvu Ridge haematites and specularites for cosmetics and pigments.

By 1968 we knew Bomvu Ridge was the world's earliest known mining site. There was skepticism of our claims, so in 1969 Beaumont and I excavated another specularite-haematite mine hundreds of miles to the west near Postmasburg. Again we recovered thousands of stone implements. But here human bones also were found—the remains of three miners killed in an accident 1,200 years earlier. They were Khoisians, a Bush-type akin to the present day Bushman of the Kalahari Desert.

Having established that the Bushmen and the Bantu-speaking blacks were the last haematite miners, we determined to identify the original Swaziland workers. Since there were no preserved bones in the acid soils of Bomvu, we picked the closest site containing bone. A deposit was 90 miles to the east in the Lebombo mountains. It was known as Border Cave because it lay across the Swaziland-Natal border.

This site had been investigated in 1934 by Dart and a team from the Johannesburg Medical School. They had uncovered Middle Stone Age artifacts similar to those at Bomvu Ridge. Six years later a prospector discovered pieces of a male adult skull while digging in the cave. In 1941-42 a team found an infant skeleton of morphologically modern type, lying in a shallow grave. It was in the upper levels of the Middle Stone Age stratum.

In 1970 Beaumont and I prepared an expedition to Border Cave. Volunteers had to be found, equipment obtained—and permits. But the Swazis were adamant. No digging. After long bickering, African Affairs agreed to allow me into the area alone to persuade the chief to reverse his negative decision.

I had stayed in the Border Cave area in 1956 and had caught snakes for their venom to earn a living. The natives had named me RraDinoga (Father of the Snakes) and later on I was initiated and accepted as—no less—a witchdoctor, about the highest honor that can be bestowed on a white man in that region. As a witchdoctor, I had status and respect among the tribes.

At the village of Ingwavuma, on top of the Lebombo mountains, I met the chief and his counselors, explaining my mission, and begged permission to start excavating. The elders said the spirits wouldn't allow it! This abruptly concluded the meeting. But during the next few days I visited headmen, witchdoctors and elders of the 35-man council.

Another meeting was arranged with the chief and an aristocratic spear-bearing Swazi dressed traditionally. All showed respect for this white-haired sage because he was the chief's uncle and had been acting chief. I knew he would be the deciding factor in our bid to explore. After heated argument, the old man inquired, "How could a man from across the sea know the things you know? It is," he said, "obviously a gift from the spirits."

I replied that most of my knowledge had been dug from the earth, described details of an archaeological excavation and my discoveries about past generations. I knew they couldn't resist the chance to learn about their forefathers. All pressed me for more details about our proposed "dig."

The chief's uncle explained the tribe's reluctance to allow us in the cave. Years ago, he said, Europeans had dug holes in the cave floor. At first the tribe didn't object, but after two visits severe droughts had withered the land. The people felt offended spirits resented the intrusion. Now more Europeans wanted to enter the cave, and again the spirits were holding back the rains. I had picked the worst time to make my plea. By late September the spring rains should have begun, but it was now December and still not a drop had fallen. Crops were destroyed and there were reports of cattle dying.

Finally I said, "You must try to appease the spirits by learning more about them." Luckily they agreed and I invited the chief, his counsellors and other tribesmen to join in the excavation, stressing that their cooperation would teach them the ways of their forefathers and earlier, unknown inhabitants of the area.

Seven days after our first meeting, the chief and his counsellors visited the magistrate's office and announced their decision to allow us to excavate. The magistrate then issued me a permit. I contacted Beaumont and the team in Johannesburg, and within three days they were at the site.

After first-day preliminaries—photographing, surveying, etc.—we decided to use the same grid-lines as the 1941-42 team had laid out. The second day we began digging—and promising clouds began piling up in the west. By noon it was completely overcast. An hour later down came the rains.

A native runner entered the cave that afternoon to say the chief was on his way to visit us. He came with his elders, all water-soaked. He said, "It is raining." I answered, "Just wait and see the rains that are still to come." This proved an accurate forecast, and the second wettest December in memory was recorded that year.

The chief was so pleased that he detailed women to carry water to the cave and ordered a headman to bring us fresh milk daily. As the rains continued, so did his favors. Soon we had laundry service twice a week, plus gifts of palm wine and fresh corn.

The site was fabulously rich. During 50 working days some 300,000 bones and stone artifacts were recovered. From an ash level above the child's grave found in 1942 we obtained charcoal. In late 1972 the testing laboratories reported the charcoal exceeded the limits of Carbon 14 dating. We knew then that the child had been buried long before 46,000 B.C.

Never has such an ancient site produced such perfectly preserved material. We found twigs, leaves, and grass probably used for bedding, and even feathers and insect wings at levels ranging from modern times to beyond 50,000 B.C. At a 35,000 year level we found notched bones, indicating that man was counting by that time. Arrowheads at levels greater than 46,000 B.C. showed that the bow had been used in that remote period. Animal hairs have been identified and we hope that human hair will be found—a discovery which would give us details about early man that have eluded modern research.

Future expeditions undoubtedly will provide further information. Even now we have proven that man's genesis was far earlier than previously supposed, and that his birthplace was in Africa, which apparently provided the perfect conditions for the development of *Homo Sapiens Sapiens*.

PART III

europe

You can go to New Zealand, or Rhodesia, or Angola, or the Netherlands Antilles, or almost any far-off place with even gossamer strands of its former colonialism woven through it, and fourth generation people from the "mother country" will talk about "going home" one day.

There's a fairly apparent reason for this. For anyone who has seen the monolithic Stone Age monuments of the British Isles, or the cave paintings of Spain, or stone implements from the Rhine valley and the Slavik countries, the meaning is clear. What's there, has been there for hundreds of generations. It is "home" for those backgrounded in it, no matter where the tides of time and fortune may have carried them adrift. And somehow the traces of "home" are in the genes, no matter how glamorous or generous the new land may be —or how tired and debilitated "home" may have grown.

But the "Old World" did not come by its title casually. What is most interesting about it, perhaps, is that its earliest days are no more clearly depicted in ancient record than are the settlements of more barbaric or primitive people. Much of the so-called civilization of Europe's "middle earth" has been lost in the miasma of undocumented oral tradition, of which few details remain. But throughout Europe the weathered remains of the works of ancient man still stand, lonely sentinels guarding the secrets of man's past. In recent years, these stones have begun to tell some stories. A few of the most interesting are recounted in the chapters that follow.

CHAPTER XIII

Are these the walls of Camelot?

In Southwest England archaeologists have found traces of an ancient fortress which some believe to be Camelot, home of King Arthur and his noble knights.

Is South Cadbury Hill, in Somerset, the site of King Arthur's legendary Camelot? Was Saint Swithin (the one who brings those wet spells) really buried outside the Cathedral at Winchester, so that "the sweet rain of heaven" would fall upon his grave? How did the Roman conquerors plan the elaborate gardens in the courtyard of their palace at Fishbourne in Sussex? What was the purpose, and the date, of the extraordinary 130-foot hill at Silbury, Wiltshire, the largest artificial mound in Europe? All over Britain, archaeologists have been digging to unravel these and other mysteries of the island's past.

The area around Cadbury Hill has been associated with the name of King Arthur ever since the 12th century monks of Glastonbury found themselves desperately short of funds to rebuild their Abbey after a fire. They needed publicity and public support—and by a piece of suspiciously good fortune, unearthed a "tomb" of King Arthur right there where they wanted it. Cadbury Hill, girdled by four impressive ramparts, lies only a dozen miles away. Quite soon after this monkish forgery, it was presumed to be the site of Arthur's palace.

The Camelot-Cadbury connection seems sketchy enough on the face of it. But there is no doubt that Arthur actually lived, 14 centuries ago, somewhere in this area of Southwest Britain—a British warrior chief whose armored cavalry had inherited Roman fighting methods, and who successfully held off the invading Saxons. The Camelot skeptics could be wrong. Even so eminent a historian as Hugh Trevor-Roper points out that "myth can be stronger than history,"—and people scoffed at Schliemann when he said he was going to discover the site of Troy.

Because of the Arthurian overtones, the excavations at Cadbury, sponsored by the British Sunday *Observer*, have had enormous news

All photos from Photo Trends

Glastonbury Abbey, north of the Salisbury plain in England, sits on foundations much older, which some people claim were Arthur's castle.

value. But, the intention in excavating the Iron Age hill fort is far broader than just looking for Arthurian traces. A microcosm of early British history, the site shows traces of occupation for some 4,000 years, from Stone Age up to medieval times, and was first heavily fortified in the Iron Age about 400 B.C. Diggers recently found that some of these walls, burned to the ground by Roman invaders, were rebuilt on a grander scale around 600 A.D.—Arthur's time.

Cadbury is an important site as much for methods as for discoveries—a testing ground for geophysical survey techniques which, already well-proved in oil prospecting, are comparatively new to archaeology. The 15-acre site was "prospected" by a team headed by Dr. Martin Aitken of the Oxford Research Laboratory for Archaeology, to see which areas would be most likely to yield results. They used a proton magnetometer, which records minute variations in the magnetic field of different types of soil; and a soil conductivity gradient detector, familiarly known as the Banjo, a sort of underground radar which measures differences in radio waves bounced off rock, disturbed soil, metal and so forth. With these machines, a couple of men could discover in a day as much as a team of diggers in six weeks.

The survey of the Cadbury site revealed large post-holes arranged

Ancient foundations shown in the foreground above date from Arthur's time. So do male and female skeletons, touted as Arthur and Guenivere.

in a circular pattern 45 feet in diameter, characteristic of the round houses of an Iron Age settlement. Much more remarkable was the one apparently square building—for a house or palace of Arthur's time would have been square. Could this be the palace of Camelot? Excitement mounted. Then came a violent storm, and on the sodden soil, the straight lines were shown to extend impossibly far—a medieval field boundary. Later, another pattern of lines emerged—a most peculiar shallow zig-zag trench. Scholarly brows were furrowed; appeals for informed guesses were sent to the public. Could anybody remember doing military service in these parts and being asked to dig a practice trench? Well—yes. So it was probably the khaki-clad Tommies of 1914 and not the armed knights of Camelot, who were, alas, responsible. Traces of a cruciform building were found, which the next summer's dig showed to be a very early Christian church—more likely 10th century than Arthurian.

The Cadbury dig yielded artifacts as well as outlines. A curious find by a gimlet-eyed 13-year-old volunteer was a bronze brooch of unmistakable Anglo-Saxon design. What was it doing in this headquarters of the Britons? It could have belonged to a captured Saxon maiden. Or it may date from the years of peace following Arthur's defeat of the Saxons, when fraternization and even intermarriage between the enemies may have taken place.

The most interesting finds of all were fragments of pottery wine jars, of a type which must have been imported all the way from the Eastern Mediterranean. These show that Cadbury was unquestionably the headquarters of a *very* important war lord and chieftain, at the time when the beleagured Britons were trying to beat off the invading Saxons. But was this Arthur's home? He *could* have been there. Learned skepticism abounds; nobody involved with the dig really wants to go further than that. Director Leslie Alcock and his team are satisfied with having established that South Cadbury was the largest hill fort in Britain in the 6th century A.D., and was heavily re-fortified in Arthur's time.

To the sorrow of legend-lovers, archaeology can destroy myths as well as reinforce them. Beside the medieval cathedral of Winchester, an Aglo-American team has been excavating the only Saxon cathedral which survived the Norman Conquest. A few years ago, Director Martin Biddle found England's earliest-known Saxon wall paintings, and made useful discoveries about the nature of Saxon architecture and liturgical ritual. More recently, the team hoped to throw some light on the legend of Winchester's native saint, Saint Swithin.

The tale goes that Saint Swithin, a humble fellow, asked not to be buried in the stately buildings of the cathedral, but in some lowly place outside in the rain, where the feet of pilgrims would tread. When the monks tried to disobey his orders and move his remains indoors on July 15th, 971, the deceased saint thwarted their plans by causing it to pour torrents for 40 days. And that, so they say, is why we still get wet when it rains on his day.

Well, until now, the site of Saint Swithin's burial certainly did appear to be out in the cold; but the new dig revealed that the plan of the Saxon cathedral at the time of his death would have embraced the shrine, proving that he was, after all, buried grandly inside without a drop falling on him.

Forty miles southeast of Winchester, at Fishbourne on the Sussex coast, the foundations of the largest Roman building in Britain have been unearthed after six years of patient research by Prof. Barry Cunliffe. Fishbourne was evidently a luxurious place, and contains the earliest mosaic floors in Britain. It measures some 500 feet by 500 feet, with four wings embracing a great central courtyard which had a magnificent formal garden.

Many of the garden's bedding trenches still contain a carefully prepared mixture of loam and crushed chalk, to counteract the acidity of the natural subsoil. In one part of the garden, climbing plants were apparently grown with their roots buried in kitchen refuse—a rose-growing method advocated by Pliny in 77 A.D.

Camelot, Winchester and Fishbourne are archaeological "big game" that have attracted most publicity. But smaller digs abound in Britain. Typical of the unspectacular, but scientifically useful, excavations was the dig at Blewburton Hill in Berkshire. This was already known to be the site of an Anglo-Saxon cemetery, but the object of the dig was to outline the shape and construction method of an Anglo-Saxon hill fort. It was also hoped to make a stratified pottery sequence of Iron Age pot-sherds. Whenever the archaeologists were getting on with seeking out revetments, skeletons kept turning up, and these had to be patiently scraped around and photographed, rather delaying the real work of the dig. One skeleton of a small child had a dagger apparently through its ribs. "Ritual murder?," asked a reporter. Scholars are not to be drawn on insufficient evidence. Director Denis Harding admitted it looked sinister, noted that the dagger was found "nearby" and proceeded with the unsensational study of revetments and post-holes. Just as the dig was scheduled to finish, the team made a rewarding discovery: a set of post-holes in the chalk ramparts showing that the fortifications had been timber-laced, the first of this type to be found in England.

Less likely Camelot contender is the crumbling abbey at Tintagel on the Cornish Coast. But it was a sprawling complex, as seen at right.

As is usual in an informal dig of this sort, local residents and unskilled volunteers flocked to the site to look around, to peer into trenches, to sit and wash and mark pottery pieces in the summer evenings. A small boy who'd been told by his volunteer parents, "Go off and play and don't be a nuisance to the scientists," returned 20 minutes later with a Roman coin he'd found on the spoil-heap, the first evidence of Roman occupation of this site. He was allowed to join the team.

Cadbury and Blewburton are natural hills which have been fortified by the addition of ramparts. Quite different is Silbury, an astonishing man-made mound some 130 feet high, with a base extending over five acres. A massive piece of civil engineering in any age, it lies only 20 miles from Stonehenge.

The mystery of Silbury has been baffling pre-historians for years. An attempt at tunneling in 1848 disclosed picks made from red deer antlers. These have just been carbon 14 dated by a New Jersey laboratory. They date from a thousand years later than the presumed time of the Silbury construction, hitherto thought to be around 1800 B.C. The dates just don't fit. And this is one of the things Prof. Richard Atkinson and a team from Cardiff University hoped to be able to clear up, in a three-year dig which British Broadcasting Corporation Television is sponsoring. So far, nothing really startling has come of it, though the project has aroused considerable interest.

An increasing number of Americans are taking part in British excavations. The Council for British Archaeology has appointed two agents who can give advance information about proposed fieldwork to help potential volunteers. They are Dr. Bernard Wailes, department of anthropology, University Museum, 33rd and Spruce Streets, Philadelphia, Pa. 19104; and E. Hunter Ross, 390 Morris Ave., New Jersey. The council also publishes a useful Calendar of Excavations which gives details about what accommodation is available, whether boys or girls are needed and whether financial help is offered. Though preference is usually given to experienced diggers, there is often scope for the unskilled volunteer who is prepared to muck in on some of the less glamorous tasks—washing pottery, pick-axing trenches or showing visitors around the site. Archaeology is thriving in Britain as never before.

CHAPTER XIV

Who built Britain's 600 stone circles—and why?

Still the most mysterious of England's antiquities, the stone circles that dot the British countryside continue to bewilder investigators as to their builders and purpose.

What have these in common: *Long Meg and Her Daughters, The Mourners, The Merry Maidens, The King's Men, The Wren's Egg, The Giants' Dance* and *The Devil's Quoits?*

They are all stone circles, those mysterious megalithic monuments which can be found all over the uplands of Britain. There are over 600 of them, ranging from the huge, impressive and complex constructions of Stonehenge and Avebury to rough, incomplete rings of stones lying half-lost in the heather in desolate moorlands. They are notoriously the least understood of all British antiquities, and no subject is more calculated to rouse archaeologists and prehistorians to heated controversy.

On one point the experts are agreed, though: these are a peculiarly British phenomenon, only a few examples—in northwest France—occurring outside the British Isles. [But circle fanciers can always take a look at the full-scale concrete replica of Stonehenge to be found in Klickitat County, Washington, U.S.A.].

When the poet Keats came upon a huge ring of weatherbeaten gray stones at Castlerigg in the English Lake District, he wrote soulfully of

"A dismal cirque
Of Druid stones upon a forlorn moor."

Keats was a good poet but a rotten archaeologist, and he couldn't have been more wrong about those Druids. They most certainly didn't build the circles. Then who did? Theories come and theories go, but the latest "answer" is that the circles were built for ceremonial purposes by the pastoral British tribes of the Neolithic and Bronze Age periods. Carbon 14 dating would place them between 2250 and 1000 B.C., whereas the Druids were Celtic priests of the Iron Age who flourished about 200 B.C., and didn't come on the scene until the stone circles had been standing for over a millenium. (Of course, they may have *used* the handy old ruins, but there is no evidence of this.) But somehow the Druid notion, invented by a handful of romantic authors, persists in the popular imagination. The myth is abetted by the odd ceremonies of a sect of present-day "Druids," complete with long white robes and bearded harpists. They gather at Stonehenge each midsummer sunrise, accompanied by folk dancers, policemen, TV cameras, reporters and a huge crowd of merrymaking modern Britons of the Plastic Age.

Apart from the Druid legend, there is no shortage of tales about how the circles came to be there . . . they were erected at dead of night by the fairies, the "Little People" of British folklore . . . the Stonehenge megaliths originated in Africa and were transported by giants to Ireland . . . the wizard Merlin obligingly lifted them from Southern Ireland and whisked them overseas to Salisbury Plain. More reasonable theories attribute the circles to Mycenean Greeks and the Bronze-Age Beaker Folk; but recent carbon dating has finally ruled these out in favor of native neolithic peoples.

Stone circles are scattered about all over the north and west of England, plus Wales, Scotland and Ireland—in other words, the stony parts of Britain where builders found materials close at hand. They are often located on lonely moorland and, in Scotland, on terraced hillsides. Usually isolated, they occasionally occur in groups of two, three or four. Their diameter ranges from eight feet to 360 feet, plus Avebury's very exceptional 1,000 feet. An "average" circle would be about 50 feet across. The height of the stones can be anything from a couple of inches to a dramatic 14 feet (some of the great stones at Avebury weigh 60 tons), and the number in the circle varies from a handful to 100. With some exceptions the stones are not "dressed," or shaped above ground, though there are indications that the builders used stone tools to shape the bases and help them stand upright.

The subject has attracted a number of enthusiasts who spend most of their spare time going round in circles. One of the most knowledgeable is Aubrey Burl, a lecturer at Hull College of Education. He has been studying circles for six years, and is writing a book about them.

Some stone circles in Britain are much bigger than Stonehenge, like the one at Avebury (top and center, opposite). Another smaller one (bottom) stands unpretentiously and unnoticed in a Welsh meadow.

Photos from Photo Trends

You can spend weeks poring over learned tomes about circles, henges and other megalithic monuments, and achieve nothing more than total confusion. For instance, many treatises refer to "stone circles" *inside* "henges". Aren't henges and circles the same thing? Most people—even in Britain—have harbored that misconception. Aubrey Burl will set you straight, promptly.

"A henge is an area of ground, roughly circular," he explains, "enclosed by a bank and inner ditch, with one or two entrances at gaps in the bank. Some of these henges have stone circles built inside them." He points out, however, that circles don't *have* to be built inside henge-type earthworks.

That's just one particular kind of stone circle. Actually, there are five main types—circles built inside henges, circles with avenues attached, circles with one or two large stones as outliers, circles with center stones, and the "recumbent stone circles" which have one stone lying flat.

These recumbent circles, found in northeast Scotland and southwest Ireland, are in many ways the most interesting of the lot. Often built on terraces on hillsides commanding wide views, they are characterized by two very tall monoliths, with a third large stone lying between them; the orientation of this gap is the southwest, the direction of the setting sun. The rest of the stones, which all stand upright, diminish in size around to the other side. The three large stones are unusual in that they are carefully shaped, and often have artificial "cup marks" made from pecking or pounding the surface. And unlike most of the other circles of Britain, they are almost invariably connected with burials.

Burl has his own theory: "I believe these circles were used for some function which included movements of the sun and the cult of the dead. At the circle called Loanhead of Daviot in Aberdeenshire, we can see the probable sequence of events. First, stones would be brought from a distance to the hillside terrace. Then they would be cut to shape, and cup marks chipped on the three main stones.

"They may have been sun emblems. When the stones were prepared, the circle was laid out in the general direction of the setting sun. A pyre would be lit near the center and bodies would be cremated; the ashes were then raked off, and a doughnut-shaped ring of stones called a Ring Cairn was built in the center. The ashes from the cremation would be deposited in the center space of the ring cairn. As to what other ceremonies went on in these circles, and the other types—who knows? But there certainly seem to have been connections with the sun."

Most controversial of all British circle buffs is Professor Alexander Thom, one-time Professor of Engineering Science at Oxford University. After 30 years spent on meticulous surveys of hundreds of circles and allied sites, Professor Thom is convinced that their true function involved sophisticated geometrical experiments by a people with advanced mathematical abilities. He feels his researches have proved the existence of an accurate unit of measurement valid all over Britain, which he has called the "Megalithic Yard," measuring 2.72 English feet.

Many of the so-called "circles," says Professor Thom, are not circles at all. Any fool can make a circle, just with a central stake-post and a piece of rope. But these geometrically minded people strove for years to perfect difficult ellipses, egg shapes and flattened circles, possibly because of an obsession with whole numbers. They wanted, perhaps, to make a near-circle where pi (the ratio between the circumference of a circle and its diameter) would equal a tidy integral three instead of the unsatisfying 3.141596 of a true circle. It looks as if they had made use of Pythagorean right-angled triangles over 1,000 years before the birth of Pythagoras.

Professor Thom goes even further and seeks to prove that Stone Age men were brilliant astronomers, and that the standing stones littered about the countryside were pointers for observing the movements of the sun and moon in order to create a calendar and predict eclipses. By successfully predicting eclipses, the astronomer priests could appear to be controlling events, thus enhancing their power.

Thom's measurements revealed several alignments corresponding with main events of the solar year. He postulates the existence of a stone-age calendar of 16 shorter months, one which would be synchronized throughout Britain, perhaps by means of beacons.

Not surprisingly, learned argument rages over Professor Thom's theories. Professor Richard Atkinson, who excavated at Stonehenge, and Dr. Glyn Daniel, leading expert in megalithic studies, feel that Thom should be taken seriously. But eminent archaeologist Jacquetta Hawkes sees Thom as a man "surrounded by loopholes, because he has so many points of observation and so many objectives." Many prehistorians are doubtful. Was stone-age man (who unlike the South

American Maya astronomer priests left no written records) really capable of such spectacular intellectual achievements? Thom says "The boys knew what they were doing."

Of the 600 stone circles in Britain, 43 percent have been excavated, but finds have not on the whole been dramatic or helpful. At Fernworthy, Dartmoor, the whole interior of the circle was found to be covered with charcoal, presumably scattered during a ceremony. At The Hurlers in Cornwall, the interior of one circle had been roughly paved. At the "Druid's Circle" at Penmaenmawr, North Wales, two children have been cremated. More agreeable, if of lesser archaeological interest, was the find at Stonehenge when a hot and thirsty excavator, in search of dating evidence lifted a fallen slab and found a bottle of vintage port generously laid down by an earlier investigator.

The curious names of the stones, "The Dancers," "The Hurlers," and so forth, are associated all over the country with legends that the stones are really merrymakers who have been magically turned to stone for the impious crime of having—or hurling—a ball on the Sabbath. It is thought that the early churchmen were worried about the continuing power of the ancient stones over the imaginations of the people, and may have fostered such alarming stories.

Fertility legends abound. The shapes of the stones in the great circle at Avebury are alternately a tall pillar and a broad lozenge, and it is suggested that these symbolize male and female. In the region of Callanish on the Scottish Isle of Lewis, there is a lingering belief that marriages consummated in the shelter of those towering stones will be exceptionally blessed, though in that wild northern clime, pneumonia seems a more likely result than fecundity. Locals will warn you that it is very important to walk around the Callanish circle "deasil" or sun-wise, and never in the unlucky or anticlockwise or Widdershins direction.

The stones at Callanish, like the Rollright Stones in Oxfordshire and many others, are reputed to be magically uncountable—the number varies whenever an attempt is made. Each stone of the "Grey Wethers," two circles on Dartmoor, is believed to revolve on its axis every morning at sunrise. There is some evidence that stone circles are still surreptitiously used today by witchcraft cults. At Sussons Common on Dartmoor, excavators opened a stone-lined grave in the center of the circle and found a coil of freshly cut human hair, pointing to contemporary black-magicky goings-on. The Rollright Stones in

Oxfordshire were, so they say, a group of soldiers turned to stone by a bad-tempered witch. Some years ago, a passerby observed a group of her descendants, a coven of naked ladies cavorting around the circle in dead of night.

Most visitors to Britain trek dutifully to Stonehenge, but many miss seeing the huge and haunting site at Avebury, only a megalith's throw away. Tourists who want to go circle-hunting should remember that the largest circles are not always the most impressive; it is worth seeking out small but perfect circles like the one at Blakeley Raise, Cumberland, or the Loupin' Stanes, Eskdalemuir, Dumfriesshire. Callanish on the Isle of Lewis in the Outer Hebrides is a magnificent circle which has been called the Scottish Stonehenge, and was well known to the ancient Greeks as "the winged temple of the Northern Isles." Although situated in one of the remotest corners of Britain, it can be reached via a two-hour flight from London. Its stones are laid out in the shape of a Celtic Cross, yet it was built 2,000 years before Christ. Intriguing groups of circles are those at Stanton Drew near Bath, Somerset, the Hurlers at Minions, Cornwall and Trecastle Mountain, Brecknockshire, Wales.

Just one thing when you're visiting circles, perching on stones, taking photographs, sighting the sunrise and measuring in megalithic yards—be circumspect and don't walk around them Widdershins, will you? You never know.

CHAPTER XIV

The stones of Wiltshire

Stonehenge today is a formidable tourist attraction. But crowds can't destroy the sense of mystery and wonder that hang over the ancient monument. It still hides many secrets.

When you enter Stonehenge for the first time it's bound to be a little disappointing. The thing is not quite as big as you had imagined, and it's jammed with tourists. Children chase one another wildly around the standing stones, and scamper over the fallen ones. Photographers bump into you while backing off to get the proper angle for a snapshot of mum and the kids in front of the sarsen trilithon. It's hard to get a feeling of antiquity under such conditions.

But if you stand around for a while looking at those stones, your feelings begin to change, and the spell of Stonehenge takes hold. You can forget all the people around, and the highway that runs just a few feet away. You begin to imagine yourself as one of the Neolithic beaker folk, the name archaeologists have given to the people who inhabited the chalk downs of Britain around 1500 B.C. when Stonehenge was being built. Then quite suddenly, the stones seem enormous!

How did people, equipped with only the simplest of tools, fashion and erect this monstrous edifice; more importantly why did they do it?

The feats are even more impressive and puzzling when you realize that Stonehenge is just one, although the most famous, of a group of prehistoric monuments in the same general area. Clearly, what is today the county of Wiltshire was, in prehistoric times, the center of a large, thriving, and as yet, little understood culture.

Next to Stonehenge, the most impressive of the Wiltshire monuments is the great stone circle at Avebury. In many ways it is even more impressive. Every visitor knows what Stonehenge looks like before he arrives, but lesser known Avebury comes as a surprise, even a shock.

You are driving along a quiet country road, when suddenly there is a huge stone shaped roughly like a diamond and standing on end stuck along the side of the road. A little farther along there is another, and another; a whole avenue of great stones. The road leads through a high bank of earth and inside there are more stones. At first no pattern can be determined.

The road takes you right into the little village of Avebury, and only after you park your car and walk around a bit, do you realize that the village is almost entirely surrounded by a double bank of earth and a circle of stones nearly a third of a mile across, with additional stones scattered inside the larger circle.

There is something freakish-looking about the Avebury stones. At Stonehenge the rock has been, in most cases, worked smooth. But at Avebury the stones are natural, except for their wildly unnatural placement. They look as though they had been stuck into the ground by some simple-minded giant. Sheep graze their way up and down the ancient earth banks, and have worn the base of some of the great stones smooth, scratching their woolly backs on them. Therein lies the real charm of Avebury—the contrast between the pastoral present and ancient times when, in the imagination at least, all manner of wild rites may have taken place inside the stone circle.

Another nice thing about Avebury is that you can have it almost all to yourself. As you walk the ridge along the top of the bank, you may meet one or two other visitors, but the place is so large you hardly notice them.

If you really want to be alone with something ancient, go a short distance from Avebury to the West Kennet Long Barrow. After you park your car you have to walk a long distance on a narrow path, enclosed on both sides by barbed wire. The path from the road to the Long Barrow runs right through a cultivated field, and you are not quite sure whether the barbed wire is meant to keep the cows off the path or the people out of the field.

The barrow is a chambered tomb; the largest in England. The mound, measuring 350 feet in length, is made up of chalk rubble dug from a ditch on either side and piled over a chamber of boulders collected from the surrounding area. The front of the mound has a facade of large upright stones. There is no doubt that the barrow was used as a tomb. Some 30 skeletons have been removed from it. The Long Barrow dates from about 2000 B.C., making it one of the earliest large monuments in the area. Archaeologists think it was used and re-used for 300 years.

Photos from Photo Trends

Despite the hordes of tourists pouring through it daily, Stonehenge still retains an air of mystery and wonder. Who built it? What was it used for?

From the Long Barrow you can get a good look at one of the latest of the prehistoric monuments of the area, built somewhere around 1400 B.C. This is Silbury Hill, the largest artificial mound in Europe. The mound is conical in shape and is some 135 feet high. The base covers five-and-a-half acres. It consists of chalk rubble excavated from a huge ditch at the base. Today the ditch is silted up.

The purpose of Silbury Hill remains a mystery. In 1777 a shaft was sunk from the top to the undisturbed chalk in the middle of the mound. Later, a tunnel was burrowed in to meet the shaft. In neither case were any significant artifacts found. Says R.J.C. Atkinson, professor of archaeology, University College, Cardiff, "It should perhaps be regarded as the largest of all round barrows, and it may be roughly of the same date as the stones of Stonehenge. All that we can be certain of is that it is earlier than the Roman road from Bath to Marlborough, which is aligned on the mound but swerves to avoid its base."

About two miles northeast of Stonehenge the early peoples of Britain built another circular monument, similar in shape to Stonehenge, although much smaller. Here, however, the builders used wood, and all obvious traces of this "Woodhenge" had decayed centuries ago. It was rediscovered by aerial photographs, and excavated in 1928. Excavators found the familiar bank and ditch, although here the boundary had been almost completely flattened by ploughing. There were six concentric rings of circular holes for wooden posts and, in some cases, the rotted stumps of the posts still survived below ground. Prof. Atkinson states, "Since nothing survived above ground, we can only guess what the remains represent. The most sensible explanation is that the posts formed the upright framework of a roofed building, like a huge barn bent round upon itself into a circle, leaving a space open to the sky in the center."

Today the sites of the original posts are marked by concrete blocks.

The Stonehenge-Avebury area is littered with barrows of various shapes and sizes and other types of prehistoric earthwork. The monuments of Wiltshire are among the largest and finest prehistoric engineering works in the world. However, we know virtually nothing about how they were built. But the scholars have been able to make some good educated guesses.

Prof. Atkinson says, "The earthworks, large and small, all seem to have been built with the simplest tools. The chalk was loosened with 'picks' made from the antlers of red deer, many of which have been found abandoned at the bottoms of ditches." The broken chalk would be raked up with rakes made from antlers, and put in baskets with shovels made from the shoulder blades of oxen.

Modern experiments with copies of ancient tools have shown that two men, working in turns, can dig about four cubic yards of chalk a day. On the basis of this experiment the archaeologists figured it would take 200 men nine years to build the earthworks around Avebury. The pile of Silbury Hill would contain nearly 50 million 30-pound baskets of chalk.

Of all the building feats, however, Stonehenge represents the most sophisticated accomplishment. Some of the stones were quarried in Wales, and transported 240 miles, probably most of the way by water. The largest of the stones did not come from so great a distance, but they still had to be hauled overland for some 20 miles. Prof. Atkinson estimates that moving these great stones with crude ropes and rollers may have occupied a thousand men for several years.

Raising the stones, and particularly the lintels that cap the huge

Possible key to the puzzle of Stonehenge is the "Heel Stone", visible through the huge stone columns. It aligns with sun and moon positions.

uprights, must have been accomplished by simple but painstaking methods, involving of man hours and human muscle power.

The most intriguing question remains; why were the monuments built? The barrows, as noted, were graves; it has even been speculated that Silbury Hill might be a gigantic barrow for a powerful chieftain.

Some of the earthworks probably represent paths or processional ways; others the sites of camps of one sort or another. At a place called Windmill Hill, about half a mile northwest of Avebury, there is an earthwork enclosure (now barely visible, but its remains have been traced archaeologically) called the "Causewayed Camp". No permanent settlements were found inside the enclosure, but traces of campfires, broken pottery and other signs of human habitation are common just outside the earth bank. This has led archaeologists to believe that the "Causewayed Camp" was used as a cattle enclosure, into which the stock was herded in autumn. The herdsmen sat outside.

It is the stone circles, however, that really excite the imagination.

Practically everyone agrees that Stonehenge was some sort of temple. The reason for such wide agreement is that everyone felt the structure had no discernible practical use, and therefore must have been dedicated to the gods.

In the last few years, however, the American astronomer Gerald H. Hawkins has advanced a theory that Stonehenge had a very practical earthly use. With the aid of a computer Hawkins found that all the important stones in the monument align with at least one other to point to some extreme position of the sun and moon. Hawkins also postulated that a group of 56 mysterious holes that lie within the monument may actually have been used as an "eclipse predictor." All in all, Hawkins found, Stonehenge was a sophisticated and brilliantly conceived astronomical observatory, used by different people over a 400 year period beginning 1900 B.C.

Hawkins was not the first to suggest the astronomical alignments at Stonehenge. For years a little cult called the Druids (their relationship to the Druidic priests of pre-Roman Britain is doubtless fictional) have been trooping to Stonehenge to celebrate the sunrise on Midsummer Day, the longest day of the year. On that day the sun rises fairly near the Heel Stone, a large rough stone which stands at the entrance of the avenue leading into Stonehenge. The people who built Stonehenge may have been sun worshippers, and some sort of Midsummer Day ritual may have been conducted there. But this cannot be proved for certain. Hawkins himself warns of "the dangers of overspeculation" and playing "the numbers game." "There are a great many numbers and alignments at Stonehenge and numbers and lines never cease to fascinate peole."

A final Stonehenge mystery was discovered in 1953. Carvings of what appear to be bronze ax heads and a bronze dagger were found on one of the stones. The axheads resemble a type made in Ireland around the time Stonehenge was being built. But, says Prof. Atkinson, "the best match for the dagger comes from the Shaft Graves of Mycenae in southern Greece, the legendary home of Agamemnon."

According to Prof. Atkinson, connections between prehistoric Britain and the civilized Mediterranean world had already been suspected, but this discovery provided "dramatic confirmation."

Many mysteries about Stonehenge and the other monuments of Wiltshire remain. This much, however, is certain: the prehistoric people who built them were no mere club-wielding savages. They were a well organized, technically sophisticated, perhaps cosmopolitan society.

CHAPTER XV

Is this Atlantis?

A gigantic explosion of Santorini volcano may have wrecked the strange Minoan civilization by sinking the island of Thera, providing Plato with the inspiration for the legend of a lost continent.

They have found Atlantis—again.

The famed "lost continent", which was populated by a near perfect race and destroyed "in a single day and night of misfortune" has been "located" many times.

The story of Atlantis was first told by Plato in about 355 B.C. He claimed that he got it from a relative who had heard it from his grandfather, who heard it from his father, who got it from the Athenian leader Solon, who had heard it from an Egyptian priest. According to the Egyptian, Atlantis had existed nine thousand years before Plato's time. This sort of hand-me-down evidence is not very convincing, and Plato was not a historian. The information about Atlantis is contained in two philosophical dialogues, *Timaios* and *Kritias*. In such works Plato often invented allegorical events to make a philosophical point. Most people have regarded Atlantis as just such a fable, for aside from Plato's dialogues there is no other source of information on Atlantis in ancient literature.

Over the centuries, however, a number of people have become convinced that there was a real Atlantis. Thousands of books, theories and articles have been produced on the subject, most of them by a wild assortment of crackpots. But during the last few years a group of respected scientists and scholars have announced discoveries which they believe cast new light on the ancient mystery of Atlantis.

Some 3,500 years ago, there was a tremendous volcanic explosion in the Aegean Sea. At the time the area was ruled by a people known as the Minoans, a great seafaring nation centered on the island of Crete. We have known about the existence of Minoan civilization for a long time. The Minoans were a highly advanced people, but their history, particularly the reasons for their sudden downfall remains

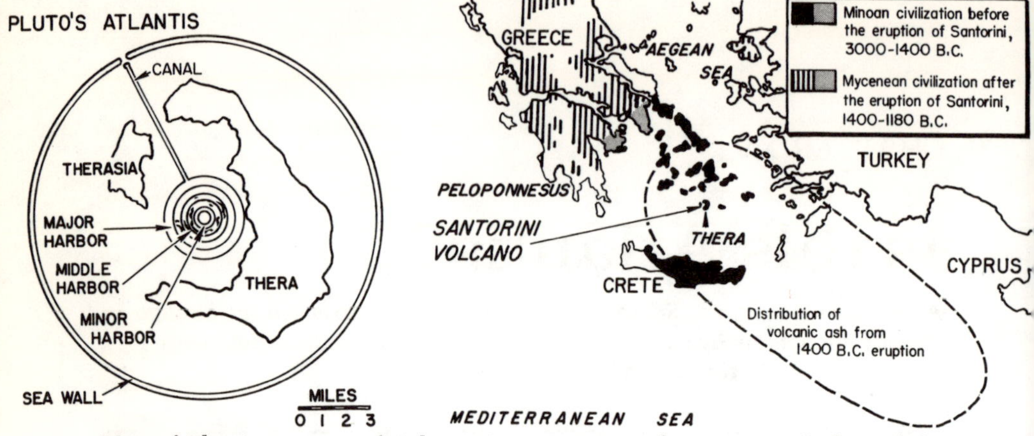

Map of Plato's concept of Atlantis is superimposed on a map of Thera, left. Explosion of Santorini affected Minoan civilization as shown in map at right.

shadowy.

What does all this have to do with Atlantis? A group of islands near Crete look as though they had been drastically altered by an explosion of the volcano Santorini. Early in the 1960s a Greek seismologist, Angelos Galanopoulos, began advancing the idea that a buried Minoan city on Thera, one of the islands, might have provided Plato with the inspiration for Atlantis.

Since then scientists from many countries have investigated Thera, a good part of which is now sunk beneath the waters of the Aegean, and decided that Prof. Galanopoulos may be right.

What they have discovered is that ancient Thera contained at least one wealthy Minoan settlement that was destroyed in the eruption.

Plato described Atlantis as a sea power where "consecrated bulls roamed at large". The Minoans did possess a great navy and bulls figured important in their religion.

Thera and the other islands of the Aegean group are part of a gigantic submerged volcanic crater. Plato describes the city of Atlantis as a fortified hill protected by alternate rings of land and water. Plato also mentions that the center area had hot springs. All this sounds rather like a fanciful description of what Thera may have been like before the catastrophe.

Dr. Galanopoulos has cleverly fitted another piece of Plato's story to Thera. Plato said the destruction of Atlantis came 9,000 years before his time and that the land was a continent hundreds of miles square, bigger than North Africa. Dr. Galanopoulos says that Plato made an error and multiplied both of these figures by 10, thus giving the impression that the relatively recent and small Minoan island civilization had been a great continent of incredible antiquity.

The destruction of Thera was not as bad as the sinking of a whole continent—but it was bad enough. Oceanographers have found ash deposits from the explosion over a wide area of the Aegean. Dr. Bruce C. Heezen, an American oceanographer who has studied the problem, believes that the Santorini explosion was similar in type to the 1883 explosion of Krakatoa, but far greater in magnitude. The Krakatoa eruption destroyed several small islands, generated tidal waves that swept around the world, killed more than 36,000 people, and released enough volcanic ash in the atmosphere to color the world's sunsets unusually red for an entire year.

Dr. Heezen thinks that the ash deposits laid down in the Aegean 3,500 years ago were so thick that they ruined Minoan agriculture, and brought the civilization to its abrupt and mysterious end, in around 1400 B.C. (However, some scholars recently have severely questioned the idea that Minoan civilization was destroyed in 1400 B.C.)

The discovery on Thera is a great one. Reporting on recent excavations at Thera, Boston University called the site "the first intact Minoan town ever discovered". Atlantis or not, this makes the discovery one of the most important archaeological finds of the century An underground museum is planned to give visitors a look at ancient Minoan life without disrupting modern life on the island.

The Minoan town covered about half a square mile by present calculations. Most of the residents dwelt in small close packed two and three story houses, although one much bigger abode, perhaps the villa of a nobleman has been uncovered.

The best thing that can happen to a city, from an archaeological point of view, is that it be completely buried by a convenient volcano. This is what happened to the Roman towns of Pompeii and Herculaneum, and why they are wonderful archaeological sites.

The volcanic ash at Thera preserved painted frescos and wooden objects that would have been lost forever if the city had been allowed to fall into natural decay. Huge pottery jars for the storage of oil and wine were dug unbroken, out of the ash. Under other circumstances they would have been smashed to fragments.

At Pompeii and Herculaneum, the eruption of Vesuvius was sudden, (people had some warnings of the impending disaster, but ignored them). A good portion of the population was buried in the ash fall.

Perfect casts of bodies caught in their final agony are among the grisliest and most compelling sights in Pompeii. No such disaster befell the people of Thera. Excavations have so far uncovered only two human bodies, although there are remains of domestic animals.

Also missing from Thera are gold and other precious objects. Apparently the volcano gave plenty of warning before it finally blew apart, one expert estimated the rumblings may have gone on for as long as fifty years. The residents of Thera were wise enough to heed the signs and depart.

So vast was the destruction that James W. Mavor Jr. of the Woods Hole Oceanographic Institute believes that several Minoan sites may have been buried.

Undoubtedly our knowledge of Minoan culture will be increased dramatically within the next few years. But all this still does not answer the intriguing question: Have we really found Atlantis?

If Plato multiplied both the size and age of the Minoan cities by 10, he committed a pretty major error. Even allowing for a systematic mistake of such magnitude, how did Plato confuse cities in the nearby Aegean with a place in the distant Atlantic? He was quite definite about the location of Atlantis, even adding that the sinking caused such a violent upheaval that for a time passage through the "Pillars of Hercules" (Straits of Gibraltar) was blocked. There are other details about Atlantis which do not agree with what we know of the destruction of Thera or of Minoan life.

It was not the historical or geographical details that were important to Plato. Primarily he was concerned with writing a moral fable. His Atlanteans were a noble race living under a perfect government. But they fell into moral decline, and came into conflict with the ancient Athenians, Plato's own ancestors. The Atlanteans had sunk so low that the gods decided to punish them. In one of the dialogues Plato briefly describes the destruction of Atlantis. In another he has a more extensive discussion of Atlantis which ends with the decision of Zeus to punish the now evil Atlanteans. Zeus calls the other gods together to discuss the punishment. ". . . and when he had assembled them, he spoke thus: . . ." The dialogue ends in mid-sentence.

The discovery of the buried Minoan cities may finish the unfinished story of Atlantis. On the other hand, many previous claims for the site of Atlantis have been made. Perahps the story of Atlantis will always remain the way Plato left it—unfinished.

CHAPTER XVII

Enigma of the lost Etruscans

The Romans regarded the Etruscans as possessors of occult knowledge. In modern times they have been regarded as just plain mysterious. Using modern techniques archaeologists are now rediscovering this lost civilization.

Some years ago archaeologists were digging at the Italian coastal town of Porto Clementino 62 miles north of Rome. Underneath Porto Clementino they found the ruins of a town built in Roman times. From ancient documents the archaeologists knew that they had found Gravisca, but it wasn't the Roman town that the archaeologists were after. Aerial photographs indicated that a city far older and far larger than Gravisca once occupied the site. The photos showed the buried traces of a vast network of roads and walls. Preliminary excavations have turned up hundreds of objects that were very clearly made by the Etruscans. The finds confirmed what the archaeologists had already strongly suspected, that under the unimportant Roman city was an important Etruscan city.

Archaeologists hope that excavations in the years to come will help clear up some of the puzzles concerning these genuinely mysterious people. Because of a series of unfortunate circumstances the Etruscans got lost in the historical shuffle. Today over two millenia after they began to disappear we are again trying to figure out who they were.

During the fifth and sixth centuries B.C., the Etruscans controlled much of the Italian peninsula. Their central power lay in the area now called Tuscany. The Greeks made some written references to the Etruscans, but these were mostly brief and unenlightening, if not downright contradictory. One Greek recorded that the Etruscans migrated to Italy from a distant land while another said they were natives of Italy. This sort of information isn't very helpful.

The Romans knew the Etruscans better than the Greeks did. The Etruscans were the chief rivals of Rome for power in Italy. At first the Etruscans had the upper hand, but they could never organize properly. Ultimately the well-disciplined Romans picked off their cities one by one. Etruscan power in Italy was completely broken by 200 B.C., but the Etruscans themselves did not disappear. During the first centuries of the Christian era there were still lots of Etruscans.

The Etruscans had been powerful, wealthy and luxury loving. The early Romans, who were quite austere, were shocked by Etruscan morals. The paintings in Etruscan tombs, which tell us most of the little we know about Etruscan life and religion display a striking contrast of vibrant sensuality combined with a gloomy and often violent view of the life after death.

After they were no longer a danger to Rome the Romans began to regard the Etruscans very highly. Many of the noblest Roman families contended that they had "Etruscan blood in their veins." They were thought of as an ancient and very wise people who possessed much magical and occult knowledge. Etruscans were commonly employed as oracles and seers, and the word Etruscan became almost a synonym for magician.

But the Etruscans were gradually losing their identity and being absorbed into the general mass of Latin people. The emperor Claudius who reigned from A.D. 41 to A.D. 54 realized that if something were not done quickly most knowledge of things Etruscan would vanish without a trace. Claudius, who was a scholar (and not the idiot that historians often say he was) personally prepared a history of the Etruscans and a dictionary of their language. Both of these works have, unfortunately, been lost. So we are forced to rely upon archaeology to fill in the details about the Etruscans, and the archaeologist's task has not been an easy one.

The first great stumbling block is that while the Etruscans had a written language of their own, we cannot read it. Most of the languages in the western world from the Sanskrit of ancient Indian to modern English belong to a family of languages called Indo-European. All these languages have a common origin and certain similarities. When scholars are confronted with an unknown language of the Indo-European family they usually can decipher it. They know, in a general way, how Indo-European languages are constructed.

Etruscan was one of the few languages used extensively in Europe that was not of the Indo-European family. In fact, as far as anyone can determine, the Etruscan language bears no relationship to any other language anywhere on earth. Repeated frustrating and unsuccessful attempts have been made to understand the language.

Photos from Metropolitan Museum of Art

Stone domes of Etruscan tombs, above left, are usually covered with centuries of earth. At right is a cleared interior of a plundered tomb. Below is an Etruscan chariot of wood, sheathed in bronze.

Nor is it likely that there will be any breakthroughs in attempts to read Etruscan without some startling new archaeological discoveries. Scholars can decipher unknown languages if they have enough samples to work with. But they are not getting anywhere with Etruscan because there are very few examples of it. The Etruscans were a highly cultured people and they almost certainly had an extensive literature but none of it has survived, or at least none of it has been found.

The ancient peoples of Mesopotamia wrote on clay tablets which are practically immortal, and a large number of their documents have survived. The Egyptians wrote on perishable papyrus, but the dry climate of Egypt preserved millions of papyrus rolls. The Etruscans must have used a perishable material and the climate of Italy was unsuitable for preservation. While the Mesopotamians and the Egyptians flourished thousands of years more distant from our own time than the Etruscans, we still know more about them.

Most of the samples of Etruscan script that we have are from hundreds of surviving tomb inscriptions. Most of these are very short, usually not more than a word or two. If they could be read they would doubtless turn out to be the name of the tomb's owner, and that wouldn't tell us much. There are only nine or ten longer inscriptions of 30 words or more in existence and that is not very much for the scholars to work with.

Where did the Etruscans and their strange language come from in the first place? Those ancient documents which hold that the Etruscans came to Italy from someplace else indicate that their original homeland was Lydia, an ancient name for part of Asia Minor. Most modern scholars tend to agree that since the Etruscan language is so utterly unlike anything found elsewhere in Europe it probably did come from Asia Minor. The finding of the Etruscan port city at Porto Clementino strengthens the theory that they were not native to Italy. It indicates they were a seafaring people whose original power seems to have been concentrated in trading cities along the coast. Only gradually did they extend their influence inland.

The sites of a number of important Etruscan cities are well known. But in the past they have not yielded too much. The Etruscans built most of their houses of wood, and these have decayed completely through the centuries. But they buried their dead in fairly elaborate stone tombs, and there are plenty of these scattered throughout Italy.

Robbing Etruscans tombs has been a major industry in parts of

Tuscany. This brings up another and rather ironic reason why the Etruscans have been "lost" in history. They have been too popular for their own good. In the early years of the 19th century Etruscan antiquities began appearing on the market in increasing numbers. People were enchanted and soon almost obsessed by the strange and beautiful Etruscan art. As a result a virtual *Etruscomania* broke out among museum curators and private collectors. Anything Etruscan would bring fabulous prices on the open market. No one was going to be too scrupulous about inquiring how the objects had been obtained. This sort of wide open market encouraged Italy's numerous tomb robbers who needed little encouragement anyway.

Etruscans were buried in huge cemeteries, virtual cities of the dead. The typical Etruscan tomb consisted of an underground chamber topped by a domed roof which projected slightly above the ground.

The inside of the tomb chamber was often decorated with brightly painted murals of Etruscan life and Etruscan visions of the life to come. The body of the dead Etruscan was placed in a stone sarcophagus. A typical sarcophagus was decorated with an image of the dead man with his head propped up on one hand, in a casual manner. These sculptures were lifelike and often rather humorous. The tomb chamber was then filled with all of those objects that were deemed necessary for life after death. In the case of a wealthy man (and there were many) the tomb might contain a considerable fortune in precious metals, jewels and art objects. The objects from the unplundered tomb of a single Etruscan couple fill an entire hall of the Vatican Museum. But of the thousands upon thousands of Etruscan tombs in Italy more than 99 percent have been throughly plundered in ancient or modern times.

The pieces from the tombs turned up in dealer's shops and ultimately in museums and private collections. Much of the exquisite Etruscan gold work was melted down for quick sale. Even an undamaged object torn from the surroundings in which it was found loses much of its value to the archaeologist. So the flood of stolen Etruscan antiquities increased the world's admiration of Etruscan art, but did little to increase our knowledge of their history and origins.

Since Etruscan objects usually turned up without any pedigree a thriving market in Etruscan forgeries quickly developed. Probably the most famous suspected fakes of modern times were the huge "Etruscan" warriors and horses that were the prized possession of the Metropolitan Museum of Art in New York City from 1933 until serious doubt was cast on their genuineness in 1961.

The Met paid $40,000 for one of the Etruscan pieces. This was a fairly low price, because some doubts about the authenticity of the statues had already been raised. The clay of Etruscan statues usually had bits of glass-like quartz scattered throughout it. Critics of the statues contended that the clay of these statues had been doctored with ground up beer bottles that were supposed to resemble quartz. As it turned out the quartz was real but the statues were still dubious.

Etruscans often made statues in which the figures were thin and elongated. One of the Met's Etruscan pieces followed this style. But the second and more impressive of the two was a warrior with a muscular and stocky build. Critics explain that probably the forgers were constructing their second fake in a rented room with a low ceiling. They originally planned to make it as elongated as the first, but when they got to the waist they realized that they would not have the room to make it as tall as they had planned. So they squashed down the upper part of the body in order to make it fit. At least that's what some experts claim.

Wall paintings of Etruscan tombs provide a wealth of information about Etruscan life and beliefs. Murals can neither be stolen nor faked. But the paintings could become innocent victims of the robbers. Once a tomb was opened the delicate paintings were exposed to the air which caused them to flake away and disappear in a few years. This after they had survived almost intact for thousands of years. Even if all possible care was taken the paintings often did not last long after a tomb was opened. In 1831 in the necropolis at Corneto, a large and lofty Etruscan tomb was opened. It was dubbed the "Tomb of the Boar Hunt" because one of the painted scenes showed an ancient boar hunt.

At the time of its discovery the colors of the wall paintings in this tomb were still reasonably fresh. In 1840, just nine years after the tomb had been opened it was visited by George Dennis, a British consul in Italy. Dennis wrote, "A descent of about 20 steps, hewn in ancient times from the solid rock, leads to the entrance of the tomb which is closed by a modern door. This opens into a spacious chamber. The first impression is one of disappointment. The chamber is in the form of an Etruscan tomb—but where are the paintings?"

Only after some time was Dennis able to perceive the dim ghosts of the paintings still on the walls. He predicted, correctly, that the murals would soon vanish.

For much of the 19th and well into the 20th century the old Etruscan region was remote and sparsely populated. Wandering among Etruscan ruins and digging up a tomb or two became popular pastime for wealthy and romantically inclined Europeans. Though a large number of books about the Etruscans resulted from these sojourns, they added little to our knowledge.

A new era in Etruscan studies opened after World War II. The RAF had taken extensive aerial photographs of Italy including the old Etruscan regions. Among the RAF photographic interpretation experts was an officer named John Bradford who had done some archaeology before the war. While studying the aerial photos taken for military purposes he realized that they could be of immense value to archaeologists. Long-buried ruins of cities, fortresses, burial mounds and the like are revealed from the air by ground patterns undiscernible on the surface.

To everyone's surprise the photos revealed that even well explored cemeteries contained hundreds of tombs that no one had ever known about. This prompted more intensive ground examinations of the cemeteries. Another surprise awaited the archaeologists. There were even more undiscovered tombs than the aerial photos had indicated.

It was almost too much of a good thing and the new discoveries presented the archaeologists of Italy with a problem. Excavating a tomb, even if you know where it is (and it is far from easy to locate a spot in an aerial photo on the ground) is both time consuming and expensive. Funds for archaeology are always extremely limited. Would the expense in time and money be justified in digging up the newly discovered tombs? Past experience indicated that the vast bulk of these tombs would be completely plundered and useless. There were plenty of empty Etruscan tombs to look at and there was no particular reason to dig up any more.

Yet not all the tombs might be empty. Even in some tombs that had been plundered the robbers left behind objects that archaeologists found valuable. Tombs with wall paintings, even if they were otherwise empty, were well worth digging up. Finally there was the chance of discovering a completely unplundered tomb.

It was C. M. Lerici, a wealthy Italian industrialist and mining engineer, who took some of the guess work out of the excavations. Lerici and his staff designed a sort of modified mine detector. Using an aerial photo as a guide the archaeologists could then use the detector to find the precise location, as well as the depth and dimension of the tomb.

Step two involved the use of a small electrically powered mining drill to sink a shaft through the earth and into the underground chamber. The third step in the Lerici process was the unique and crucial one. A miniature camera and photoflash were inserted in the tube and lowered down the shaft into a tomb. Photos could then be taken of the inside of a closed tomb to see if anything in the interior justified the expense of excavation.

One set of photos revealed writing on the tomb walls. Nothing like it had ever been encountered before. But, alas it was not an Etruscan inscription for the words were in modern Italian. Robbers had entered the tomb, and not content with merely stealing what was inside they scribbled their names all over the wall. Then they filled in the hole they had dug, so no one would know the tomb had been plundered.

A later refinement of the Lerici process involved the use of a television camera so the archaeologists would not have to wait for photos to be developed. The interior of an Etruscan tomb was even shown live on Italian television.

At one cemetery alone some 50 new painted tombs were discovered in ten years. That was more than had been found in over a century of previous archaeological exploration. And now aerial photography has located an unknown Etruscan city.

Once the field of Etruscan archaeology seemed at a complete dead end. The puzzles surrounding these mysterious people appeared doomed to remain unsolved forever. Now modern science has given Etruscan studies a new lease on life. Today, next week, or next year a find might provide the key that will unlock the mystery of the Etruscan language and origins.

CHAPTER XVIII

Saint Peter's bones—are they or aren't they?

Pope Paul accepted Vatican archaeologists' theories that St. Peter's remains have been found deep beneath the floor of the great cathedral. Other experts aren't so sure.

Are a box of bones without a skull, a jumble of faint inscriptions and a buried shrine important clues in the solution of an ancient archaeological mystery? Or are they unrelated facts juxtaposed to prove a theory?

Early in 1968, Pope Paul VI declared that bones unearthed in an area below St. Peter's Basilica in the Vatican had been identified to his satisfaction as the bones of St. Peter, first Pope of the Roman Catholic Church, who died in either 64 or 67 A.D. The evidence was provided by a team of archaeological experts who had analyzed the grave site and the artifacts it contained.

The most important evidence was provided by Dr. Venerando Correnti, a University of Rome anthropologist, who identified a box of bones found below the basilica as those of a robust man about 5 feet, 4 inches tall, and from 60 to 70 years of age. Only about 60 percent of the skeleton was found and the skull was missing. But the description of the remaining bones tallies with what little is known about Peter.

The bones came from a site near a small monument uncovered earlier in the excavations and identified as St. Peter's tomb in 1950. On a wall near the shrine are a number of faintly scratched inscriptions—"graffiti"—that overlap each other and are written, for the most part, in a kind of code. The name "Peter" would appear to be conspicuously missing from the wall in fully spelled out clarity.

However, Professor Margherita Guarducci of Rome University, who is an expert at reading ancient Roman and Greek inscriptions, believes that the graffiti scratched on the wall near the bones *does* include the name of Peter "dozens of times," either abbreviated or symbolized. She translates one inscription as "Peter is buried within."

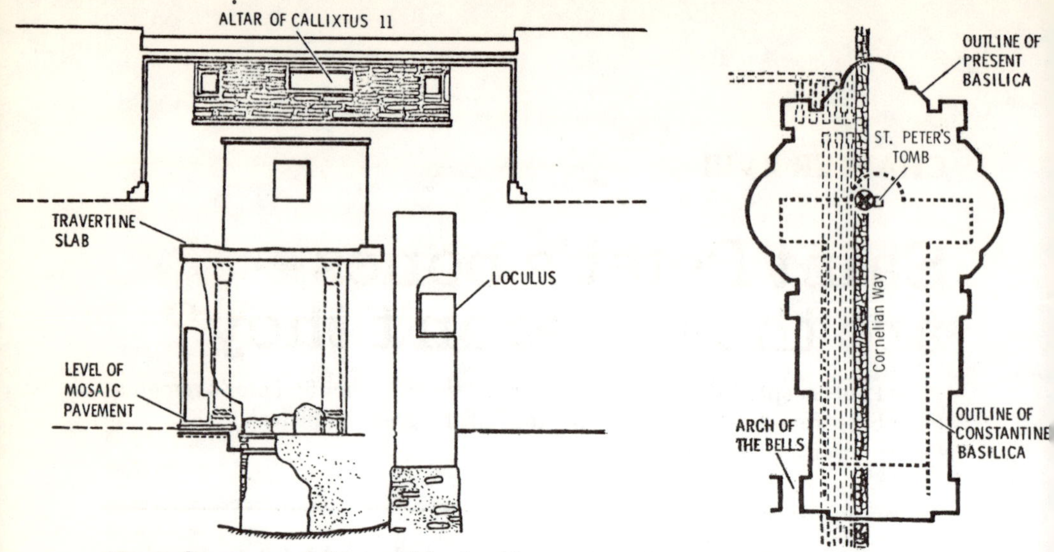

Second-century shrine within fourth-century shrine built by Constantine contained three niches from top to bottom. Current bones came from loculus in the wall at right. Cross marks niche (right) where Peter's bones were found.

Although this evidence has apparently convinced Pope Paul, experts not involved in the excavation work are still not sure. Their doubts revolve around certain points:

Why was a medieval coin found in the niche with the bones? (It's suggested that the bones were placed in the niche later or, at least, that the niche was opened long after Constantine's time.) Why was only half of a skeleton found of the presumably highly-valued remains of the first Pope? Why were the bones found to one side of the monument and not within it?

The strongest objection to the Peter's bones theory is that so little is known of St. Peter. Without some clues to his physique, such as a bone deformity, say many scientists, it's impossible to identify his bones. "The bones could be anybody's," says Dr. Judice Cordiglia, professor of forensic medicine at Turin, pointing out that the area below the Vatican was a cemetery in Roman times.

"You couldn't identify Peter absolutely on the basis of the bones themselves," maintains Dr. William A. MacDonald, a professor of classical archaeology at George Washington University in Washington, D.C. "The *context* is the important thing. If you could definitely establish that the graffiti was connected with the shrine, I might say, 'Yes, the bones are Peter's.' But you'd have to have some evidence from Peter's time."

For that matter, some experts doubt that Peter was even in Rome. According to ancient tradition, Peter lived his last years in Rome and was martyred there. The tradition is widely accepted, and not only by Catholics. "I don't see why Peter couldn't have been in Rome—the city was full of people from the East at that time," points out Professor Alfred Frazer, who teaches classical art and archaeology at Columbia University. But conclusive proof is lacking.

Dr. Guarducci, the spokesman for the Vatican archaeological group, vehemently rebuts objections to the identification of the bones. "These are tortured explanations unsupported by evidence. They imply a series of coincidences—for example, that this other person buried there was of the same stature and age as St. Peter."

She notes that the medieval coin found with the bones could have dropped to the sealed niche by the same cracks that let in a mouse whose skelelton was found in the box. Pilgrims to St. Peter's Basilica often dropped coins in the vicinity which has long been associated with the first Pope. The missing bones, Miss Guarducci continues, could have been lost when a wall was constructed near the original grave. As for the location of the bones, she and her colleagues say simply that the niche is the only possible container anywhere on the monument other than the dirt-filled opening underneath it, so it *must* contain the bones.

To put both sides of the argument in perspective, let's go back to the first period of Vatican excavations, which began in 1939. Directly under the altar of the confession in St. Peter's Basilica, archaeologists encountered, first, an altar erected by Pope Callistus (1119-1124), then one put up by Pope Gregory (590-604). Still lower, they found the monument built by Constantine in the fourth century. Within this fourth-century shrine are the remains of a still earlier shrine dating from the second century.

The second-century shrine, from what can be learned of it in its present state, is a small structure with three niches set one above the other. Underneath the bottom niche was a cache of bones which turned out not to be the right age, size or, in one case, sex for St. Peter. In the wall at the side of shrine, however, is a small, box-like opening that was apparently added to the wall before Constantine's basilica was built. When it was opened, the marble-lined interior held bones, a medieval coin and scraps of cloth. It is these bones that have been identified as Peter's.

The bones in the wall were held in so little regard when they were first discovered that a Vatican workman was told to put them in a box and store them out of the way. They lay in the storeroom for 13 years until Miss Guarducci became interested in the wall niche. The workman led her to the storeroom and the bones. "As soon as I saw the cloth remnants, I knew that these bones must have been important," she says. "The cloth was of rich purple material and was worked with pure gold."

She thinks that Constantine removed the Apostle's remains from the earth grave where they were found—possibly directly under the shrine—wrapped them in the cloth and stored them in the marble-lined compartment in the wall "to insure their permanence."

It could have happened that way. The area below the basilica was used as a graveyard by the Romans, very possibly as early as the first century, when Peter died. A number of anonymous early graves have been discovered in and around the shrine identified as Peter's tomb. All of these burials were "inhumations" or burial of the whole body instead of cremation, the normal Roman rite at that time. Since Christians all practiced inhumation, the graves may well be those of Christians, and one of them could have been Peter's.

Adding support to this theory is the tradition that Peter met his martyr's death in Nero's Circus, or arena. Recent evidence, including an inscription on the tomb of a wealthy Roman unearthed in the Vatican excavations, indicates that part of the arena was actually on the site of St. Peter's Basilica.

But if Constantine did find Peter's grave and placed the remains in the shrine, they may not have stayed there. One archaeologist, who prefers to be anonymous, says he has no doubts that the site is the tomb and that Peter's remains were buried there. But he thinks the body was put in the logical place, under the floor of the shine, and that the shrine was then opened by barbarian invaders and the casket with the bones stolen. The Saracens occupied and looted St. Peter's in 846, and one source says the invaders, "bore off all ornaments and treasures, together with the very altar which had been placed over the tomb of the said Prince of the Apostles."

Whether or not the bones are St. Peter's, the Vatican excavators have undoubtedly uncovered some of the most fascinating archaeological material found in this century. Constantine built his fourth-century church over a Roman graveyard of the second and third century and the present church occupies the same site, so the excavations revealed monuments that had been hidden for some 1,600 years. Some, like the ones in the immediate vicinity of Peter's shrine, probably consisted only of a stone slab laid on top of the body, but others were ornate structures, resembling modern mausoleums, attesting to their owners' wealth and culture.

The most important mausoleum uncovered in the long-hidden cemetery is probably the tomb of the Valerii family, which boasts an assortment of white stucco carvings. Every niche and recess in the upper part of the large structure is occupied by a full-size stucco carving representing either a god or goddess or a human. Stucco portrait busts commemorate members of the family, while low relief figures of satyrs, maenads and pans fill the back walls, and sculptured heads support the cornice. When the tomb was intact these sculptures were probably enlivened with splashes of polychrome and gilt.

The Valerii tomb is important for another reason besides its fine stucco carving. Professor Guarducci found two primitive portraits scratched into a wall of the mausoleum; one of Christ and the other, she says, of Peter. Peter is shown as an old, bald man with a long beard. One tradition *does* indicate that he was bald. To the left of the head are the letters "PETRV" and to the right, an inscription that is translated by Miss Guarducci as "Peter, pray for the pious Christian men buried near your body." When she first saw the inscriptions in 1952, she says, they were quite visible, but now, unfortunately for her case, they have almost vanished.

Why would Constantine build a basilica right over a graveyard, undoubtedly angering the wealthy owners of the tombs? The evidence shows that the mausoleums were in use up until the time they were covered by the foundations of the church. The considerable slope of the ground here, too, is unsuitable for a large building, making it necessary for the architects to dump tons of earth on the site to level it out. Nearby on Vatican hill at that time were any number of open, flat spaces on which the emperor could have erected a church. The reason for the choice of the site seems inescapable: Constantine had to build his basilica there because the site held something he wished to incorporate within the building.

Was that something the tomb of St. Peter? Accepting the graffiti as translated by Miss Guarducci, a good circumstantial case can be made for the second-century shrine being dedicated to Peter and, perhaps, for its being his tomb. But the presence of the bones within the shrine is another matter. The identification of the remains will have to remain uncertain, at least until the complete scientific evidence compiled by the Vatican archaeologists is made public.

PART IV

north america

Somehow the northern half of the "Western World" has never been considered much of a "seed bed" of mankind by anyone interested in such matters. This may be because other places are more exotic or, perhaps, because much of it was beset by glaciers for so long, making it an untenable area for construction of stone cities or barbaric empires of any consequence. Everybody (if there was anybody around those parts in pre-Roman times) was far too busy trying to stay alive than to fuss around enslaving folk, piling up rocks, and otherwise "civilizing" things.

At any rate, it wasn't until recently that historians, archaeologists, anthropologists, cryptographers and other authorities began to deploy their antennae seriously for reports of artifacts, runes and ruins other than those associated with North American Indian mounds and early colonial settlements.

Today, the usual professional battle lines are drawn on a number of archaeological curiosities in North America—Viking runestones in Minnesota and even in Oklahoma; Mayan glyphs in coral caves on a Caribbean island; unlikely flints in an unlikely citadel of earthworks in Louisiana. In some of these discoveries the authenticity of the artifacts is in contention. Though none have yet been *proved* fraudulent, neither have they been *proved* valid beyond question.

These chapters bring up to date the on-going studies of investigators in the field, along with a few other accounts of the more interesting new digs involving Indian and Colonial settlements.

CHAPTER XIX

Riddle of the 'Viking' cryptograms

Did Vikings or pranksters carve the American runestones? Clues may lie in accurate deciphering of the runic messages—and anyone can take a crack at it, including you.

The battle over who discovered the New World first—Christopher Columbus or Scandinavian explorers—started at the turn of the century when Olaf Ohman, a Scandinavian immigrant farmer, claimed that he had unearthed, enmeshed in the roots of a yew tree on his woodlot, a large stone that was carved with medieval runes (alphabetic symbols used by ancient Teutonic peoples, particularly the Scandinavians). The stone was discovered near Kensington, Minn.—an area heavily populated by Scandinavian descendents and immigrants —and has come to be known as the Kensington Stone.

Since the Swedish farmer's discovery, opposing camps of opinion have sprung up all over the country—for that matter, all over the world. The fire of controversy, involving experts and laymen alike, has been fed, in part, by unscholarly investigation techniques and a glossing-over of unexplained aspects of the Kensington find.

Erik Wehlgren, in his book *The Kensington Stone, a mystery solved*, is representative of the skeptics of the stone's validity. His book does not particularly set out to prove that Columbus was indeed first to the New World. Rather, it systematically goes about the business of disclaiming the stone as having been carved by Swedes or Norwegians in the year 1362 (over 100 years before Columbus) as members of the opposite camp believe. The Scandinavians may have been first—but the Kensington Stone, according to his evidence, is not legitimate proof.

The other side of the argument is fought just as vehemently. The principal champion of the Kensington Stone's authenticity has been the Norwegian-American writer, Hjalmar Rued Holand. His articles, essays and other writings have persistently defended the stone since 1907. And though he has been accused of sloppy or unscientific tech-

Painting by George Kelvin

The Poteau runestone, once part of a hillside ledge, was found in Poteau, Oklahoma. The question is whether the runes on it were carved by Scandinavian explorers before Columbus, or by nineteenth century pranksters.

niques in his investigation, it is through him that much of the initial information was obtained—some of it quite substantial.

There is still just too much unexplained evidence—sloppy or not—that supports the "Scandinavians First" theory to let the matter be buried. To make the matters more perplexing, the Kensington Stone is not the only discovery of its kind in North America.

Through the years, two other runestones have been discovered, one in Nova Scota and another near Bourne, Mass. Skeptics have also had to contend with a carving of a 14th century knight of the Orkney islands upon a stone near Westford, Mass., and two rather similar medieval axes found in separate locations: Beardmore, Ontario, and Rocky Nook Point, Mass.

Only a few years ago, a Laval University exploration team discovered indisputable evidence of a Viking longhouse on the Ungava peninsula in northern Canada, which they have dated between the 11th and 12th centuries.

Add to this one of the most persuasive arguments of proponents of Viking exploration of North America—the World Map of A.D. 1440, allegedly drawn by Scandinavian explorers. Known commonly as the Yale Vinland Map (found in 1957 in Europe by a New Haven, Conn., rare book dealer, Laurence Witten), it now is part of the rare document collection in the Beinecke Library of Yale University.

The map, 11 by 16 inches, was discovered bound in with 21 manuscript pages; but five holes in the parchment map, inflicted by bookworms, did not coincide with holes in other manuscript pages—indicating that the map belonged to some other volume. Later when the rare volume *Tartar Relation* was discovered, it was proven that the map belonged within. The wormholes matched exactly, the notations were determined authentic by some authorities, and the map was dated at about A.D. 1440.

Vinland, as the Vikings called it, began at the most northern part of Labrador and extended 2,200 miles south—or as far as Florida. There is no dispute over the belief that the Vikings were great explorers, but even the Yale Vinland Map has been questioned by certain authorities on the subject.

But now the battle must turn far inland, for in Oklahoma there are not one but two major runestones. The location of these runestones is in East-Central Oklahoma, near the Arkansas border. One lies within a cliff-enclosed vale high up on a mountain near the town of Heavener.

The second stone was removed from a hill near Poteau, Okla.

For those skeptics of Norse exploration inland to Minnesota, the runestones in Oklahoma already have proven to be a tougher nut to crack than the Kensington Stone in several ways.

As with Yale's Vinland map, nature provided an aid in giving an air of authenticity to Oklahoma's runestones—in this case the lowly lichen. Lichen is particularly slow in growth. The inscriptions on both stones contained a solid lichen growth within and on the edges.

The discovery of the Heavener Runestone was made by Choctaw indians in the 1830s when Oklahoma was "Indian Territory." The Choctaws did not think the runes looked like anything indian, but then the "civilized" white man arrived on the scene and explained to them that the inscription was indian writing. With that conclusion, the Heavener Runestone passed into the 20th century with the label of "Indian Rock."

In 1923, C. F. Kemmerer of Heavener wrote the Smithsonian Institution for information about the inscription on "Indian Rock." Though ethnologists at the Smithsonian were interested enough to exhibit the Kensington Stone in 1948-49 at the institution, the staff in 1923 brushed off the Heavener inscription as being done by someone with a "Scandinavian Grammar" as a guide (that is the current argument being used against the Kensington Stone).

Had it not been for the work of Mrs. Gloria Farley, the Heavener Runestone might well have passed into another century known as "Indian Rock." In 1948, she also inquired for information from the Smithsonian and was referred to the answer given Mr. Kemmerer. But, she asked, just how would a Choctaw or an even earlier indian have had access to a Scandinavian Grammar? Mrs. Farley began to dig deeper into the riddle: She studied runic writing, Norse history and, above all, made the local citizens aware that "Indian Rock" might be much more than it seemed.

Rediscovering the stone was quite another matter. It is 12 feet high, 10 feet wide and 16 inches thick, standing upright like a monolithic billboard not much more than two miles from Heavener. However, this runestone stands in the center of a deep ravine, surrounded by steep cliff-like walls, and the ravine is situated on an upper crest of 2,500-foot-high Poteau mountain.

The major turning point in the work occurred on September 28, 1959, when at the invitation of Mrs. Farley, representatives of the

The Heavener runestone, found by Choctaw Indians in the 1830s, was considered an Indian artifact. Detail of runes at right show them to be deeply cut.

Oklahoma Historical Society met with Frederick Pohl, noted Norse scholar who published a translation of the Kensington Stone in his book *The Viking Explorers.* The meeting concluded with official recognition that the inscription was composed of valid rune characters and was "of sufficient credibility" to warrant intense investigation.

The following years brought the expected amount of criticism, but the work of verifying the runestone's authenticity, according to its investigators, easily outpaced its opponents. In fact, the only "modern" explanation that could be found involved a French expedition operating under John Law's colonization scheme for the Mississippi Valley. A portion of that expedition entered the Arkansas River area in 1718-20, and one group was led by a Swedish captain. Just as the Kensington critics made much of Olaf Ohman's ancestry, the theory of the critics seems to be "a Swede found is a runestone explained."

But again, easy explanations do not stick that easily to the Oklahoma runestones. In September 1967, two junior high school boys, Henry McBride and Mike Griffeth, discovered the second runic inscription on a hill near Poteau, Okla., about 10 miles from Heavener. Knowledge of the combined runes of the two inscriptions would certainly have made that Swedish captain a most unusually advanced scholar in the 18th century.

Now, to an unusual aspect of the Oklahoma runestones: Though the Kensington Stone is still subject to academic attack, everybody agrees that one possible translation was completed, (with some unfortunately critical grammatical errors and dubious assumptions) by Hjalmar Holand. Such is not the case with the runestones in Oklahoma. Though there have been several plausible translations offered on the Heavener inscription, there is still a good possibility that the message has yet to be translated. And with the more recently discovered Poteau Runestone, there has been only one serious attempt at translation.

Translating and deciphering is the one field of science always open to the armchair-amateur, and they have scored some notable achievements, too. Michael Ventris, an architect, deciphered the Minoan Linear B. script; and a major contribution in the deciphering of Cuneiform was accomplished by Henry Rawlinson, a military advisor. So—let's get on with the problems and techniques of runic cryptography on the following pages.

How good is your cryptography?

These pages provide three basic runic alphabets, along with attempted translations of the questionable inscriptions by several scholars. If you're a word puzzle fan, here's a chance to try your hand.

The task of translating runic symbols is not an easy one, but if you like word puzzles it can be fascinating. Here are a few of the problems that make even the most expert cryptographers' work subject to doubt—and give credence to the work of almost any amateur who knows what he's doing:

There are at least a dozen runic alphabets, all distinctively different (the three provided here are the ones important to the inscriptions in question, the Heavener and Poteau Runestones, since they were most often used during the period when Vikings would have had to carve the American runestones to make them valid. It doesn't mean that other runes might not have been used, however).

Once runic characters are deciphered into letters, they can't just be strung together into tidy English equivalents. You must run through a labyrinth of medieval language forms: a variety of ancient Scandinavian forms; Germanic; early and middle Anglo-Saxon—of which every island in the North Sea and Atlantic had its own variation.

Each of these language forms carried different meanings and shades of meanings for similar symbols. Hence the cryptographer must go through all of them in a wide variety of combinations to arrive at the most logical translation for a given runic message.

In many cases, the oral language carried quite different meanings

The Kensington Stone

Kensington Stone translations tell story of exploration and death. "AVM" has been shown to mean "Ave Maria." This, as well as the date at the end, has been questioned.

8 göter ok 22 norrmen pa
8 Goths and 22 Norwegians on

oppaselse farp fro
exploration-journey from

winland of west wi
Vinland over West We

hape lager wep 2 skjar en
had camp by 2 skerries one

pags rise norr fro peno sten
day's journey north from this stone

wi war ok fiske en pagh äptir
We were and fished one day. After

wi kam hem fan 10 man rope
We came home found 10 men red

af blop og pep AVM
with blood and dead AV(e)M(aria)

fräelse af illy
Save from evil.

har 10 mans we hawet at se
have 10 men we have at the sea

äptir wore skip 14 pagh rise
to look after our ship 14 days' journey

fram peno öh ahr 1362
from this island year 1362

All-Germanic Runes—3rd century

f u th a r k g w h n i j e n R s t b e m l ng o d

Danish Runes—6th century

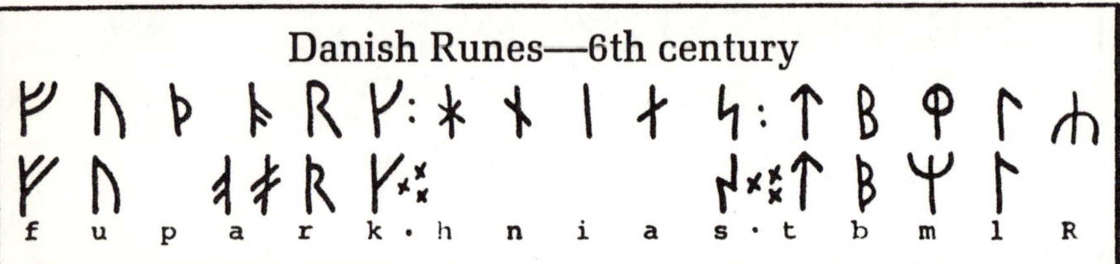

Swedish-Norwegian Runes—6th century

f u p ą r k h n I a s • t b m l R

Three runic alphabets, above, from separate geographical areas and times show how complex runes can be; there are a dozen such alphabets.

Heavener Runestone

The Heavener stone has been translated to mean "Sun Dial Valley."

Poteau Runestone

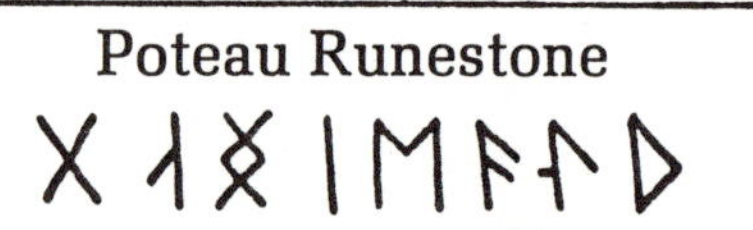

The Poteau runes could spell "November 11, 1017" among other things.

from the formal written (engraved) symbols. Hence, literal translations make little sense and often contribute to serious error.

To complicate matters, in many early Scandinavian runic inscriptions, each rune was used not as a letter in the alphabet, but as a symbol for a complete word—a sort of Viking shorthand, which might involve the entire inscription, or combine with alphabetical usage.

Once you are over this morass of problems, and have come up with a mysterious, or senseless jumble, you may suddenly find that it does indeed make sense if you turn everything backwards and start over—because *some* runic inscriptions were made from right to left!

While space limitations do not permit the kind of course material necessary to provide complete history and instruction for this sort of thing (books have been written on the subject), the basic data on these pages will be enough to get you started. The bibliography at the end of the chapter is designed to start anyone who is really interested in pursing the puzzle seriously off on a fascinating quest.

Perhaps the author's experience with the Oklahoma runestones will help to give you an idea of where to start. First, the limited number of runes in the Heavener and Poteau inscriptions offers a strong possibility that the messages were written in a "shorthand" or code. One translation by Alf Monge and O. G. Landsverk is a cryptographic solution involving calendar dates rather than words. The solution is explained in their book, *Norse Medieval Cryptography in Runic Carvings* by Norseman Press. The author's approach to translating the Heavener Stone was an example of a shorthand solution:

The X which leads off both inscriptions was taken as a monogram for St. Andrew, a logical patron saint for such an exploration. The 1 — deciphered as "N," by others, but which the author disputes and translates as "A." And in old Anglo-Saxon, "A" stands for "always." The real guessing game in shorthand runes comes with ᛟ, which is usually "O." The author uses "O" as shorthand for Old English "on," which stood for "with."And projects it further (with reason based on accepted meanings of the time) to stand for "on Ealdor," which would mean "with king" in more modern English. And so we eventually come up with something like: "(May) St. Andrew always (be) with King Medoth." Where's the logic in this? There are many old tales of a Prince Medoc of Wales who led his people to a new land far west across the sea. Unless it is confirmed through translation of another inscription, such as the Poteau stone, the author's is a calculated guess. But it was fun, and the goal merits the effort. It indicates, here, the free-association—involving language, history and anthropology—that must be brought to bear in this kind of cryptography. The key to an answer may come from anywhere.

As impossible as the task appears, there is little doubt that future translations will be made that will help solve the riddle of American runestones. Even if no new stones are discovered, the Vinland argument will most certainly be expanded further than either side of it ever anticipated. Perhaps your own efforts will shed new light, or at least expose an overlooked corner of the mystery.

So, if cryptography intrigues you, start deciphering. And good luck!

CHAPTER XX

Mayan mystery of the Onima Caves

On an Island in the Dutch Antilles, walls of sea-worn caves known to have been inhabited by Arawak Indians, are adorned with unmistakable Mayan glyphs. How did they get there and what do they mean? This chapter offers an answer.

A few years ago, a lone man with a flashlight was prowling through a labyrinth of coral caves on Bonaire, a remote island in the southern Caribbean. Playing the light beam across the cave walls, he noticed what appeared to be markings. Curiosity aroused, he picked his way carefully across the sea-worn cave bottom and stopped dead in his tracks. What he saw was not possible, but there it was. Unmistakably, the marks on the wall were distinct symbols—not so remarkable of itself in an ancient cave. What was remarkable was that several were —Mayan glyphs!

The man was Charles Lacombe, a Miami, Florida expert on Mayan writing, whose published works on Mayan hieroglyphics had recently appeared in the University of Miami's *Journal of Inter-American Studies*. Lacombe knew that "Indian inscriptions" were said to adorn the walls of some of these caves, and he'd expected to find Arawak doodling here and there. But not Mayan!

Bonaire, about 24 miles long and five wide, lies in the Dutch Antilles, some 60 miles off Venezuela and far from known Mayan haunts. Among naturalists the isle is known for the salt lake at its southern tip—a breeding ground for thousands of flamingoes. Aside from that, it hosts a modest parade of scuba divers, fishermen, bird watchers, honeymooners and other escapees from the more bustling, commercial Caribbean resorts. Few visitors have explored the coral caves, carved by receding ocean waters over thousands of years. Fewer still knew about the mysterious markings on walls and ceilings, painted in a reddish brown. Dutch archaeologists visiting several caves on Aruba, Bonaire and Curacao in 1890 had copied what they termed "Indian inscriptions," and left for home. Everyone agreed they were of Caiquetios origin and about 500 years old. The *Caiquetios*, an

Arawak tribe, reportedly lived a stone-age existence when Amerigo Vespucci discovered Bonaire in 1499. The Dutch discovery caused a flurry of interest and was quickly forgotten. So were the caves. Local urchins added their graffiti to the "Indian script" and there matters had stood until Charles Lacombe's recent visit. How did he know that Arawak Indians might not use symbols similar to the Mayans? He explains that the Mayans were the only known people to write in *cartouches,* in circles. Their script is the only one known to utilize dots and circles—and so do the Indian inscriptions in the caves on Bonaire.

"When I first saw what looked like the Mayan *glyph* (sign) for *Lamat,* one of the 20 days in the Mayan week, I simply didn't trust my eyes. Then I knew I had a reason for looking further," Lacombe said.

Using a reproduction of the *Madrid Codex,* one of the few surviving Mayan documents, he points to the frequent use of spirals, inverted S formations, *cartouches,* dots, and the *Lamat* sign. This *glyph* not only represents a day but also the Planet Venus in Mayan script.

He has photographs and slides taken in the caves he visited. The similarity between Mayan script and some of the cave inscriptions is hard to deny.

There is another possible link between the caves in the Dutch Antilles and the Mayan civilization. In the entrance to the caves of Onima, on the island's North coast, stands the so-called "Guardian of Onima," a stalagmite with clear indication of having once been carved. It doesn't resemble other stalagmites which are usually very rough and jagged on top. This one is smoothly rounded and eyes and nose indications are unmistakable. The Guardian of Onima stands in the exact center of a community of caves.

Carved stalagmites are rare. One, in the Yucatan cave at Loltun, has a bearded face carved on it. This one seems to have been smoothly shaven.

None of the many caves in the Dutch Antilles bearing Indian inscriptions have been properly investigated and explored. Charles Lacombe says there are at least ten of these caves on Bonaire.

Lacombe believes that some of the caves may have been used for religious ceremonies. Several of the so-called inscriptions may even indicate directions in which the caves seem to be spreading. At one time Caiquetios and other Arawaks may have made their homes in some of them.

We know little about the Arawaks of the Caribbean. In 1512, the

Spanish returned to colonize the island, and the entire native population, reportedly shrunk by wars to only several hundred, was deported to Santa Domingo into slavery.

Could this primitive culture develop the complicated script? Stone-age cavemen in other parts of the world have left us some intricate and beautiful cave-wall paintings of the animals which shared their environment. However, the signs found in the caves of the Dutch Antilles seem script rather than art. Moreover, on Curacao, *cartouches* are carved into the rocks of *Hato Caverns.*

Oddly, no other indications of ancient cultures have been found on the islands at this time. No monuments, no sculpture, not even the usual artifacts, such as projectile points, pot-sherds, etc.

Do the mysterious inscriptions, including the sacred Mayan symbol of the circled cross, point to Mayan influence? Charles Lacombe says that one similar configuration could simply be coincidental. However, four or five of the unusual configurations in the caves are clearly based on Mayan script. Others resemble it. Lacombe feels this is too much of a coincidence to be dismissed lightly.

The Mayan civilization, already in decline when the Spanish arrived, stretched from the Yucatan Peninsula to what today is Honduras in the south. There is little doubt that Mayan traders shipped their wares farther south. While exploring the waters southwest of Cuba on his second voyage, Christopher Columbus picked up a canoe loaded with brightly colored cotton garments. The natives indicated they were tradesmen from the land of Maia.

But as far as we know, the only Mayans able to read and write were those of the scholarly and educated priest-class, not the reportedly uneducated merchants. Does this account for the clumsy handwriting on the cave walls of the Dutch Antilles?

Charles Lacombe is personally convinced that some of the writings in the caves on Aruba, Bonaire and Curacao are based on Mayan hieroglyphics. Other scientists do not exactly doubt that Mayan trade influence may have reached much further south, but are not quite prepared to accept the long jump into the Dutch Antilles.

One of the outstanding experts on the Mayan civilization is Dr. Alan Craig of Florida Atlantic University in Boca Raton. Dr. Craig has told one journalist that while he does not doubt Mayan trade influence in the Antilles, he does not believe that the Mayan hieroglyphics would have traveled along with them.

"It wouldn't be too surprising," he admits, however, "to find Mayan influence that far from the Mayan mainland." Dr. Craig goes on to explain that on his fourth voyage during 1503-1504, Christopher Columbus found Mayan traders on an island more than 1,000 miles from their shore. Can such successful, far-ranging businessmen be expected to be entirely ignorant of reading and writing? (Or arithmetic and astrology to navigate their trade routes?)

About ten years ago, a Russian mathematician claimed he had solved the riddle of the Mayan script through computer use, and Lacombe studied this report at the University of Miami. He feels the Russian scientist is on the wrong track. He accepted as a premise for his study the information Spanish priests who followed Cortez obtained from their Mayan colleagues.

"They talked to the people who actually knew the hieroglyphics. But I am certain the Mayan priests gave the Spaniards a bum steer.

"As a matter of fact, when these Spanish priests first saw one of the sacred Mayan symbols, the circled cross, they actually believed they had found a relationship to Christianity.

"The Mayan priests told the invaders about their calendar structure but the nature of reading and understanding the hieroglyphic structure remains a secret. It died with them."

Lacombe agrees with other scientists who feel that the Mayans will talk again. Many attempts at deciphering their script are being made. Each seems to add a little to our understanding of the meaning of the mysterious and fascinating hieroglyphics.

Some 50 years ago, a glyph student named S. G. Morley, wrote in the Smithsonian Institution, Bureau of American Ethology, Bulletin 57, about the study of the Mayan script: "That we have succeeded in deciphering . . . only the calendric parts . . . the chronological skeleton on Maya history . . . should not discourage the student . . . Thirty years ago, the inscriptions were a sealed book. . . ." (That would have been around 1890, when the caves in the Dutch Antilles were visited by Dutch scientists.)

We have learned a little bit more since Morley's report. Bishop Diego de Landa, the first bishop of Yucatan in the mid-1500s during the Inquisition, was a fanatic young priest. He wrote a book on Mayan customs, use of hieroglyphics, their amazing knowledge of astrology, etc., while in jail, awaiting trial in Madrid.

Charles Lacombe says, "Actually, the Inquisition had ordered

Diego de Landa back to Spain, charging him with cruelty. Landa considered the Maya children of the devil and tortured them mercilessly because they refused to convert. He burned all their books as works of the devil. It was Landa's duty to send the books back to Spain for study, so the Spaniards could evaluate the Mayan books and pass judgment on them."

Bishop Landa's book, lost for some 300 years, helped modern scholars to understand the Mayan calendars, but the hieroglyphics are still a puzzle. Most scholars expect that the few Mayan documents (*codices*) that escaped destruction by Landa and have reached Europe will contain only agricultural and astronomical information. They are not expected to shed further light on Mayan life and culture.

However, modern Mayans in Yucatan believe the priests of their ancestors may have hidden the sacred books in the safest possible places—caves. Yucatan caves offered dry storage for the books, and the gods were believed to live in them. That should have made them a safe refuge from the book-burners of the Inquisition.

Michel D'Obrenovic, FRAI (Fellow of the Royal Anthropological Institute in London), discovered some Mayan ceremonial caves in Yucatan during 1961-1962. They contain unexplored passages which, it is hoped, will eventually yield at least some of the Mayan books.

Dr. D'Obrenovic introduced Charles Lacombe to the Mayans and the two men became scientific collaborators, working on parts of the *Madrid Codex*. Eventually Charles Lacombe, cryptographer, and Michel D'Obrenovic, FRAI, archaeologist and anthropologist, published "Project 'Xoc' Some Keys to Maya Hieroglyphics," in 1968.

It seems unlikely that an expert like Charles Lacombe would make an error in calling the indian signs in the caverns and caves of Aruba, Bonaire and Curacao "of Mayan origin."

There is now hope that the autonomous Government of the Netherland Antilles will preserve the caves. Charles Lacombe reported his discovery to the Dutch officials who plan to send a part of an indian sign to the U.S. for carbon dating. The officials are also planning an educational campaign at home, to acquaint inhabitants with the historic significance of the caves. There are plans to interest modern archaeologists and anthropologists in evaluating the caves for possible diggings to unearth their secret. Whether these activities will lead to our understanding of the Mayan hieroglyphics remains to be seen.

CHAPTER XXI

They're digging up witch lore in Salem

Twenty Puritans were executed as witches in Salem, Massachusetts, in 1692. Now archaeologists are unearthing the ruins where the trials took place. Anyone who wishes may help, and buffs are making exciting discoveries.

The Sins of Salem

At Danvers, Massachusetts—originally Salem Village, archaeologists and historians have joined forces in an attempt to reconstruct a significant but little-known phase of America's colonial history.

It all began in the year 1692. The people of Salem Village were about to enter a time of fear, confusion and terror. There were witches in Salem. They would be discovered, tried and executed to save the Christian village from "diabolical workings of the devil."

Even great scientists of the day—men like John Locke and Francis Bacon—believed in an invisible world and experimented in the occult. The *Holy Bible*, basis of their religion, dictated the punishment for the convicted: "Thou shalt not suffer a witch to live."

All over the world witch hunts were taking place. New England, by comparison, was only mildly involved in the witch-hunt frenzy. In the first half of the 17th century, 900 witches were burned in the city of Bamberg, Germany and 5,000 in the province of Alsace. But the 23 deaths in Salem were, nevertheless, part and parcel of an intercontinental mass fear of the powers of witchcraft.

It began in the home of John Parris, the minister of Salem, whose West Indian slave Tituba led his daughter (9) and niece (11) in experiments with the occult. They are believed to have used an egg white in a glass, in the way side show "spirit mediums" use a crystal ball today to tell fortunes. When the girls and their friends who joined them in this experimentation became sick, a doctor was called, and pronounced them "bewitched." In the midst of hysterical fits, they named their tormentors—Tituba, and two other irascible old townswomen.

This was the event that set off a witch hunt that was to last nearly a year, and reverberate grimly through the corridors of American colonial history. More and more townspeople were accused by the afflicted girls during their fits as the "trials" progressed.

One of the first women accused was Sarah Good, known in Salem as a mean old woman. When the presiding magistrate asked her at her trial to look at the girls, they went into fits, crying out that they saw her spirit coming after them. The court took this to mean that Sarah Good was inflicting them for accusing her of witchcraft. Mass self-hypnosis ran riot. When the girls claimed they saw Sarah's spirit creeping toward other women in the courtroom, these ladies, too, were stricken with hysterical fits. When Sarah was made to touch the girls, the fits ceased; "proof," it seemed, that she had supernatural powers.

The spreading suspicions might have subsided except for one frightening event. Tituba, Parris' servant, confessed to being a witch. She said she and several others had made a mark in blood in "the devil's book," allowing themselves to be used as his messengers. She could not name the others, and this set the town agog with wonder and worry about who the other witches among them were.

It didn't take long to find out. The afflicted girls continued to make accusations, and the court continued to take their alarming and convincing convulsive fits as proof that the accused were guilty. It was difficult to believe otherwise when the presence of a suspect caused some ten young girls to suffer violent convulsions, contortions of arms and legs, loss of sight and speech and—according to witnesses—even levitation.

Martha Corey, another townswoman, was jailed when her husband mentioned that she read strange books—books of the devil, no doubt. While one of the magistrates—one judge Hathorne—badgered her with questions and accusations, she became nervous and distraught. When she bit her lip, the girls went into fits, screaming that Martha's spirit was biting them, and when she clenched her hands, they cried that they were being pinched. When the girls were examined, some had bite marks and pinch marks on their bodies. What more proof was needed? Martha Corey was convicted.

Another arrest was that of five-year-old Dorcas Good, Sarah Good's daughter. She confessed to the court without any prodding that she was a witch, and that she had a snake that sucked on her finger and hurt people. (The devil was believed to take over the bodies of animals and suck the blood of witches, leaving a "Devil's Mark.") The judge found a deep red spot on Dorcas' finger. With such "strong physical evidence," there was no alternative but to convict the child.

On another occasion, Parris' niece Abigail had a fit in her home and cried out that Elizabeth Proctor was tormenting her, causing terrible pain in her stomach. When her uncle went to her aid, he found a pin in her stomach—with the point sticking out. Since Elizabeth Proctor could not explain this strange occurrence, she was judged as being used by the devil to afflict the girls. Shortly she, too, was imprisoned.

It appears to some that one convicted woman, Bridget Bishop, possibly *was* practicing witchcraft. She had put curses on neighbors, and dolls with pins in them, the most telling tools of the trade, were found buried in the walls of her cellar.

Not all of the accused were women. One of the male suspects was John Willard. He had been a deputy-marshall in charge of going to the homes of the accused and arresting them. He resigned, however, when he began to believe that innocent people were being arrested. This put him under suspicion, and the afflicted girls began crying out his name in their fits. His grandfather also testified that Willard "put the evil eye on him," causing him to become ill. Willard was convicted of being a wizard and hanged with the others.

Although the courts depended on the afflicted girls' testimony of seeing the spirits of the suspects as their prime convicting evidence, there were other popular tests for witches. Ironically, some of these actually were charms and tools popularly associated with witchcraft. One was the presence of a "Devil's Mark," which was supposed to lack sensation. By sticking a pin in it and observing the suspect's reaction, he could be cleared or accused. Another method, a favorite of the crowds, was the water-ordeal, in which the suspect was dragged by a rope through a body of water. If she floated she was a witch because the water was rejecting her as she had presumably rejected her Christian baptism; if she sank she was innocent, and promptly rescued.

The judges, especially Hathorne, were far less than impartial in their investigations. Added to this was their strong feeling of "public service" in weeding out the witches, plus the then extant legal tenet that accused were guilty unless proven innocent. Under such frightening circumstances, this was rarely possible.

Many of the accused confessed, after badgering and pleading by the judges and even their own relatives. Others went to the gallows vowing their innocence. If a simple confession would have saved their lives, why did they remain silent? In Puritan New England, lying was a grave offense, a mortal sin, and a good Christian would not commit it under the direst circumstances. Besides, the devil was known as the Prince of Lies, and if one were caught in a false confession, he would incriminate himself as really being a witch or a wizard.

What brought these traumatic trials to an end? Several books by prominent people appeared at that time condemning the kind of evidence used. The public was growing more skeptical of the proceedings, and the girls' accusations were becoming preposterous. It was rumored that they had mentioned the governor's wife!

Finally, in October 1692, the trials were ordered halted. The infamous witch hunt was over, but the effects of the previous months did not end as easily. John Parris was removed from his ministry because he had helped to gain convictions against people in his own congregation. The people of New England fasted and prayed in an attempt to reconcile their hysterical actions of the past year, during which they came to believe they had executed many innocent people who were unknowingly possessed by the devil but were not actually witches.

The bizarre events may seem unexplainable, and the powers of witchcraft that were manifest in Salem unbelievable. But even then there were some who understood how such strange events could take place. The Reverend John Hale of Beverly, who examined the afflicted girls and witnessed the frenzied courtroom scenes, wrote in a book published a few years later: "In matters of malice the devil suits his actions to man's belief about them." Chadwick Hansen, in his book *Witchcraft at Salem*, has put it another way: "In a society that believes in witchcraft, it works." In Salem, Massachusetts, this was sadly but surely true.

Digging up the Witchlore

Today, the diggers into Salem's past have located and partially excavated foundations of the home of the Reverend Samuel Parris. The Danvers team also has located the site of the crude lean-to once occupied by Tituba, the West indian slave woman.

In addition, investigators have recovered nearly 60 bags of colonial artifacts, some of which are directly traceable to the Parris household.

The Danvers witch-dig began when Richard B. Trask, the energetic young historian who serves as curator for the Danvers Historical

Society, decided to initiate a community-involvement program that would bring forth new knowledge of the town's colorful history and provide new local educational possibilities.

Because the Parris house—described in historical records, but never definitely located—offered a crucial link to the origins of the 1692 witch-craze, Trask chose it as the primary focus of his initial investigations.

The search began with an intensive examination of historical documents. Trask checked early First Church record books, which gave church votes concerning the building of the parsonage as well as subsequent repairs and additions, and pursued house title through age-yellowed public records. Various accounts of the location of the house were found in published and unpublished papers held by the Danvers Historical Society. A map dating from 1730 helped to locate the general area in which the house once stood.

According to numerous accounts, the Parris home was built in 1681 and measured 42 feet by 20 feet with "four chimlies and no gable ends." From testimony given during the Salem witchcraft trials, Trask knew that the lean-to occupied by Tituba was attached at the back of the house. And First Church records indicated that an addition measuring 23 feet by 18 feet was constructed, also at the rear, in 1734. By that time, the trials and executions had ended. But guilt on the part of Salem Village townspeople precluded any mention of the great witch-hunt for decades afterward—hence the spottiness of the historical record during this era.

Hoping to fill gaps left by guilt-laden and reluctant historians of that troubled time, Trask enlisted the aid of archaeologist Roland W. Robbins of Lincoln, Massachusetts. Robbins—best known for his excavations of such colonial sites as the 17th-century Saugus Iron Works, Thoreau's cabin at Walden, Thomas Jefferson's birthplace and the John Alden house at Duxbury—showed a keen interest in the proposed project.

Field work began in late July, 1970. By mid-October, test probes and peek-holes pinpointed the location of the Parris house foundations in a field owned by Mr. and Mrs. Alfred Hutchinson of Danvers. Mr. Hutchinson, who has permitted excavation without charge, is a descendant of Rebecca Nurse, one of the women hanged in 1692 as a witch.

Trask's enthusiastic invitation to Town Manager Robert E. Curtis to view the site resulted in authorization to use Department of Public Works equipment and a skilled operator for a period of five days. Backhoe operator Charles Cahill, working under the direction of archaeologist Robbins, dug out the major amount of cellar debris, heaping it beside the site for careful screening later. Areas adjacent to foundation walls and the cellar bottom were dug by hand. Photographers stood by to record all developments as the excavation proceeded. After digging and sifting began, a master grid was charted to plot the location, placement and elevation of each foundation stone and artifact.

Work continues today at the Parris site, but it is already apparent that foundation measurements match exactly with historically-recorded dimensions. The house faced to the south, with chimney and bulkhead to the east. Tituba's lean-to and the 1734 addition are located at the rear.

From the area of the lean-to, about three inches below the soil surface, workers recovered their grandest prize so far: a fragment of a metal tray engraved with the initials "SPE"—indicating ownership by the Reverend Parris and his wife Elizabeth.

Other treasures include gold coins dating from 1684, clay pipes, earthenware, buckles, food remnants and animal bones, 17th-century window-glass, brass spoons, knives, forks, oxen shoes, slipware pieces, a portion of an early lice-comb, and more than 250 whole bricks together with countless fragmentary ones.

"All the material," says Trask, "appears to date from the mid-17th to the mid-18th century"—a time period that encompasses the full duration of the Parris occupation of the parsonage.

Cataloguing of retrieved artifacts is not yet complete. But even the initial finds give heady glimpses into the lives of the people who inhabited Salem Village at the time of the 17th-century witch trials. The vast number of shattered beverage bottles, unearthed at the site tells us that the Puritans—not nearly so prudish as history portrays them—were prodigious drinkers of wine and ale. Fragmentary animal bones sifted from kitchen debris suggest that the Salem villagers preferred domestic beef and pork over the meat of game animals. The broken lice-comb makes an interesting comment on the state of personal hygiene in 17th-century New England.

Small insights, and random ones—but they provide precisely the sort of historical foot-notes, seldom found in written records, that

Trask and Robbins hoped to uncover. Facts like these help to reconstruct an entire cultural context against which the people and the events of history can be viewed.

And herein lies the real significance of the Danvers witch-dig. Trask and Robbins have demonstrated that an inter-disciplinary approach—a planned pooling of skills by experts in the fields of history and archaeology—yields greater information for both by broadening the perspective of the investigation.

The Danvers project is an important milestone in the formulation of a new scientific attitude, one based on the unending search for new and improved research methods. Increasingly, the trend is toward cross-disciplinary studies in which resources af authorities in diverse fields are brought to bear on a particular research problem.

Scientific specialization is by no means obsolete. In archaeology alone, modern investigations demand skills so highly specialized that no one individual can locate, excavate, and interpret a site single-handedly. At Danvers, for example, Robbins turned to earthenware expert Laura Watkins for assistance in dating and reconstructing the base of a colonial vase that still bore markings left by a potter's wheel more than two centuries ago. Archaeologists and anthropologists will continue to concentrate on their chosen fields of specialization—whether these be pottery type, bone morphology or colonial architecture—just as historians will continue to earn their expertise by conducting long-term, in-depth studies of specific historical events, personages or time periods.

At the Danvers dig, Trask has added a new dimension to his inter-disciplinary investigations by initiating a "dig-it-yourself" program for interested townspeople. Individuals and groups may come to the site and, under supervision, sift debris heaps in search of colonial artifacts.

"At the same time," says Trask, "they are given information concerning the history and significance of the site and archaeological methods used in its excavation."

By opening the site to the public, Trask hoped to establish a healthy rapport with townspeople and to educate them in the use and value of inter-disciplinary study—goals he has obviously attained. The first "dig-it-yourself" day brought over 500 eager volunteers to the Parris site. To demonstrate the worth of history and archaeology for education and recreation, Trask plans to enclose the cellar and rebuild foundation walls—thus creating an institutional device whereby students can learn history through on-site study and archaeology through actual excavation.

Danvers, scene of the weirdest events in colonial history, is rich in archaeological potential. Since local response has been overwhelming, Trask hopes to continue his excavation of city sites. Next on his list of priorities: the 1672 Meeting House, where the witchcraft trials took place, and the John Putnam house, where one of the "bewitched" girls lived.

CHAPTER XXII

Mysterious mounds at Poverty Point

Ancient builders constructed terraces at Poverty Point, Louisiana? When? Why? For 15 years, archaeologists have been digging into the concentric earth hummocks to find out. The secrets they've uncovered are surprising.

For as long as anyone can remember, unusual indian artifacts have been turning up on an old plantation known as Poverty Point in northern Louisiana. Local citizens made collections of the "relics." A few professional archaeologists took an interest in Poverty Point stone tools, especially the tiny flint knives and curious little baked clay objects.

Some of this material came from the place where a road crossed a series of long, low earthen hummocks or ridges. The hummocks themselves seemed in no way remarkable—until an archaeologist happened to notice how they looked when viewed from above. Aerial photography revealed that the ridges formed a very definite geometric pattern. They could only be a series of well-planned terraces built by man in the form of six huge concentric octagons. The configuration measures three-quarters of a mile across, and its huge size conceals its real nature.

Fifteen years of archaeological-work at the site then answered some mysteries. It also presented baffling questions: Who built the terraces? What for? When?

The statistics of Poverty Point are staggering. To form the terraces, men and women and no doubt children carried earth in baskets and heaped it to a height of six feet or more. Each terrace measured about 80 feet wide at the base. The total linear measurement of the six concentric earthen ridges was 11 miles.

Nor was that the end of the earth-moving operation. On the west side of the terrace-complex these same people built a tremendous mound 640 feet by 700 feet at the base and 70 feet high. Although it is much eroded, there is some indication that they shaped the mound to resemble a colossal bird, and they connected it to one of the outer terraces by a huge sloping ramp. About a mile away stands another large mound and, close by, is a smaller cone-shaped one more than 20 feet high and almost 200 feet in diameter at the base.

In all, the builders of the mounds and terraces dug up and transported, perhaps 50 pounds at a time, at least 20,000,000 basketloads of soil. Why? Were the large mounds associated in some way with religious ceremonies? That was certainly true of mounds which the first Spanish invaders actually saw in use elsewhere in the South.

What beliefs did the Poverty Point people hold? What cult, if any, did they follow? A hint came from the cone-shaped heap of earth near the terraces. Excavation in this relatively small mound uncovered the remains of fires and remnants of burned human bone. Here the dead may have been cremated with elaborate rites and ceremonies of a kind that was very common north of Louisiana, especially in Ohio, 2,500 years ago.

Could the mounds be that old? The experts thought so.

As for the terraces, the first digs at the site unearthed fragments of household debris, suggesting that dwellings once stood along the tops of these man-made ridges. Perhaps as many as 600 homes sheltered a population of several thousand.

Such a big population could have furnished the manpower needed for the vast building projects. But how was that manpower nourished? Early excavators found little or no convincing evidence that these people grew any crops. If they had been efficient farmers, they might have supported so large a village. But as a rule people had to live in small groups in the days when men followed game and when women gathered seeds or fruit as it ripened in place after place. Could seasonal hunters and gatherers have afforded the time and energy both to feed themselves and to work at gigantic building projects?

For answers an archaeologist has to depend mostly on man-made objects that he digs up—or on traces of objects. For example, the earth in a mound can show him the imprint of the weaving in a discarded carrying-basket even after the basket itself has rotted away. The most numerous artifacts at Poverty Point were the intriguing little baked clay objects, many of them roughly spherical in shape. In clusters of five or ten, even as many as 200, these Poverty Point balls were often associated with signs of fires.

Cooking fires? That seemed to be the only explanation. First a woman would dig a pit in the ground. Then, one after another, she molded small handfuls of damp clay into convenient shapes, laid them in the pit and built a fire over them. Presently she raked out the coals and the balls of clay, now hardened by fire. After lining the hot pit with grass, she laid in food, covered it with the heated balls and left it to cook, clam-bake style.

The heated balls may also have been used in the way hot stones were used elsewhere—dropped into a vessel containing stew or mush to make it boil. In the days before women had sturdy cooking pots to set directly over the fire, they stone-boiled their food in watertight baskets or skin pouches or wooden vessels.

Because rocks were scarce in country near the Mississippi River, women had to improvise. They made an estimated 24,000,000 of the little Poverty Point objects during the 1,000 or more years the village was occupied. Some of the objects were rough and formless—as if a woman in haste merely pinched a gob of clay with her fingers and laid it in the pit. Others were twisted, grooved, melon-shaped, biconical like a child's top or patted into biscuit form. In some places the objects found in any one fire pit were all made alike—as if each woman had her own special style.

Other artifacts that turned up in abundance at Poverty Point were very small sharp stone tools called microflints. Outside of Alaska, such tools were not common in the United States. Where did Poverty Point people learn the art of microflint working?

Still other unusual discoveries included a large curved stone blade, small baked clay figurines (always women, never men) and little figurine heads with deep notches modeled in the top or grooves across the forehead. What these signified no one could say.

Strangest of all was the early date of the earthworks and mounds. Elsewhere in the Mississippi Valley great ceremonial mounds were built—but much later. The Poverty Point people seemed to be hundreds of years ahead of their time, and their village had long been deserted when other mound construction was just beginning.

Such an assemblage of oddities was bound to call attention to Poverty Point. In 1956, archaeologists James A. Ford and Clarence H. Webb made a scholarly report on the site. Before long, similar ancient sites were being reported elsewhere in Louisiana, Arkansas and Mississippi. Caches of Poverty Point balls also turned up at these sites.

Over the years, Ford and Webb and others examined scores of thousands of artifacts and put together masses of evidence. One thing became increasingly clear: The Poverty Point people did raise crops, probably including corn. So did the neighbors who borrowed Poverty Point ideas. They were productive farmers at a time when other North Americans were only just learning how to cultivate small garden plots.

These people did not, however, invent agriculture. That had been done long before in Mexico. Did some adventurous Mexican travelers reach the Mississippi River Valley and stay to teach their arts to local residents? Here are some clues to the answer:

Food-grinding tools eventually turned up at the Poverty Point site. Some were of the type used by women in ancient Mexico to grind corn.

The female figurines discovered at the site were typical of farming people. Here, as in Mexico, farmers must have made them, hoping to encourage fertility in crops. The figurine heads were particularly interesting because the clefts in forehead or crown duplicated those in figurine heads found at several farming centers in Mexico.

The innumerable microflint tools were also characteristic of many groups in Middle America, and it was reasonable to suppose that the art of making them came with travelers from Mexico.

Town-planning flourished in ancient Mexico, along with agriculture and the building of great pyramids. Often there was a strong link between farming, astronomy and certain Middle-American religious practices. Priests knew a good deal about the heavens and could forecast the right times for planting crops. With this in mind, James A. Ford has now studied the large Poverty Point mound and its ramp. They were, he found, oriented in a special way. If a man stood on top of the mound and sighted along the ramp, he would be in direct line with the rising sun at two times a year—about March 21 and September 21, the equinoxes. As in Mexico, dates were important to farmers who needed to know when to put seeds into the earth.

The ability to lay out a calendar-mound may very well have accompanied religious beliefs, ceremonies and all the other imports from Middle America. Just how or when these foreign influences reached Poverty Point is still unknown. Nor can an archaeologist tell the exact spot where the important Poverty Point traits originated. Did they come perhaps at different times and from different sources? How was mound-building here related to the construction of earthworks elsewhere in the Mississippi Valley? Why, in the end, did Poverty Point people leave this place which had cost them so much effort? Where did they go? These puzzling questions still await answers.

The Poverty Point site itself awaits Congressional action that will make it a National Monument, complete with exhibits giving visitors an idea of its remarkable and still mysterious past. Meanwhile, the best thing available is a reconstruction of the village, together with a display of Poverty Point artifacts, which can be seen at Louisiana State Exhibit Museum in Shreveport.

CHAPTER XXIII

Who carved the hand-prints on prayer rock?

A chunk of granite with hand prints and crude carvings was found in South Dakota nearly a century ago. Recently experts have decided that it may be a clue to a previously unknown civilization.

The old-timers of Marshall County, South Dakota, are amazed at all the fuss being made over a grayish-brown chunk of granite discovered amid the Coteau des Prairies Hills on top of a butte called Windy Mound. Men like Newton Jones, an attorney, can recall the rock's existence from their boyhoods, as far back as 60 years ago. Even then, the 1,870-pound rock was interesting, but nobody thought (or did) much about its strange carvings.

Prayer Rock, as it is now known, has been positively identified as an ancient indian artifact; its possible historic importance was first recognized about five years ago.

Perhaps the most significant things about Prayer Rock are the pictographic symbols chiseled into its smooth face. At each side are handprints. The thumbs are on the outside, suggesting that hands might have rested on the rock with palms turned upward in a gesture of supplication.

At the left edge is a sun disk with its rays directed across the top to the right. The disk, with its radiating lines, bears a strong resemblance to the foot of a large bird. On either side of the disk are two smaller figures that are difficult to read.

This disk appears to act much like a sun dial. It casts a shadow at sunset on the winter and summer solstices, the equinoxes and three other dates that have no meaning to researchers.

To the left of the sun dial is a cross with two crossbars and vertical bar with forked bottom. Here lies the first controversy over Prayer Rock. The figure is quite similar to a Chinese number nine.

Although Prayer Rock's significance is still being debated, acknowledgment of its authenticity was fast in coming from two sources. A. Z. Nelson, a student of indian rock art from Grand Forks, N. D.,

The carved handprints, with thumbs out, suggest the carver intended "palms-up" supplication to a diety—hence, the name Prayer Rock.

called Prayer Rock aboriginal Chinese and at least 4,500 years old.

No doubt the oriental looking figure had something to do with Nelson's decision, but no other authority has been willing to climb out on the same limb.

The Nelson theory hangs on one thread of possibility. Archaeologists have found traces of mound civilizations forming a pattern across the continent from the west coast. Most notable are ruins of an almost modern city in Alaska. Its artifacts show traces of an Asiatic culture. The nearby Bering Straits would be a logical route for migrating Asians.

Henry B. Collins, then acting director of the Smithsonian Institution, was less specific in his analysis. He called the rock a prehistoric indian petroglyph (rock picture). Collins did not choose to speculate on an exact age or the significance of the double barred cross.

Current speculation is that Prayer Rock and the Windy Mound area may pinpoint the center of a very ancient civilization. The mound itself would be the logical center of any theocratic (religiously oriented) government.

Other mound dwelling societies chose with exactness the highest ground for their religious shrines. Windy Mound fulfills this requirement, and Prayer Rock implies the existence of a religious center.

Who were these mound dwellers? Chinese or Indian? Only time will tell, but it is safe to say that residents in southeastern North Dakota and northeastern South Dakota may be sitting on top of a very old and surprisingly advanced civilization. Exploration of other mound dwelling civilizations reveal that they did have a written language, did build their cities on a complex pattern, did understand basic mathematics and a form of geometry. They kept records and maintained census figures.

Tepee rings and ruins of what appear to be mound dwellings are known to have been unearthed at Windy Mound by an expedition in 1926. Further digging would no doubt provide additional clues.

The proud Sioux roamed these hills long before the white man. Yet there is a time gap between them and anything close to 4,500 years ago, and their folklore does not fully explain the rock's symbols.

They do know that Windy Mound has long been a Wakan, or sacred place. The William D. Neill papers at Macalester College in St. Paul contain the manuscript of a Sioux translated into French at Paris in 1719. It describes the land of the Thunderbird 30 miles northwest of Big Stone Lake on the Minnesota-South Dakota border. An 18th century explorer's map puts the home of the Thunderbird in the same region which is one and a half miles directly northeast of Windy Mound.

This Thunderbird legend is one that is found in varying forms in indian cultures throughout North America. Some speculate that it had its origin at Windy Mound. There is an ancient Sioux legend telling of a Sioux chieftain coming to the rock because it was the dwelling place of this Thunderbird. In Sioux mythology the Thunderbird symbolized the power of their god on earth.

The old chief knelt before the rock, praying from dawn until dusk, pressing his hands against the rock with the palms turned upward. It was a gesture of giving and also one of receiving.

Possibly he prayed for rain, or good fortune in battle, or even for an end to disease within his trible. At sunset, completely exhausted, he arose; but his handprints remained imbedded on the rock. Later chieftains came to this same rock to pray, each placing his hands on the prints left by this leader of so long ago.

What will happen to Prayer Rock? Residents of Britton, S.D., 125 miles west of Minneapolis-St. Paul, suddenly find their locality abounds in indian and frontier history. A museum has been opened to house these artifacts and Prayer Rock is a main attraction.

And one thing is certain. Prayer Rock has escaped charges of fake so often leveled at similar discoveries, but controversy will most assuredly swirl around its significance.

Chinese? Indian? One time center of the Continent? Home of the Thunderbird? You can pay your money and take your choice.

CHAPTER XXIV

Brawl over a "2,000-year-old" archaeological site

Did the old stone structures in North Salem, New Hampshire hold bootleg whiskey, runaway slaves, loot from stage coaches—or are they evidence of a pre-Columbian invasion from megalithic European cultures?

Our guide pointed to the groove running around the edge of the 6 x 10 foot granite table in front of him and explained to the attentive tourists that it was probably used by an ancient people for sacrifice, human and animal. The groove, he said, served as a collection channel for the victim's blood which could be drained off at a cut leading to the edge of the stone. The tourists spoke in church whispers as they walked past the four-and-one-half-ton slab, giving it wide berth.

The explanation seemed plausible in that the table is on a heavily wooded hilltop in the midst of an apparently random assembly of strange stone structures, some collapsed into a jumble of rock, some still standing. These occupy about three quarters of an acre on a 12-acre plot of land crisscrossed with a grid of low walls interrupted here and there with upright slabs. The additional fact that this is located about 40 miles from Boston in the small New England town of North Salem, New Hampshire is a jolt to one's sense of American history.

The place is Mystery Hill and it is being preserved and studied by a nonprofit organization of amateur archaeologists called NEARA—an acronym for New England Antiquities Research Association. This group maintains the site with admission fees charged to an interested public.

NEARA's explanation for the origins of the site holds that the ruins were ceremonial grounds built about 4,000 years ago by a megalithic people whose cultural roots probably originated in Europe. Most professional archaeologists are unconvinced and consider Mystery Hill merely the remains of a colonial farm.

There was not always such confusion or concern about the origin and purpose of the hill. For years few people outside the natives of North Salem knew or cared about the stone-littered hilltop. In those days the place was called "Pattee's Caves" after a French Huguenot farmer, Jonathan Pattee, who occupied the land between 1823 and 1849. Local people believed he was responsible for the odd constructions and had built them to hold everything from bootleg whiskey and runaway slaves to loot from mail robberies. Research, however, revealed he was not a scoundrel. Three times he was elected trustee of town funds and he once donated a building for the town schoolhouse. Also nothing could be found mentioning construction of these buildings. If he had built and used them for shady purposes, it was a secret.

Pattee's hill wasn't "discovered" until 1936 when William B. Goodwin, a retired insurance executive and amateur archaeologist from Hartford, Conn., came upon the site and bought the land to excavate it.

It had not survived the years too gracefully. Quarry operations in Pattee's time and later in the 1920s had carried off or destroyed much of the stone originally used.

After reading about a band of Irish monks in an 800-year-old history of the Vikings in Iceland, Goodwin decided that what he had found was the site of a monastery built by these monks 1,000 years ago. He spent thousands of dollars during the next 14 years seeking proof of this.

Ignorant of the delicate brush and trowel technique of the meticulous archaeologist, he carelessly dug up the hill destroying dating sources, soil profiles and throwing away valuable artifacts that didn't support his monk theory. In some places he took the stone rubble and rebuilt structures the way he saw fit, destroying the original site in favor of the one that existed in his imagination. Nothing was ever discovered to prove Goodwin's monks had lived there; yet he clung to his theory until he died in 1950.

The hill remained untouched until 1955 when the Early Sites Foundation, an association of amateur archaeologists, commissioned Dr. Junius Bird of the American Museum of Natural History, and Gary Vescelius, a young Yale-educated archaeologist, to excavate the hill. Both had visited the site in Goodwin's days.

Vescelius supervised the digs, sinking 10 test pits which yielded thousands of artifacts, all colonial or post colonial. After six weeks he reported and evaluated his findings. He concluded that there was no evidence of anything but a colonial occupation.

Goodwin's theory was disproved and all members of the Early Sites Foundation agreed with the findings except a member of the

Photos by Douglas Colligan

Most dramatic piece of stonework on Mystery Hill is the "Sacrificial" table, below. Above, a word to the wise, and John Whittal, archaeologist.

amateur team named Frank Glynn who felt the report had not fully answered all questions. He continued investigating on his own. In 1956 he was joined by another amateur, Robert E. Stone.

Fascinated, Stone opened the site to the public in 1958 intending to stir interest in it and also providc funds to preserve it. He later established the corporation that owned and operated it. He agreed with Glynn that Mystery Hill was one of several examples of pre-Columbian settlings along the eastern seaboard, and founded NEARA in 1964 to investigate it.

NEARA's theory about Mystery Hill began with Glynn who sent photographs and queries to Professor T. C. Lethbridge of the University Museum of Archaeology and Ethology at Cambridge, England. Seeing similarities between the New Hampshire structures and some found on the island Malta and on the Iberian peninsula, he encouraged Glynn.

Research has provided interesting parallels. James Whittall Jr., chief archaeologist for NEARA, visited some of these sites and found that stonework style is similar and grooved stone tables are also present. But Whittall admits it's difficult to link the European constructions and their possible American cousin because of lack of evidence. Between Goodwin's haphazard excavations and previous destruction, about 80 percent of what originally stood on that land may have been removed or destroyed.

NEARA declares with certainty that the site is pre-Columbian, likely European in origin; that it is one of many traces left behind by a megalithic culture; that the site was used for some ceremonial purpose, and that it is 3,000-4,000 years old.

As supporting evidence Stone offers the structures themselves and carbon datings made at the site. Assembled from unmortared granite stones and roofed with massive slabs, the constructions, he says, resemble no stone handiwork of a colonial farmer.

Although the ruins of farmer Pattee's house, which burned down in 1855, now stand in the midst of the other buildings, Stone disagrees that Pattee was an eccentric who built them in secret with the help of his 11 children. Of Pattee's 11 offspring, nine were girls and only one boy survived beyond infancy. Furthermore, the pure mass of the rocks, ranging in weight from four to 14 tons, is an argument itself against this being a family project.

NEARA also points out monoliths and dolmens, or stone monuments, on the site. Some now are being investigated as having astronomical alignments with a point overlooking the sacrificial table. This has been complicated by vandals who have changed their original positions.

The four-and-a-half ton slab, NEARA says, was used for sacrifices and is positioned to conceal a "speaking tube," a hole in the wall of the oracle chamber that amplifies voices speaking into it. Whatever the exact purpose of these features, Stone feels they make no sense in a colonial context.

"We've also got seven good carbon dates at Mystery Hill," he points out, and these form added proof of the site being non-colonial. The first test produced colonial dates but earlier than Pattee's occupation.

One sample, made up of pieces of a rotted pine root imbedded in a wall, was dated 1690, 33 years before known settlers were in the area. Material from a lower level in the same location produced the startling date of 1000 B.C. with an error factor of plus or minus 180 years.

In the summer of 1971, tests on carbon from chinks in one wall produced the incredible date of 1525 B.C. with an error factor of plus or minus 210 years. When correlated to a more exact dating method called the bristle cone pine method, Stone says this is corrected to almost 2000 B.C.

When these results were published there was little interest among professional archaeologists. Stone says they refuse to budge from their colonial view because they discount the possibility of pre-Columbian contact with the New World by a number of European cultures, and because they take the findings of an amateur organization lightly.

Of the archaeologists who have made contact with Mystery Hill, most are unconvinced that there is any mystery at all. Dr. Bird, for example, has not returned since his excavations in 1955, and doesn't feel any urge to do so. "Everything pointed to colonial occupation. There was not one thing found to contradict this conclusion," he says.

Bird claims there is no reason a colonial farmer couldn't have built the structures and finds no trouble placing such oddities as the stone table in an Early American context. What is now called the sacrificial table might have been used for leaching lye for soap making, via water-soaked barrels of ashes placed atop the table. The whole megalithic speculation he dismisses as "a lot of wishful thinking."

Of Dr. Bird's colleague on the 1955 excavation, Stone says, "Vescelius set out to disprove Goodwin's monk theory and he did; but he still wasn't sure it was colonial."

Vescelius remembers his attitude differently. "I went in there with no preconceptions. I wasn't particularly adverse to the notion that a pre-Columbia culture may have lived there." And he was not aware of any doubt about the age of the buildings. He feels the stonework is no older than the 19th century.

According to Vescelius, the mysterious buildings were used for storage purposes, the "oracle chamber" in particular for holding cider barrels with the table serving as the base of a cider press. The "speaking tube," he says, actually served as a shortcut for piping the freshly pressed cider from the stone table to the barrels.

Vescelius did find the stone work unusual but has an explanation. Pattee's forefathers had come to America from the French province of Brittany on the English channel, where Vescelius says there are hundreds of megalithic structures similar to those at Mystery Hill. He feels Pattee's transplanted ancestors may have passed on that style of stoneworking.

He refused to consider the carbon dating at face value. A specialist in carbon dating himself, Vescelius claims there are too many variables to be weighed before acceptance.

More recently involved are Glyn Daniel, an expert in European archaeology and editor of the British archaeological magazine *Antiquity*, and Dr. Stephen Williams, an expert in North American archaeology and director of Harvard's Peabody Museum. Both went to New Hampshire shortly after the 1971 dating was pubilicized—Williams out of professional curiosity and Daniel as part of a BBC film crew.

As a colleague of Professor Lethbridge who corresponded with Frank Glynn, Daniel was unimpressed by what he saw and says as much in an editorial: ". . . it (Mystery Hill) certainly bears no morphological or constructional remEmblance to the great megalithic monuments of prehistoric Western Europe, apart from, of course, the coincidental resemblances that occur when dry stone is used in construction, and large stone slabs for trabeate roofing. . . . The real interest of Mystery Hill is not that it is a great archaeological mystery, but that it is built up as such."

Similarly in an interview at the time of the 1971 carbon dating, Dr. Williams' opinion was: "It's a very good colonial construction. It's my professional opinion that there's nothing of the age and connection they suggest." During the same interview he also admitted that no one from Harvard had been to the site in over 20 years. In the fall of that year he rectified this and examined the area where the dated carbon material was found.

"I went over the site and over the evidence with them," he recalls. "They apparently dug down and out away from the wall so that where the material was extracted was not near the wall. It's obvious something once burned there but there is no way that charcoal can date the wall above it."

As for the structures themselves, Williams says that it is difficult to know where everything belongs on the site, exactly what Goodwin reconstructed. He thinks NEARA underestimates both this and the extent of the quarry operations, and points out that no artifacts other than colonial have been found to support the megalithic theory.

Not everyone in the academic community opposes NEARA. One sympathizer is Professor Ross T. Christensen of the Department of Anthropology and Archaeology at Brigham Young University, who believes: "The constructions were plainly not built by New England Indians or their ancestors of any known variety. They clearly do not fit into the pattern of prehistoric cultural development usually assigned to the Eastern Woodlands area by professional archaeologists."

Another is Cyrus Gordon, Professor of Mediterranean Studies at Brandeis University, who made news with his pronouncement that a small inscribed stone found in a burial mound in Tennessee in 1885 was evidence that Semites had landed in America 1,000 years before Columbus. Gordon concludes that Mystery Hill is "definitely pre-Columbian, mainly due to the use of megaliths at the site."

Like Stone, he feels there are other examples of pre-Columbian, European culture throughout the northeastern U.S. and that people able to work in stone crossed the oceans many centuries before 1492.

"Professionals shy away from it (Mystery Hill) because it's skating on thin ice," says Gordon.

As things now stand it appears that Mystery Hill will continue to puzzle some people, and prick like a thorn in the sides of others.

Whatever the difference of opinion, most probably will agree with one observation made by Gary Vescelius: "The buildings have the look of something designed to be secret. All the structures were at least semisubterranean at one time and were built with the apparent motive of making them as unobtrusive as possible. Whoever was there had something to hide."

PART V

asia and the pacific

The continent that boasts—with justification—some of mankind's most ancient, complex civilizations and written languages, should have relatively few dark archaeological mysteries. Yet it has many, and those it has are deeper and more exotically mysterious than those in other, more primitive lands.

The intricately carved limestone towers and atrium-like courts of stone fretwork in Cambodia's long-deserted jungle cities of Angkor, and the newly opened tombs of Han and Chou dynasty royal folk in the Changsha region of Red China, still pose more questions than answers. So do the ruins of the once proud citadel of Nan Matol on an island in the Western Pacific; not to mention the incredible stone heads of Easter Island.

These and other brooding Asian monuments to earlier men have been partially explained in some instances, but this serves only to heighten scientists' curiosity about the things that still remain unanswered. With the mounting interest of many current Asian governments in preserving the cultural beginnings of their people, archaeological exploration and digging has become an on-going program. China and Indo China now are rigidly enforcing laws to prevent looting of historical sites. New digs are carefully policed. Hopefully, it will result in one of the world's greatest contributions to the uncovering and preservation of the heritage of mankind.

CHAPTER XXV

Angkor—jungle city of the dead

Snarled in llianas and verdure of the northern Cambodian jungle, an elaborate city has stood totally abandoned for centuries. Who built it? What is it doing there? What became of the builders? Archaeologists now have unearthed part of the dramatic story of Angkor Wat and Angkor Thom.

On a day in February, 1860, a seasoned, sun-hardened explorer headed out from New Angkor, in Battambang Province of Siam. He traveled down the Battambang River to the place where several streams join to form the Tonle Sap River.

Thirty-odd miles down the Tonle Sap, the river widened out into a lake with the same name as the river. Coated with lily pads, lined with rattan palms and the white trunks of fromager trees, the lake was crossed by the explorer and his Indo-Chinese crew. They had heard rumors of vast ruined cities north of the Tonle Sap and were eager to discover the remains of a highly sophisticated ancient civilization that had mysteriously abandoned its great cities to monkeys, snakes and jungle centuries before.

The traveler was Henri Mouhot, a naturalist who specialized in tropical butterflies. A French Protestant from Montbeliard, he had been sent by the British Geographic and Zoological societies to brave swarms of mosquitoes and leeches on a scientific reconnaissance of Indo-China.

On all sides rose a dense forest, spreading out across the wide plain. Butterflies flapped through the steamy air; lizards scuttled out of the path. Gibbons and monkeys chattered in the treetops; flocks of parakeets rushed by, screaming. Vultures hung in the sky.

The path followed the course of a creek, the Siemreap. After a two-hour hike, signs of tumbledown, man-made masonry appeared. Towers of sandstone blocks, intricately carved, loomed over the greenery.

As far as Mouhot's eager eye could reach into the shadowy distances, there stretched megalithic walls adorned with sculptured reliefs. A maze of galleries served as boundaries for overgrown courtyards.

Mouhot asked the Indo-Chinese about the city but got replies like: "It is the work of giants." "It built itself." "It is the work of Pra-Eun, the king of the angels."

For three weeks, Mouhot lingered at "Ongcor" (as he spelled it), sketching, measuring and writing. The temple on which he stumbled, he learned, was but one of a vast complex of ruins. Then he returned to Bangkok and set out northward into Laos. Near the Chinese border, malignant malaria struck him down, and he died almost immediately, leaving many questions unanswered. But when his journal and letters were assembled the excitement of his discovery sent several other French explorers on his track.

These and other visitors carried away many statues, stelae and other parts of the ruins for private collections and European museums. The plundering continued until checked, at the end of the 19th century, by the newly formed *Ecole Française d'Extreme-Orient.*

During this period, ownership of Angkor switched back and forth between Siam and Cambodia until 1907 when the ruins became finally Cambodian as a result of French protection of that country. (In 1949 Siam became officially known as Thailand.)

Given a free hand, French archaeologists swarmed over the ruins, hacking away the jungle, putting fallen stones back into place and studying inscriptions.

For decades, men wondered who built Angkor. Cambodian history did not say. But then, Cambodian history only went back to the 15th century; and, like most traditional histories, it began in a mass of myth. According to the myths, an Indian hero named Kambu Svayambhuva wandered into a desert, where he was befriended by the Nagas, a race of genii in the form of seven-headed cobras. Kambu wedded the Nagaraja's daughter, who considerately took human form for the occasion. The serpent king was so pleased by Kambu's account of India that he cast a spell, which turned his land, too, into a well-watered country. From Kambu and his serpent princess sprang the ruling house of the land, called Kambuja, of which "Cambodia" is merely a modern Latinized form. Being immortal, the princess made herself the permanent first wife of the Kambujan kings.

The legend conceals a grain of fact: that, long before the *Chronicles of Cambodia* were written, Indian adventurers, traders and missionaries came by sea to Cambodia, where they gained control of the

Funerary temple of Suya-Varman II, built in 1300s, is the most spectacular part of Angkor Wat ruins. Elephants once carried monarchs down the approach.

barbarous Khmer people and imposed a veneer of Indian civilization upon them. Hence the early kings of Kambuja bore Indian names and put up inscriptions in Sanskrit, while the common people continued to speak the very different Khmer tongue.

The early decades of this century saw a lot of mystification about the builders of Angkor. Why had they walked out of their capital *en masse*, leaving it to the jungle? What became of them? Had they simply disappeared, or were the modern Cambodians their descendants? In the latter case, what caused the downfall of this once pretentious civilization?

Sir Osbert Sitwell suggested that the Angkorians' prosperity depended upon the export of kingfisher plumes to China, and the kingdom fell when Chinese fashions changed. Others surmised that the proletariat had revolted, slain their overloads and gone back to simple village life.

During the century since Mouhot, many French archaeologists have deciphered the numerous inscriptions on monuments of the Khmer kingdom. Hence, although there are still many gaps and doubtful points, the outlines of Khmer history have been well established.

Angkor Wat, the best-known part of the ruins, is the funerary temple of Surya-Varnan II, built in the early 1300s. This temple, connected with the worship of the Hinduist god Vishnu, has been called "the largest religious edifice ever built by man." (Another Cambodian temple, still in ruins, may be larger.)

If you were exploring Angkor Wat, you would probably approach from the west along a thousand-foot causeway, the railing of which are a pair of sculptured Nagas, or seven-headed cobras, rearing up to a height of 13 feet. You would pass over a moat and under a great wall to find yourself in a vast enclosure. There are three concentric enclosures, each in the form of a hollow square. Loving squares and straight lines, the Khmers shaped their buildings as hollow squares, sometimes divided into four smaller squares by cruciform structures. These squares and sub-squares are made up of long galleries, whose walls are covered with reliefs of bare-breasted dancing girls, kings and gods of Hinduism.

The builders of Angkor Wat erected towers in the form of lotus buds at the center and at each corner of the large hollow squares. The central and tallest tower—over 200 feet high—and the four towers of the innermost square are still in good shape; the others are partly or wholly delapidated. Where the causeway enters the outer square through an ornate gateway, there were special entrances for chariots and elephants.

Half a mile north of Angkor Wat lies Angkor Thom, a capital city in the form of a square about two miles on a side. Jaya-Varman VII built it in the late 12th century. This was the fifth capital city on this site. The first had been erected in the 11th century by King Yasho-Varman I, after whom it was, before modern times, called Yashodharapura.

At the center of Angkor Thom rises the Bayon, a great Buddhist temple built by Jaya-Varman VII, Cambodia's Rameses II. Although much smaller than Angkor Wat, the Bayon is still the second largest building in the area. Crowded into its 56 acres were 54 great towers, each bearing a sculptured face on each of its four sides. The faces represent the Buddhist divinity Lokeshvara; the features, however, may actually be those of Jaya-Varman VII, who fancied himself a Living Buddha. Like much late Khmer construction, it was built in a hasty, slipshod fashion. Hence, although half a century or more younger than Angkor Wat, it is more delapidated.

According to the Chinese, civilization first appeared in Indo-China in the first century of the Christian Era, in the form of a kingdom they called Funan. The Chinese found many Funanese customs barbarous. Trial, for instance, was by ordeal. The accused had to carry a piece of red-hot metal, or pick something out of a boiling cauldron. If he was burned, he was presumed guilty and was thrown to the crocodiles in the moats of cities and palaces.

On the other hand, women enjoyed a comparatively high position. The Indo-Chinese took a permissive attitude towards sex, which has not much changed. An 18th-century British diplomat posted to Indo-China complained that he could not enjoy a stroll in the evening because of the "horrible fornications" he was compelled to witness. Even centuries before, in the 1290s, a Chinese visitor was revolted by the troops of homosexuals who wandered about.

The Khmer kings were deified. Although Shaivism (worship of Shiva) was the state religion, Vaishnavism (worship of Vishnu), Buddhism, ancestor worship and the veneration of a horde of petty godlets and demons also flourished. Each king built a special temple to house his *lingam* the symbol of his authority. A lingam is a pillar carved in the likeness of an erect phallus; it is one of the forms under which Shiva is worshipped. Jaya-Varman IV put up one 100 feet high, but it has vanished.

In the 10th century, Yasho-Varman I built the first city of Yashodharapura on the site now called Angkor Thom. He also dug the first of a series of immense reservoirs, the five-mile East Baray. In the next century, Surya-Varman I dug the West Baray and rebuilt the city. These colossal waterworks, which irrigated rice fields for miles around, were actually a greater and more costly achievement than all the temples. It was customary to build a temple in connection with each reservoir.

Jaya-Varman VII, who reigned from A.D. 1181 to after 1215, was the greatest Khmer builder. Besides once more rebuilding Yashodharapura, he erected a multitude of Buddhist temples elsewhere. He also constructed roads, hospitals and healing shrines. Obsessed with his own divinity, he overdid the whole thing. Since ancient public works were usually executed by forced labor, the amount of labor needed for the vast projects of this Living Buddha impoverished and wore out his subjects.

Medieval Kambuja was a prosperous land of gleaming, gold-plated temple towers. The Khmers wore breech-clouts or skirts but went bare above the waist, with much use of perfumes and golden bangles. All the more prosperous citizens owned slaves, who were captives from the barbarous hill tribes. Women controlled most trade. Trial was still by ordeal. Convicted felons, were punished by cutting off toes, fingers, noses or other members. Capital punishment was by burial alive or being thrown to the crocodiles.

The king gave audience while standing at a palace window with a golden frame. When he left the palace, riding the royal elephant and grasping the sacred sword, he went clad in iron armor against assassins and surrounded by troops of his soldiers, war elephants and women. On the New Year's festival, the Khmers set off rockets and huge firecrackers, whose explosions shook the city. Other festivals featured dancing tournaments, boxing matches, cockfights and combats of elephants.

The once-mysterious downfall of Angkor was, however, fast approaching. Under the weak successors of Jaya-Varman VII, the empire shrank as outlying provinces revolted and broke away. The building of public works ceased. The spread of the pacifistic Theravada or southern Buddhism, brought by missionaries from Ceylon, militarily weakened the Khmers.

Pushed on by the growth of the great Mongol Empire, the Thais swarmed down from southern China into the valley of the Menam River west of Kambuja. In 1941 a Thai king, Paramaraja of Ayuthia, invaded Kambuja and sacked Angkor Thom. An enormous booty was carried off, including the Khmer king's own royal troupe of dancing girls and as many of the Indian- descended intelligentsia as the Thais could catch. Rumors still waft of treasure hidden from the invaders beneath the Bayon.

The Khmers soon rallied and drove the Thais out of Angkor. But, finding the city uncomfortably close to the border, the kings moved the capital to its present site of Phnom Penh. Now a border province exposed to raids, the Angkor region was abandoned to the prowling leopard and the wandering hunter, until in the present century the French cleared the ruins and recovered much of Cambodia's lost history.

CHAPTER XXVI

A 2,000-year-old chinese lady returns

A four-foot layer of clay and charcoal may be the secret of the remarkable preservation of an ancient lady and her belongings in a Red Chinese tomb that still has archaeologists puzzled.

One of the most intriguing news stories to come out of China since the People's Republic again began exchanging information with the West is the discovery of a 2,100-year-old tomb containing a remarkably well-preserved body. In photographs the corpse is easily recognizable as a woman. Chinese doctors say she was probably 50 years old at her death. The connective tissue beneath her skin is still soft, the tissue fibers distinct and the color of her femoral artery like that of a person who has just died.

Not only the tomb's occupant, but also more than 1,000 objects buried with her have weathered the centuries amazingly well, the Chinese report. Silk and linen items of clothing in the Chinese style have retained their colors and patterns and, judging from photographs, still are wearable. Glowing lacquer trays and dishes look elegant, ideal for serving a Chinese dinner. Some of the lacquerware, in fact, did contain food such as chicken, pears, eggs and flour—all perfectly recognizable if not edible. A bamboo musical instrument called the *yu* is in such fine condition it might still be playable.

Artifacts like these have occasionally survived in good condition for millennia in Chinese tombs, but a well-preserved 2,100-year-old corpse is unique! Nothing like it has ever been found in China, or indeed elsewhere in such magnificent preservation. Other Chinese tombs from the same period, the Western Han Dynasty, 206 B.C. to A.D. 24, yield only skeletons at best. How did the occupant of this tomb and most of her goods retain their original appearance so well? No Western scientists have examined the tomb and its contents, but accounts of the discovery reported by the Chinese offer some clues.

When the body was unearthed on the outskirts of Changsha, the capital of Hunan Province, it was half immersed in a "reddish pre-

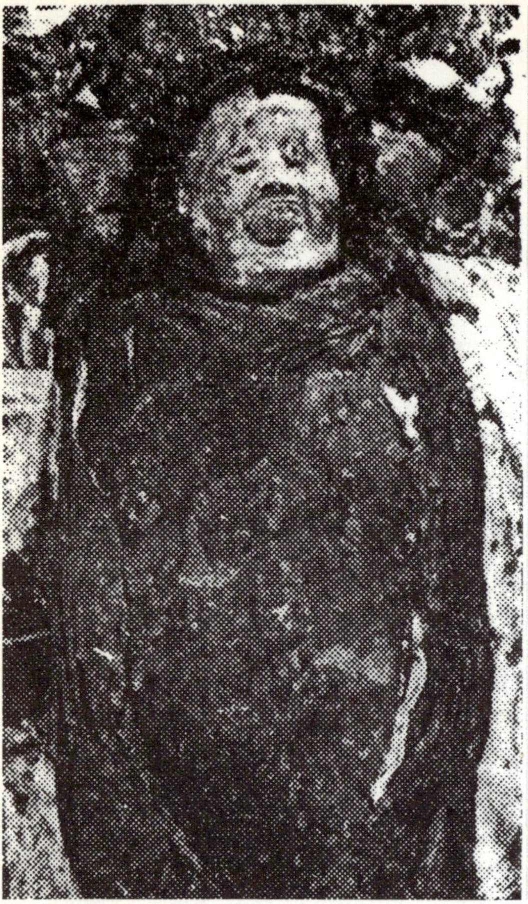

Though 2,100 years old, the body tissues of the Chinese lady above left were soft and pliable as though she had just died; the 1,000 items buried with her were equally well preserved, like the garment above and service below.

servative fluid." Six wooden coffins, one inside the other, encased the body. Except for the outer coffin, more of a wooden tomb chamber than a coffin, the other coffins fit tightly together. The tomb chamber was located at the bottom of a 50-foot-deep pit. Five tons of charcoal were piled on and around the tomb chamber then a four-foot layer of sticky white clay put over that. The rest of the pit was filled with red clay and earth. Finally, a 65-foot high mound was raised above the ground.

Chinese archaeologists suggest that the main reason for the well-preserved state of the contents is the white clay, which keeps out moisture. Changsha has a sub-tropical climate and the ground is damp. Many ancient tombs have been excavated in the area, but bodies and wooden coffins buried without the protective layer of clay have long since decomposed.

Nevertheless, no well-preserved bodies have ever been found in other clay-sealed tombs, indicating that some special factor operated in this instance. According to Dr. A. Gutkind Bulling, research associate in art and archaeology at Columbia University and author of some 60 articles and reviews on Chinese archaeology, that factor might have been charcoal. "No other tombs in this area had charcoal," she says, "so that might have contributed to the preservation of the body." Also, she notes, the "reddish preservative fluid" may have played a role. Analysis of the fluid hasn't yet appeared in Chinese journals but Dr. Bulling expects it will be published soon.

The tomb, she notes, is more typical of the earlier Chou Dynasty (B.C. 1122-1249) than the Han. The smallness of the tomb chamber, the multiple coffins, the space between the outer coffin and the inner ones, and the use of clay for sealing are common in the tombs of Chou aristocrats. "The number of coffins depended on your rank," says Dr. Bulling. "The more coffins, the higher the rank."

A number of objects in the tomb of the Changsha lady bear inscriptions indicating the owner was the Marquis of Tai, or Ta, a title conferred by the Emperor Hui of the Western Han Dynasty for the first time in 193 B.C. and withdrawn a few generations later. The woman, Chinese scholars believe, was probably the first wife of the first Marquis of Tai, Li Tsang. Despite his wealth, as indicated by his wife's tomb, Li Tsang is not believed to have been a powerful noble since he ruled over a small fief of about 700 households. The Han period was rich in material goods, however, and even a petty nobleman could bury his wife in a princely style.

Accounts from China are not clear on how the tomb was found, but one source indicates it was discovered early in 1972 when workmen were digging a tunnel. Once the site was determined an ancient tomb, it was given high priority for excavation, possibly because Chairman Mao Tsetung comes from Hunan Province. When the tomb's contents were revealed, they apparently caught the imagination of Chinese leaders, who have encouraged wide publicity. The official Communist party newspaper and other journals have published illustrated accounts of the excavation in Chinese and English.

According to these journals, the coffins and the grave goods are of exceptionally fine quality. The exteriors of some of the coffins are lacquered with brilliantly colored designs showing monsters and animals. Cloud motifs float over most of the scenes. The lid and sides of the inner coffin are covered with embroidered silk and colored feathers. Draped over it was a large piece of silk in a T-shape with tassels hanging from its corners, in the opinion of Chinese experts the finest single item from the tomb. The T-cloth is covered with painted scenes, some taken from legends and others depicting the life of the society to which the tomb's occupant belonged.

Between the outermost coffin and the one beneath it is a space where most of the objects were placed. The ancient Chinese did not subscribe to the slogan, "You can't take it with you," so the trove includes almost everything a wealthy woman might need in afterlife: clothes, dishes, cups, jars, toilet boxes, benches, screens, pillows, food, walking sticks, musical instruments, medicine and money. Among the clothes are some 50 different items including shoes, stockings, gloves, garments and lengths of material. Most are silk and in spite of their delicacy (some are so light they resemble nylon net) they have survived with colors and fibers intact.

"Silk has been found in Chinese tombs before but this clothing is better preserved than any found in China except in the desert regions of Sinkiang," says Dr. Bulling.

Many of the objects are interesting for their artistic excellence, as well as the light they throw on life among the wealthy in early Han times. During the Han Dynasty, factories produced much fine lacquerware, examples of which are found in this tomb. The lacquer used was the juice of a tree, *Rhus vernicefera.* When applied in thin layers to wood and allowed to dry, the juice provides a hard, shiny surface that

Not only was the strength and texture of the silk garment above in a perfect state of preservation after 2,000 years, but the colors had held up as well.

Site of grave, outside of Changsha in Hunan Province is shown here after removal of earth mound remains.

Five coffins were encased one within the other inside this outer one, and lacquered in brilliant colors.

can be polished and painted. Among the 200 or so lacquered items are dishes, trays, cups, a zither and toilet boxes, all gleaming as if newly arrived from the factory. Most are black on the inside and red on the outside, with stylized designs traced in a contrasting color.

One thing a wealthy woman needs that is difficult to provide in a tomb is servants. In earlier times in China, servants were simply killed when their master died and buried along with him. During the Han period, however, a more humane practice prevailed. Small wooden and pottery figures were placed in tombs to serve the occupants. In this particular tomb, there are about 150 little figures, some dressed in silk garments and others painted. One group of 23 forms a song and dance group, that was possibly to play the life-size musical instruments in the tomb.

Glorious as the Changsha tomb is, its grave goods and architecture are surpassed by the most spectacular Han Dynasty tomb discovered in China in recent years. In 1968, Chinese archaeologists dynamited the iron walls of a tomb in Hopei Province that belonged to Liu Sheng, a prince and a son of Emperor Chin Ti of the Western Han Dynasty. The prince and his wife were dressed in suits made of thousands of small rectangles of jade sewn together with gold thread. Their heads rested on jade pillows and they held jade crescents. The suits, the first complete ones ever found, were worn only after death and were reserved for those of high rank. They were meant to preserve the body, but inside the suits Liu Sheng and his wife were skeletons.

Liu Sheng's tomb and that of his wife are spacious structures with several rooms that resemble underground palaces. Both have four rooms, plus a "bathing room." Construction is typical of that of later times, when tombs were built to resemble the houses in which wealthy Chinese actually lived. In the Liu Sheng tomb, one big room held a dozen horses and several chariots. Another contained hundreds of pieces of pottery filled with food and wine. When the tomb was completed, the doors were sealed by pouring molten iron between two parallel walls.

The excavation of tombs is not unusual in China today. Since 1949, when the People's Republic was established, the Chinese may have excavated more sites than any other country in the world. Most excavations have been tombs, but some cities and villages also have been uncovered. According to Dr. Bulling, who has followed Chinese publications closely since 1949, the new finds have "completely changed our picture of the development of China." The excavated sites range from the prehistoric to the last imperial dynasty, with current emphasis placed on early historic periods like the Han.

"In China, as in many other countries undergoing a redefinition of nationhood, archaeology has become a necessity," says Dr. Judith M. Treistman, an associate professor of anthropology at the City University of New York and an authority on Chinese prehistory. The pursuit of the Chinese past, she notes, is encouraged by Chairman Mao, whose dictum "Let the past serve the present" is often quoted by Chinese archaeologists.

When tombs are opened, they not only supply rich stores of beautiful objects but history lessons as well. A recent Chinese book describes some of the archaeological finds made since 1949. The author ends his account of Liu Sheng's jade suit with this statement: "The two specimens serve as evidence of the crimes committed by the feudal ruling class in cruelly exploiting the people and at the same time show the skill and hard work of the laboring people in such early times." This theme is reiterated throughout the book.

When the People's Republic was formed in 1949, the government placed sites known to be rich in archaeological remains under special protection and alloted funds to restore them. It also created many museums to receive archaeological objects. In 1958, China claimed she ranked third in the world in number of museums. Today the number undoubtedly has grown. Funds also have been made available to conduct new excavations at sites turned up accidentally, a frequent occurrence. "The massive presence of the past is revealed whenever the Chinese earth is disturbed to any depth," says Dr. Bulling.

When a tomb such as that at Changsha is discovered, the government has a set procedure to follow, according to Dr. Bulling. The finder notifies authorities who, in turn, inform members of the provincial museums or a central institution such as the Office of Culture. Representatives from these organizations visit the site and, if it seems promising, make recommendations that it be excavated. If the site looks unusually good, members of the Archaeological Institute of the Academia Sinica in Peking will do the work; otherwise it falls to local archaeologists.

One result of the strict laws: there are no legitimate private dealers and archaeological looting that plagues other countries is dangerous. A recent Chinese book tells about a group of peasants who turned over to the state some valuable artifacts they had found. They were publicly praised and given a "certificate of commendation." The new reverence for the national heritage is striking in China because before 1949 that country was notorious for its enterprising archaeological looters, some of them Westerners. While "loot" still comes out of China it is relatively little.

Because of our long involvements in the looting of the Chinese past, some archaeologists here believe the Chinese government will be reluctant to let Western scientists participate in the excavations now underway. "I doubt if American archaeologists will ever be able to work with their Chinese counterparts, but we may be taken to some sites to be shown finds made by the Chinese," says Dr. Treistman.

If the warming relationship between the United States and the People's Republic continues, archaeologists may even get to see a Han tomb that may rival that of the Marquis of Tai's wife. Next to the Changsha tomb is a similar mound. Does it, too, contain a well-preserved body and a treasury of grave objects? The visible evidence looks promising.

CHAPTER XXVII

City of the sacred turtle: Nan Matol

The strange ruins of a once proud city stand silent and dark in the Pacific, a monument to the almost forgotten cult of the sacred sea turtle. Oral histories still describe the kings who once ruled it.

From the tropical waters of the western Pacific, the steep peaks of a mountainous, jungled island rise more than half a mile into the sky. Around the 164 square miles of this island lies a necklace of coral reefs and small islets. This is Ponapé, the largest of the Carolines.

A broad bay gapes in the southeastern coast of Ponapé. Scattered about this bay are scores of small islands, the largest of which is called Temuen. At high tide, the eastern end of Temuen is sea-washed into nearly a hundred low-lying islets, on which stand a vast array of huge, dark, strange, silent ruins of deep blue stone. Such is Nan Matol, one of the world's citadels of archaeological mystery.

Nan Matol is an awesome ruin despite damage from hurricanes, treasure hunters and the prying action of tropical vegetation. Most of the islets are bounded by enormous walls up to 30 feet high.

Lying a few degrees north of the equator, Ponapé is warm and dank, with frequent rains and some hurricanes. Like other Micronesian islands, it has birds and insects but no native mammals save those, like pigs and rats, brought in by man.

White men first saw Ponapé on December 23, 1595, when a Spanish ship under Pedro Fernández de Quiros touched there on its way from the Solomon Islands, just discovered, to Manila.

There is no record of other foreigners' landing for several centuries, until in 1826 when an Irish sailor, James O'Connell, arrived with a few survivors from a shipwreck. By dancing an Irish jig and by his fortitude in letting himself be tattooed all over, O'Connell made a hit with the Ponapeans, who married him to the king of Net's 14-year-old daughter before he knew what was happening. He stayed on the island for 11 years and fathered two children by his native wife, until a passing ship offered him a chance to return to civilization.

At this time, the island was divided into five warring kingdoms: Jokaz, U, Metalanim, Net and Kiti. (These strange Micronesian names have many spellings: Chokach, Matolenim, Not, etc.) Temuen and its ruins lay in the district of Metalanim. O'Connell and one of his fellow-castaways, paddled by a Ponapean terrified of spirits, twice visited Nan Matol. O'Connell described them:

"At the entrance we passed for many yards through two walls, so near each other that, without changing the boat from side to side, we could have touched either of them with a paddle. They were about ten feet high, in some places dilapidated, and in others in very good preservation. Over the tops of the wall, coconut trees and occasionally a bread fruit spread their branches, making a deeper and refreshing shade. . . ."

O'Connell found no trace of inscriptions. The walls were built of a prismatic basalt which, crystallizing slowly from lava deep in the earth, forms large prisms, usually six-sided. (The best-known formation of this kind is the Giant's Causeway in Ireland.) The island of Jokaz, off the northern coast of Ponapé, has an exposed cliff of these rocks, with heaps of broken prisms at its foot. The builders of Nan Matol must have hauled these prisms down to the shore, loaded them on rafts and towed them 15 miles along the coast.

The walls look as if they were made of black logs, with courses piled alternately parallel to the axis of the wall and then at right angles to it. The "logs," however, are columns of basalt. The stonework is very crude, with gaping holes.

In 1886, during the last great scramble for colonies, Spain annexed Ponapé. But the Spaniards never controlled much of the island, and the warlike Ponapeans rose several times against them. The islanders had a stern, Spartan culture, which went in for self-mutilation as a sign of bravery. Before missionaries, traders and adventurers demoralized them (as they did all the South Sea Islanders during the 19th century), they were also deemed a notably cheerful and honest people, albeit formal, with a caste system and a passion for titles.

During the past hundred years, the Ponapeans have been handed about among the powers. In the Spanish-American War, the United States seized the Carolines but later gave them back to Spain, which then sold them to Germany. When the Ponapeans rose against German rule in 1910-11, the Germans crushed the rebellion with a bombardment from the famous cruiser *Emden* and hanged the leaders. In the

First World War, the Japanese took the Carolines and kept them under an ill-observed League of Nations mandate. Today the United States governs them under a United Nations trusteeship.

Ever since its discovery, Nan Matol has been a subject of mystified speculation. Some have said it was a fortified base built by Spanish pirates; others, that it was the capital of a once-great Pacific empire; still others, that it was a relic of a lost continent. Occultists have averred that it was a remnant of Lemuria, a former continent in the Pacific, which sank as they thought Atlantis had sunk in the Atlantic.

The idea of Lemuria began a century ago as a sober scientific hypothesis. Certain British scientists tried to explain resemblances between geological formations in India and South Africa by supposing that they had once been connected by a land bridge across the Indian Ocean.

Other geologists surmised that Lemuria was a remnant of a much larger and earlier continent, which they called "Gondwanaland" after the tract of Gondwana in India. They supposed that Gondwanaland once reached three-quarters of the way around the earth in the Southern Hemisphere, with a gap in the Pacific, and that it "broke up" by the sinking of various parts. More recently, this theory has been revived in connection with Alfred L. Wegener's hypothesis of continental drift. In the new version, Gondwanaland broke up, not by partial sinking, but by the horizontal drifting apart of its various component pieces.

These hypothetical continents, however, have no bearing whatever on human history. Even if they once existed—which is possible in the light of recent discoveries in Antarctica, and in the cores brought up by the *Glomar Challenger*—the world's main land masses had reached about their relative places many millions of years before man arose from the lower primates.

Most of the mysteries of Nan Matol turn out to be man-made. The facts about it were lost as those who knew them died off without recording them in writing.

Most of what is now known about the pre-colonial history of Ponapé was gathered by Dr. Paul Hambruch, of the Thilenius expedition of 1908-10 from Germany. Hambruch's native informants told him that two young wizards, Olo-Sipe and Olo-Sopa, set out from Jokaz to build a great cult center to the gods, demons and ghosts. When they found Temuen, they cast a mighty spell which caused the basaltic prisms on Jokaz to fly through the air and settle down in the right positions to form Nan Matol.

Hambruch also heard of the conquest of Ponapé by the king of Kusae, an island several hundred miles to the east. At that time, a single king, called the Satalur, ruled all of Ponapé. According to several highly mythological versions of the tale, the king of Kusae, Iso-Kalakal, defeated and drove out the Satalur, and Iso-Kalakal's successors ruled as the Nan-Markis. They failed to keep control of the whole island, which split into five kingdoms. Of these, the Nan-Markis ruled Metalanim. There were 12 Satalurs, followed by 17 Nan-Markis. Hambruch guessed that the two dynasties together reigned for about 500 years, and no better estimates are yet to be had.

Nan Matol consisted of several groups of structures. The main center was Matol-Pa, the lower city, where dwelt the king. The upper city, Matol-Pa-Ue, includes the tallest building: Nan Towas, where the Satalurs were buried. It also includes Es-Een-Tau, the house of the high priests, and Pei-En-Kitel, the burial place of Iso-Kalakal. Near the southern end of the ruins lies Pan Katera, the sacred governmental center, including a palace and altars for offerings.

Nanpei of Metalanim told Hambruch that, until recent times, Nan Matol was used as a center for the worship of the turtle god Nanusunsap. When the Ponapeans caught a sea turtle, they brought it to Nan Matol and kept it in one of the buildings. When the tribe was assembled, the priests annointed the turtle with coconut oil and hung it with ornaments. They took it with much ceremony to Pan Katera, killed it, cooked it, and served it to themselves and the king.

About 1800, in the reign of Luk-En-Mueiu, the ceremony ended in farce. At one ritual, a priest got no roast turtle. He walked out in a rage, howling curses, and went off to live by himself on a sand bank and eat eels. The Metalaminians feared he had so profaned the ceremony that they dared no longer hold it.

The crudity of the stonework and the lack of any writing or relics of civilization rule out the idea that Nan Matol was built by men of advanced culture. Likewise, the lack of native mammals shows that Ponapé was never part of a continent or joined to a continent. Everything indicates that Nan Matol was a religious or cult center rather than a true city. Other Micronesians built similar centers, although never on so vast a scale.

Sifting fact from legend, the history of Ponapé runs as follows:

About 1400 A.D., after many migrations and conquests, the population of Ponapé was much as it is now. Then a single chief made himself high king of Ponapé, with the title of Satalur. He or one of his successors began Nan Matol as a cult center.

About 1600, the Satalur demanded tribute from King Iso-Kalakal of Kusae. Instead of paying, Iso-Kalakal conquered Ponapé. His successors ruled Metalanim as the Nan-Markis. They lived on another island but continued to use Nan Matol as a cult center. There were probably several cults, but the turtle cult is the only one we know about.

Although the Nan-Markis may have added somewhat to Nan Matol, when they lost control of much of Ponapé they no longer commanded enough manpower for such grandiose building projects. Therefore Nan Matol ceased to grow. The other kingdoms built their own, smaller cult centers, whose ruins still exist. The last active cult at Nan Matol was the Nan-Markis' personal cult of the sacred turtle, which ended around 1800 when that hot-tempered priest profaned its ceremonies.

Then came the white men, and Nan Matol was left forlorn, to be covered with mangroves and to mock later visitors with its dark, silently frowning walls and empty, overgrown courts.

CHAPTER XXVIII

Isle of eyeless watchers

The huge 'heads' of remote Easter Island have fascinated people for centuries. Who built the awesome statues and what purpose did they serve?

One of the loneliest places on earth is Easter Island, or Rapa Nui as its dwellers call it. One must travel 2,200 miles eastward to reach the South American coast; or, in the other direction, 1,200 miles to find Pitcairn Island. The desolate isolation of Easter Island makes its ruins all the more astonishing.

From the sea, the island appears as a green, grassy land, rolling away behind tall, black cliffs. It is roughly triangular, about 35 miles around, with an area of 45 square miles. Near the points of the triangle stand the cones of three extinct volcanoes: Rano Raraku, Rano Kao and Rano Aroi. Smaller cones rise elsewhere. The climate is mild and windy, with gusty rains. There are no native mammals, but insects are bothersome.

The soil of Rapa Nui is decomposed lava, fertile but very porous. Hence the island has no rivers and only a few springs. The natives had to work hard to clear stones from their fields and to carry water to irrigate their simple crops, mainly sweet potatoes.

The island is famous for its huge-headed statues. Although many have been taken away to museums, or have been used for building materials, or have fallen into the sea, there are still over 600 of them on Rapa Nui. Completed statues range from 3 to 6 feet in height. Some larger ones, up to 66 feet long, were begun in the quarry of Rano Raraku but never finished. The sculptures, although often called "heads" or "busts", are for the most part complete statues. The size of the heads, however, is so exaggerated in proportion to the squat bodies that the latter pass unnoticed.

The Dutch admiral Jaakob Rogeveen landed on Rapa Nui on Easter Sunday, 1722, and named the place Paasch Eyland or Easter Island; hence the name "Pascuans" for the Easter Islanders. These people are

All photos from Photo Trends

Along the volcanic ridges of Rapa Nui, early inhabitants had carved highly creative forms in the native rock. Their significance is still unknown.

Polynesians—big, handsome folk with brown skins and straight or wavy black hair. They speak a dialect of the Marquesan language of the Polynesian family, and nowadays they also know Spanish. They farm, fish, and work on the sheep ranch run by the Chilean government. They wear western-style clothing, some of it stolen from visitors.

Scientists, adventurers and cultists have all tried to solve the problem of how and when these folk came to Easter Island. Some have said that Rapa Nui was the remnant of a sunken Pacific continent, or that it was once joined by a land bridge to other land masses. Geology has, however, completely discredited such ideas. Others have asserted that the island was settled by venturesome Vikings although there is nothing to suggest such an origin.

Scientists are now convinced that the Pascuans are of purely Poly-

Megalithic walls of unmortared block of volcanic rock were painstakingly laid up and fitted by the early Polynesian settlers of Easter Island.

nesian origin, and that the Polynesians once lived along the southeast coasts of Asia. The rise of a powerful Chinese Empire in the second millennium B.C. touched off a general movement of peoples. Each tribe on the fringes of Chinese civilization, fleeing advancing Chinese imperialism, crowded its neighbors outward. Because the Polynesians were already spread along the coast, they could go nowhere but across the sea. Language, culture, and archaeology all indicate that the Pascuans came from the Marquesas Islands.

The Polynesians, the most accomplished of all barbarian seafarers, may have occasionally reached the coast of South America. It is less likely—although not entirely impossible—that any Peruvian indians ever got to Polynesia. There may have been many such unrecorded transoceanic voyages in the history of mankind.

In the vast majority of cases, however, the voyagers probably perished, either on the voyage, or at the time of landing, or soon thereafter, without leaving any trace of their voyage. The best they could hope for would be that a local tribe, instead of instantly killing and perhaps eating them, would take them in. But, to survive, the voyagers would have to adopt the ways of the locals, and not vice versa. Living on suffrance in strange surroundings where most of their previous knowledge would be useless, they could not be "enlighteners" of their hosts.

Early in this century, Juan Tepano, a Pascuan who collected tribal lore, told the following tradition of the settlement of Rapa Nui:

The land of our fathers was a great island to the west called Marae Ranga. The climate was warm and many trees grew there, of which our ancestors made large boats or gathered together to build themselves houses. . . .

Hotu Matu'a was a chief of this island, but he was forced to leave it after a quarrel with his brother Te Ira-ka-tea.

There was in the island a certain Hau Maka, who had tattooed King Hotu Matu'a. Hau Maka had a dream: his soul journeyed across the sea to an island where there were holes [craters] and fine beaches . . . Hotu Matu'a understood that Hau Maka's dream was a promise. He chose six men, gave them a canoe, and told them to sail straight ahead until they reached the land Hau Maka's soul had seen.

The pioneers found Rapa Nui, and Hotu Matu'a followed close behind.

For a defeated Polynesian chief to set out with his henchmen to look for new land was usual; otherwise he was liable to be eaten by the victors. While most such expeditions perished at sea, some succeeded, and thus the isles were peopled. The so-called Polynesian "canoes" were sailing catamarans up to 150 feet long, carrying up to 400 people. Radiocarbon dates show that the settlement of the western Polynesian islands began several centuries before the Christian Era, and of Rapa Nui not later than the ninth century of this era and possibly several centuries earlier.

In the millennium following the settlement of Rapa Nui, the Pascuans farmed, fished, fought tribal wars, carved hundreds of awesome statues, and then saw their culture crushed by the all-conquering white man.

In 1576, the Spanish seaman Juan Fernández reported land in the area of Rapa Nui; in 1687 an English buccaneer, Edward Davis, made a similar report. In 1722 came Admiral Roggeveen. Naked natives came aboard bearing food. When they had presented their gifts, they stole whatever they could lay their hands on, including several sailors' caps and the admiral's tablecloth, and dived overboard.

When Roggeveen sent a party ashore, hundreds of Pascuans gathered on the beach. Some made friendly gestures; others threatened the visitors. When they began throwing stones, a volley of musketry littered the sand with dead and wounded. The Pascuans scattered but soon returned with servile gestures. A few hours later, Roggeveen sailed away.

In 1774, Captain Cook arrived. To him the Pascuans seemed few, poor and miserable. The probable reason is that they had been having terrific intertribal wars. Survivors of a losing side hid in their underground storerooms, hoping to avoid being roasted for a victory dinner.

In the ninteenth century, foreign pressure on the Pascuans rose. American whalers stopped to kidnap natives for slaves or to shoot a few for target practice. Hence the Pascuans became increasingly hostile to strangers, and their hostility caused more clashes. A group of French missionaries who landed in 1843 were massacred.

The Pascuans presented a formidable sight. Like other Polynesians, they were a tall, powerful, heavily-built folk, the men being notably taller than the women. Many went entirely naked, although some men wore a G-string and many women a grass skirt, and all donned barkcloth cloaks against the chill winds.

The men were bearded, tied up their hair in topknots, and wore large wooden plugs in their ear lobes. They tattooed themselves all over, and the men were painted over the tattooing in gaudy patterns of red and black. When a visitor arrived, they crowded down the beach, capering, dancing, and yelling. Many would be friendly, but others at the least provocation would throw stones with alarming accuracy.

Rapa Nui's culture received its fatal blow in 1862. One day, Peruvian ships anchored off the island, attacked the islanders, killed some, and rounded up about a thousand others, whom they carried off as slaves. After Bishop Jaussen of Tahiti protested, the Peruvian government ordered the victims returned. By this time nine tenths of them had perished. Of the remaining hundred, all but fifteen died of smallpox on their way home, and the survivors spread the disease among those who had remained on the island. So the population shrank from several thousand to a few hundred.

The dead included King Kamakoi and nearly all the priests and nobles. Since these were the people who had kept the records and knew the procedures, the culture fell to pieces. Then Catholic missionaries landed and took up their work, made easier by the disappearance of the native leaders and the decay of traditions.

The modern ideal of benevolence towards the backward, however, at length made its way to Chile. Today, although poor by western standards and bereft of most of their ancient culture, the Pascuans seem healthy and fairly happy. In 1955 the population was 842.

The Pascuans were much more than just a cannibal tribe. Despite their isolation, they developed a complex culture. They carved pictures on rocks, engaged in sports like surfboard riding, and observed complicated religious ceremonials.

They also had a system of writing, unique among Polynesians. They incised lines of characters on wooden boards. A special class of reciters, called *tangata rongorongo*, kept the boards and read them.

With the destruction of the ruling class in 1862, this system of writing was practically forgotten. By the 1870s, when scholars began to take an interest in their writing, the Pascuans were using the last of their tablets for firewood or for building canoes. They said the missionaries had urged them to burn the tablets as relics of paganism.

Many efforts have been made since then to decipher Pascuan writing, and some quite fantastic theories have been advanced. One such cryptographer was Bishop Jaussen, who tried to rescue the Pascuans from Peruvian slavery.

In the 1950s a German scholar, Thomas Barthel, after a world-wide search, found Bishop Jaussen's linguistic notes in an Italian monastery. He also rounded up copies of the two dozen surviving rongorongo boards, scattered in museums around the world. He claimed to have deciphered the writing, which he said consisted of hymns and other ritualistic material. More recently, Russian and Norwegian scholars have denied Barthel's claims. So the problem of the rongorongo boards has not yet been settled—if, indeed, it ever will be.

The most spectacular Pascuan achievement was the famous statues. The Pascuans built sacred inclosures called *ahu*—rectangular, pyramidal, or ship-shaped—as burial platforms. Some ahu were as much as 300 feet long. Around each platform they erected statues, facing inward. When a Pascuan died, his kin wrapped his body in bark cloth and placed it on a scaffold on the ahu, where it remained for months before being buried. There were once about 260 ahu, with a varying number of statues—up to sixteen—apiece. Many ahu were demolished for their stone.

The Pascuan ahu and their statue were used also for religious rites; Roggeveen saw the natives squatting around fires in front of the statues and going through the motions of praying. Possibly they thought the spirits of their ancestors entered the statues during these rites, but of this we cannot be sure.

Competition for prestige led each chief to build bigger and bigger statues. In many parts of Polynesia, chiefs used megalithic building as a way to gain honor. Thus Tonga acquired its famous trilithon, consisting of two uprights of coral rock weighing thirty-odd tons each, supporting a lintel of the same material. Other Polynesia peoples also built sacred inclosures and carved gigantic statues of wood or stone.

The Pascuan statues were made of volcanic tufa from one quarry in the crater of Rano Raraku. Everything about them indicates that they were made, not by men of some vanished Lemuria nor yet by Peruvian explorers, but by the ancestors of the present Pascuans. While there is no exact way to date individual statues, the custom of erecting them probably lasted down to the eighteenth or early nineteenth century.

Aside from nearly 200 unfinished statues in the quarry and a few scattered along the roads leading thence to the coast, the statues fall into two groups. One comprises the ahu statues, which were sledded from the quarry by grass ropes. They were then erected by prying up one end, shoving stones under it, prying it up a little more, and so on until it lay at a slant against a heap of stones. The final erection was done with ropes. The ahu statues were also given cylindrical "hats" of red volcanic rock from another crater, representing the Pascuan man's topknot.

Another group, between 250 and 300, were erected on the slopes of Rano Raraku. These statues lacked topknots. Instead of having flat bases for standing on the pavement of an ahu, they end in tapering stone pegs, driven into the soft volcanic soil to support the statue.

Their carving also differs from that of the ahu statues, suggesting that they were made at a different period. Whereas the ahu statues have the orbits of the eyes sculptured all the way round, the volcano statues have no distinct eyes. The planes of the cheeks are carried right

Illustration from a 19th century book shows sailors measuring the few remaining Aku statues still standing and wearing top knots. The picture indicates no hint of "taboo" on the part of natives; the statue cult was dead.

up to the eyebrow ridges, whose shadows look like eyes.

One theory is that the volcano statues are unfinished ahu statues. They were erected, it is said, on the slopes of Rano Raraku to finish the carving on their backs. Then they were hauled to their sites, where their pegs were cut off so that they could stand on their ahu. Lastly, the carving around the eyes was completed so that the statue could see.

During the intertribal wars from 1722 to 1840, all the ahu statues (save one, badly weathered and partly buried) were overturned. Along with burning their houses and destroying their exposed corpses, each tribe upset the statues of its foes to insult them. Now every ahu statue lies flat on the ruins of its platform, save the weathered one and one other re-erected in 1956.

The volcano statues, however, were not vandalized. Although many have been upset and buried by landslides, more than half still stand, frowning forever across the rolling land and the pounding sea. Whether the volcano statues were made before, or after, or at the same time as the ahu statues; why they were set up on Rano Raraku; why they were not toppled with the rest; when and why the Pascuans stopped making statues—these questions may never be answered.

One may wonder why the Pascuans went about everything so frantically, whether erecting colossal statues, welcoming visitors, or butchering and devouring one another in relentless wars. Perhaps the boredom of utter isolation is the answer. Having settled on an almost treeless island, they could not leave because there was no timber for shipbuilding.

The isle gave its people a good living—at least until they became too numerous—but no variety. There were only the grassy fields and volcanic knolls, and beyond them the booming sea. There were no wild beasts to hunt or be hunted by; no neighboring tribes to fight or trade with; no other lands they could reach in their flimsy little canoes, patched together from driftwood; no traders to stop by with trinkets and news.

So, to relieve the tedium, they went in for games and sports, for fantastic rites and ceremonies, for bizarre forms of personal adornment, for megalithic construction projects, and finally warfare.

PART VI
archaeological crime-old and new

On the face of it, most people seem to think of archaeology and anthropology as fairly remote, dusty pursuits, performed by somewhat offbeat people wearing safari suits and wielding picks, shovels and camels hair brushes. It is certainly true that these two professions are hardly as exotic or glamorous as you'd guess from the novels and screen plays about them. Like all pastures seen from the other side of the fence, the nettles, briars and crabgrass are hidden by the usual modest clumps of juicy clover.

Work in the field, as anthropologists Thomas and Sharon McKern have described it, ". . . allows a man to grow a scraggly beard without fear of criticism, and to chatter aimlessly to himself without disgracing the family. But tossed into the balance go the echoing silence of loneliness; the painful inconveniences of life in the wilderness; the perpetual itch of unwashed, sweaty skin; the communal intimacy with snakes, spiders and biting bugs; the celebration of holidays with a cold can of baked beans, a salt tablet and a cup of gritty coffee."

Whatever his characteristics, however, you'd hardly conjure up the image of an antiquities digger as one involving violence and crime, including murder. Yet in the past, and even today, the field has had more than its share of violent crime. Even more curious, archaeologists have been called upon to play detective and try to solve murders that were committed thousands of years ago. On the pages that follow, the authors report on a broad spectrum of case histories of archaeological misbehavior and ancient mystery.

CHAPTER XXIX

Looters even kill for pre-Columbian treasures

A growing market for ancient artifacts has encouraged a new crime wave of murder and looting that threatens the archaeological finds of the world and the lives of the scientists investigating them.

It was nearly dusk one hot March day in 1971 when Harvard research fellow Ian Graham and three companions reached the Mayan ruins of La Naya in the Guatemalan jungle. The party put up their tent, slung hammocks and began preparing dinner. On the following day Graham, a young British-born student of the Mayan culture, planned to record the details of the inscribed stone slabs that La Naya was reported to contain. These large slabs (most rise to a height of 12 to 15 feet, may weigh a ton or more) are called stelae. They are found in many areas of Guatemala and Mexico. The hieroglyphics the Mayans carved on them over 1,000 years ago have not yet been deciphered by scholars but progress is being made. Certain signs, for instance, have been linked to specific Mayan rulers.

The more inscriptions that are recorded, the greater the possibility of finally unlocking the secret of the Mayan hieroglyphics. Graham had been photographing, drawing and recording all the inscriptions he could find in Central America. From reports he had heard, the La Naya site appeared promising.

As one of Graham's party set out the dinner, Pedro Sierra, a Guatemalan guide who was a member of the group, stepped to the door of the tent. Two shots rang out. Sierra fell to the ground dead at Graham's feet. Terrified, the other members of the party huddled in the tent until dawn, then dashed into the jungle. Graham returned to La Naya later, accompanied by members of the local police force. A number of the stelae, they found, had recently been removed. Graham had stumbled on a party of armed looters who were sawing up the stelae for easy transport. Sierra was probably shot because he had already helped send several men to prison for plundering La Naya.

By the time Graham had reached La Naya with the police, the stelae fragments were undoubtedly on their way through the jungle to a dealer in a Guatemalan city, who had probably "commissioned" the plunder. The dealer might sell the stelae within the country but, more likely, he would smuggle them into the United States, where stelae bring a much higher price.

If Graham managed somehow to locate the La Naya stelae in a United States collection, they would probably be of little use for his purpose. Stelae are so massive and located in such remote areas that thieves must dismember them for transport. They use chisels, saws and even acid. The inscriptions on a stela are on the sides and back of the slab; the face contains a sculpture. Since the sculptured face is more appealing to most collectors, looters try to removed that portion, usually destroying the inscriptions in the process.

But even the rare whole stela on display in a museum or a collection is not particularly valuable to Graham or other students of the Mayana culture. Clemency Coggins, an art historian who specializes in the art and archaeology of ancient America, pointed out in *Science* that the Mayans placed their stelae in highly symbolic locations. A stela removed from its context thus loses much of its historical meaning.

Archaeological looting is an old story. Thieves plundered the tombs of the early Egyptian kings thousands of years ago. Today, however, the boom in the antiquities market has led to an increase in the looting of ancient objects all over the world. Many of modern robbers carry guns.

Unauthorized removal of archaeological items as well as their sale and export is now illegal in most countries. But the illegality does not seem to slow the pillaging. Stories of looting keep coming from many areas, but particularly the New World since antiquities from our hemisphere are "in".

At Tikal in Guatemala, anthropologist Dennis E. Puleston of the University of Minnesota, found a well-preserved Mayan stela in 1965. The date carved on it revealed it was one of the last monuments erected before the collapse of the classic Mayan civilization in the ninth century A.D. Three strange signs carved on it were the same as those from a calendar used in Mexico, indicating that Mexican invaders may have obtained a foothold here. Puleston made a mold of the stela but held up publication of his find for fear looters would get to it before a complete study could be made. His precautions were useless.

On a return visit in 1970, he discovered that much of the stela had been destroyed in an attempt to remove two small figures on its face.

In Keams Canyon, Ariz., U.S. ranger Elmer Randolph, assigned to the Hopi indian reservation, pointed out recent damage to an ancient Hopi village. "That was just done," he said, noting a wall that had been hacked down to expose an underground chamber. The empty chamber had contained pots, dishes and bowls. "Two days ago when I was here, that wall was still standing and a week ago, I found another room that had been broken into. As I was going into the area, I passed a jeep full of people going out. I think they probably had just left with a load of loot."

At the remote site of Machaquila in Guatemala, according to Stephen Williams, director of Harvard University's Peabody Museum, a large stela was broken into many pieces and taken out on muleback. A shrimp boat carried the fragments to the southeastern U.S. Last fall the pieces, cemented together by a dealer, were on sale in California at an asking price of $350,000. During its travels, however, the stela had been well publicized. Ian Graham, the Harvard researcher whose companion was killed at La Naya, recognized the fragments as those of a stela he had last seen on site in Guatemala. Using this identification, FBI and U.S. Treasury Department agents seized the stela last winter.

In Nigeria the director of the National Museum at Logas reported, just before the Nigeria-Biafra conflict broke out in 1967, that rare wooden statues carved by the Ibibio tribe were being stolen from villages. Known as "Ekpu figures," they stand three to four feet high and represent Ibibio ancestors. During the war, the rest of the statues were carried off by soldiers. According to the magazine *African Arts*, quantities of African sculpture from Nigeria have appeared on the international art market in spite of strict Nigerian laws against their export.

In many instances, even if the looted object is undamaged the wreckage the thieves leave behind is enormous. Clemency Coggins describes an exhibition of some 50 carved and polychromed Mayan vessels, all of them whole, on display in New York City in 1971. "Very likely such a concentration of superlative objects represents countless unproductive excavations and burials discarded at the site by looters," she says. The destruction inevitable in the search for small objects like these, she adds, may be worse than that associated with the plundering of large monuments.

But from a scientist's point of view, the greatest damage done to an archaeological site by looters is "the tearing of the gossamer threads of context," as Dennis Puleston puts it. He is particularly concerned about the uprooting of Mayan stelae like those of La Naya, which are particularly popular among American collectors. "Removed from the context of other monuments and the buildings with which they were associated, the fragments of dynastic or military history on a single piece become essentially meaningless," he told a recent meeting of the American Association for the Advancement of Science. "The chances of tracing an unrecorded monument back to its site of origin once it has made its appearance in a collection in another country are almost zero."

Scientists lose in a number of ways when an archaeological site is robbed but collectors of the looted objects win, at least in the short-term sense. In the past, museums were the big collectors of archaeological objects, not a few of them looted. But today, anthropologist Richard I. Ford of the University of Michigan estimates, only about two percent of the items entering this country are bought by museums. Private collectors purchase the rest. Many of these simply want to put a fragment of a Mayan stela or a Turkish vase on their coffee table or bookcase as a status symbol.

Some collectors of looted objects, however, should know better. They are students and even teachers of art and archaeology. A professor of African art at a large university, who buys many items, says: "They are already stolen, so why shouldn't I buy them?" His students also are good customers for the dealers.

In time, some of the wiser purchases may pay off for private collectors. A Mayan stela purchased for $5,000 a decade ago, for instance, brings about $80,000 today. Some private collectors, in fact, are now amassing archaeological collections for investment rather than for pleasure. But the real winners are the dealers and the looters who supply the dealers. David I. Owen of the University of Pennsylvania cites one sale of a Turkish antiquity that netted the seller a $15,000 profit on a single small item.

A typical transaction involving looted antiquities was described to a AAAS meeting by Dwight B. Heath, a Brown University anthropologist. Two Costa Ricans took gold and jade objects to New York City on consignment, spent $7,500 on "living high," paid off $11,500 to the actual looters—and each kept $4,000.

Dealers buy items from a small army of looters, many of whom rob ruins on a part-time basis. In little Costa Rica there are more of these "huaqueros," or grave robbers, than there are professional archaeologists in the entire world, according to Heath. The approximately 4,400 huaqueros make up about one percent of the total economically active population. Huaqueros make more money looting than they could legitimately. Like treasure hunters everywhere they dream of the "big strike." Three men picked up gold items worth $12,400 in a single day; in the next month, the same trio got $13,800 more in gold.

If the looting, sale or export of antiquities is illegal in most countries, why are the huaqueros and dealers so successful? The laws are difficult to enforce. In the jungles of Central America, for instance, the government simply cannot keep track of looters, who often know the territory better than the police. And the poorly paid officials are eminently bribable.

The picture doesn't look quite as bright for dealers as it did, though. In the last two years, moves have been made to curb the trade in stolen antiquities. In 1970, the U.S. and Mexico signed a treaty under which Mexico, on request, can get back any "important" artifacts stolen after 1970. The treaty isn't foolproof, mostly because small objects like pots are excepted, but at least it is a step in the right direction. So are recent resolutions by Harvard University and the University of Pennsylvania, which have large archaeological collections, that they no longer will purchase, and, in the case of Harvard, even accept as gifts, objects that have not been legally exported.

Meanwhile, a convention passed in 1970 by UNESCO, the United Nations Educational, Scientific and Cultural Organization, to control archaeological looting will eventually have some good effect.

Like the Harvard and University of Pennsylvania resolutions, however, the UNESCO convention mainly affects museums, not the much larger private market. To control that market, says Richard Ford of the University of Michigan, additional measures are needed. Among other things, he suggested educational programs in the United States and abroad, a halting of tax-exemption for donations of stolen antiquities to public institutions, compensation of citizens for donating objects they find to museums, and lawsuits by concerned organizations. One of his more imaginative proposals was the encouragement of the replication of antiquities by local craftsmen to fulfill the human desire to collect. The idea has already worked in some Mediterranean countries.

Whatever action is taken, it should be taken quickly. "Must we wait for the near destruction of ancient sites before we act?" asked David Owen. "The answer is obvious!"

CHAPTER XXX

Crackpots and forgeries

Forgers of Egyptian antiquities usually are neither successful or totally sane, but whoever forged the famous Etruscan pieces was clever enough so his work was exhibited for 30 years before it was found fraudulent.

As the old saying goes: You don't have to be crazy to be an Egyptologist, but it helps. Perhaps Hindu philosophy and Druidism have attracted an equal proportion of crackpots, but Egyptology has an undue fascination for the unhinged.

Once the curator of Egyptian antiquities in an eastern museum was working in his office when the guard ushered in a visitor. This was obviously a gentleman by his dress, his neat beard and his old-fashioned spectacles. The visitor produced from his pocket a large scarab and laid it down upon the table. The curator saw immediately that it was one of those crudely made paperweight scarabs that are sold on Egyptian streets. "I am sorry, sir," he said, "but I'm afraid that that is a modern forgery." "No," said the old gentleman, "that is a genuine ancient Egyptian scarab." He then produced from another pocket a glazed figurine. The curator took more time to examine this, but soon satisfied himself. "And this too, sir," he said, "is a forgery. The inscriptions is impossible." "No," repeated the visitor, "that is a genuine ancient Egyptian servant figurine."

"Well, sir," said the curator, "do you mind telling me why you are so certain that these pieces are genuine?" "Not at all," the gentleman answered with quiet pride. "I am the god Amon Ra."

When the curator recovered from his astonishment, he decided to make the best of the situation. He said: "Well, sir, this a great honor, and—if I may say so—a great opportunity. As you probably know, we can do reasonably well in translating hieroglyphic, but we cannot pronounce Egyptian. They never wrote the vowels, and we are not always sure about the values of the consonants. Would you do me the favor of reading some Egyptian aloud?"

The visitor graciously accepted the invitation, and the curator took a book of inscriptions off the shelf. The gentleman adjusted his glasses and ran his finger along a line of hieroglyphs. Then he went back and started over again, his lips moving silently. Then a third time. Then he closed the book regretfully. "I am sorry," he said, "but it has been a very long time!"

The macabre appearance of a mummy excites the imagination of the superstitious, and there are stories about a mummy making a gesture or moving around at night. The only mummy that I ever heard of that did move was Peruvian, and not Egyptian. The story goes that Chicago's Field Museum many years ago received a shipment of mummies from Peru. They had been crammed down into barrels, tightly flexed inside the wooden containers. The foreman of the basement workers said: "Jim, knock the head off of one of those barrels. Let's see what's in them." Jim went to work and loosened the head of a barrel. He had just succeeded in getting it free all the way around, when the head of the barrel flew off, a mummy rose up before him, making a wooshing noise as the air rushed into its body. With the release of pressure, the body resumed its outstretched position. Jim left suddenly without discovering what the shipment was.

An otherwise reputable scholar, whose field was not Egyptology, wrote that he visited the Tomb of Tut-ankh-Amon in the early years of its clearance and read with awe the inscription carved over the door: "Death to those who enter this tomb." There never was any inscription carved over the door of that tomb, and there never was any curse carved or written anywhere in the tomb. But the legend of the Curse of King Tut has a kind of manufactured credence, because so many people repeated the nonsense that they came to believe it despite all protests.

When we visit an Egyptian temple at night, it is quite common for the government guards to hand us a lantern and then stay safely outside. Some years ago a local peasant climbed over the rear wall of the temple of Medinet Habu, fell and broke his leg. He set up howls of pain, but the guards stayed trembling outside. They thought that he was the *afrit* (bad spirits) which haunted the temple. Only after the sun had risen did they go in and rescue him.

North of the great temple at Karnak there is a small temple sacred to the god Ptah. Modern archaeologists have mounted in that temple a black standing statue of the goddess Sekhmet, with a woman's body and a lion's head. She stands in such a way that she is generally in the shadow, but the entering light picks out her features in a horribly dramatic way. She is particularly forbidding in the moonlight. So a body of terrible lore has gathered around that statue. She bites the heads off men. Years ago an Egyptian peasant attributed a run of bad luck to that statue and smashed it. The authorities had it restored, and it is a pet of the dragomans, who love to tell tales about its baneful influence and then suddenly bring their tourists into startling confrontation with it.

The forging of Egyptian antiquities is about 125 years old. For some categories, such as scarabs, it has become a skilled craft. Egyptologists, when shown a forged scarab, sometimes made the mistake of rejecting it and pointing out the errors in the carving. The forger would not repeat the blunders the next time.

Legend says that a provincial judge in Upper Egypt sat in court two days a week and made scarabs the rest of the time. He had the scholarly books on scarabs, so that he copied faithfully and made no mistakes. Another legend says that ancient glaze of broken figurines is used for scarabs. This is quite fresh looking when the piece is finished, so that the scarab is then fed to a turkey, and the bird's gizzard "ages" it.

Forgers in other materials have learned the tricks of the trade. Some ancient timbers may still be found here and there. They can be carved into statuettes and figurines, which would date back to ancient time if subjected to the carbon-14 test.

Since traffic in antiquities is legal only under government license, both the finders of genuine pieces and the makers of forgeries try to make their sales at night. Characteristically they will come with an air of furtive mystery and terror of the police and try to sell a piece in a subdued light and a haste which does not permit close examination or careful consideration. At the old Chicago House in Luxor in the 1920s a man once brought two stone heads under these conditions. It was impossible to look at them carefully, and he first insisted that he would not leave them. He was finally persuaded to let them stay with us for twenty-four hours. In the light of day it became evident that they were probably made by the same hand. The break at the neck and a smash on the cheek were identical on each piece. When the man was charged with making them, he finally broke down and admitted it.

Among the most famous archaeological forgery *suspects* are the New York Metropolitan Museum's pieces of Etruscan statuary men-

This famous 'Etruscan' warrior was accepted as genuine for years. Today it is known to be a clever forgery, but still a work of art.
Metropolitan Museum of Art

tioned in a previous chapter. Today, the warrior shown on the left is labeled by the museum as a "XX Century piece executed in the style of 500 BC". An Etruscan horse, beautifully rendered in classic form, still remains unproven as a fraud, but remains in doubt.

Just because a piece of artwork is copied doesn't necessarily mean that the copier is a bum artist, either. Some copies are as good or better than the originals. Michelangelo once admitted to sculpting a "Greek" piece, "antiqueing" it and selling it to a rich Roman family as the real thing, when he was hard put for cash. He knew he could sell the "old" sculpture, though his new work, under his own name, wasn't going.

One of the treasures of the Metropolitan Museum is the Benvenuto Cellini chalice, a delicate cup of gold and enamel, in which the basic element is a seashell mounted on the back of a turtle.

In the 1920s museum security was not as careful as it later became. One morning the chalice was missing from its case. At the same time it was found that a young guard, recently hired, was also missing. The museum went through its customary forms of notifying the police and advertising the theft throughout the world of museums and art dealers.

In the next three or four months only one pertinent incident was reported. An art dealer in Amsterdam, Holland, had a visitor, a young man carrying a shabby suitcase. The young man opened the suitcase, unwrapped an elaborate object of gold and enamel, and handed it to the dealer. The dealer examined it carefully and at length, and finally handed it back to the young man, shaking his head. The young man began to protest: "It's genuine! It's very valuable! It's a piece that you can sell for a fortune!" The dealer continued to shake his head: "Young man, I know exactly what it is, and I cannot afford to touch it! In fact, for my reputation, I shall have to report that I have seen it." The young man hastily put the chalice back into the suitcase and left.

A few months later a curator of the Metropolitan Museum was working at his desk, when an unkempt and seedy-looking man entered his office. The intruder dramatically pulled out of his overcoat pocket a newspaper-wrapped object, and then set the chalice upon the desk. The curator glanced at it, finished what he was writing, pushed up his glasses, picked up the chalice, and examined it carefully. "Well," he said, "you brought it back. We thought you would.

The young man said: "What are you going to do with me?" The curator answered: "Do with you? We're not going to do anything with you. Of course, you'll never get another job. But we're not going to *do* anything with you. You don't think that a museum like the Metropolitan would leave anything so valuable out for the likes of you to carry off, do you? We always have replicas. You don't think that you actually stole the original Cellini chalice, do you?"

The young man said: "So I can go?" The curator nodded: "Certainly you may go."

As soon as the young fellow had left, the curator pushed a buzzer on his desk, and the assistant curator came in. "Oh!" cried the assistant, "he brought it back after all."

"Yes," growled the curator, "and I didn't give him the satisfaction of knowing that he had it!"

In the spring of 1919 a German scholar appeared at the British Museum in London and asked to see an ancient coin in their collections. It was a unique piece, so that the British Museum specimen was the only recorded example. For the purpose of this story, let us call it the Cilician stater. At that time, just after World War I, Germans were not at all popular in England, but this man's credentials were in perfect order, so that he was given a cold but correct acceptance and taken to the room where the coin collection was stored.

A sub-curator checked a list, went to a cabinet and pulled out a drawer. It was full of coins, each in its own little circular depression set into the floor of the drawer. The sub-curator carried the drawer to a table, pointed out the Cilician stater to the German and went away. The German picked up the stater, got out his notebook and magnifying glass and went to work.

After some time the German scholar picked up the drawer and sought out the sub-curator: "Thank you very much. Now I return the coin in its drawer." The sub-curator took the drawer, looked down into it, and said: "Very good. Would you mind putting that coin back again?" The slot where the Cilician stater should have rested was empty. "But I did put it back!" cried the German, "right in that empty hole!" They went back to the table which was bare. The German kept insisting that he had returned the coin to the slot.

The chief curator and the deputy curator were summoned. The war-time habit of hostility to Germans was still in the atmosphere. There was a heated argument. The chief curator insisted that the German scholar turn out his pockets, "just in case you might accidentally have put the coin with your notebook or reading glass." The German flatly refused to turn out his pockets. Voices rose, as both sides became more excited.

Another man came into the room, heard the argument, and came over to the indignant group. When he heard what the debate was about, he identified himself as a museum carpenter, reached out and took the drawer. "I made these drawers myself, and once in a while we have trouble with them, you know. The thin strip of wood at the bottom of the drawer, the one with the holes in it, is glued to the flooring of the drawer. Sometimes it warps and lifts away, so that there is room for a coin to slip in under the flat strip." Then he gave the drawer a quick little jerk, and the coin, which had been hidden under the flat strip, slid back into its little hole.

The German scholar sighed and mopped his brow. "Thank God!" he cried. "Everybody says that the British Museum Cilician stater is the only surviving example of its kind. But I have found another Cilician stater, and I came here to compare it with yours. I have mine right here in my pocket!"

CHAPTER XXXI

Ancient murders in the digs

What was the crime rate in ancient Egypt? Nobody knows for sure, but in digging their artifacts, archaeologists often uncover evidence of antiquarian foul play.

It was obviously murder. Bloodstains were still plainly visible on the wound and on her dress. Even a cursory examination showed that the girl's throat had been cut. Robbery couldn't have been the motive for nearby lay a leather satchel crammed with jewelry and other valuable objects, and alongside the body was a bundle of brightly colored cloth also containing jewelry.

There wasn't much point in calling the police, however, for the girl had been dead for 1500 years. The body was discovered in the twentieth century; the murder had been committed in the sixth century.

Archaeology is often compared with detective work. The archaeologist collects various clues to build up a picture of what has happened in the past. But usually the essential element of traditional detective work is missing—no crime is involved. Every once in a while, though, archaeologists run across evidence of a real or suspected crime committed in ancient times. The result of such a discovery is often a fascinating archaeological puzzle. The solutions are of necessity speculative, and no accused murderer dead for centuries is ever going to have to stand trial. But the fact that no firm solution will be found does not lessen the fascination of the puzzle.

In addition, these ancient crimes often convey most dramatically the feeling that the people of ancient days were human like ourselves. So often in the excavation of ancient tombs, the bodies have been buried amid such strange customs that the people seem barely to have been human at all. But evidence of a crime, like the one of the murdered girl, present these long dead people in a human rather than a ceremonial light. In a sense they make the ancient dead seem more alive.

The girl with her throat cut was found by archaeologists excavating burial mounds at Qustol, in Nubia, during the 1930s. There had been plenty of bodies found in the mounds. These mounds had been raised as burial places for the royalty of a people named by archaeologists (for lack of a better term), the X-Group.

The X-Group people were no great world power, but they were an interesting and significant indigenous African culture that had been heavily influenced by the Egyptians to the north. The X-Group kingdom flourished from the second to the fifth centuries A.D.

Perhaps the best way to describe the burials of the X-Group kings is to say that they took place amid barbaric splendor. The term has been overused, but here it is quite accurate. The X-Group tombs, at least those which had not been emptied in some past age by robbers, were crammed with jewelry and other precious objects, often made in the Egyptian style. The dead kings and queens were loaded with gold and silver ornaments encrusted with precious and semi-precious stones before they were put into their tombs. Small wonder that most of these tombs had been robbed. Only the remote and inhospitable nature of the land (summer temperatures average 110°) had kept the mounds at Qustol from being emptied completely.

The jewelry was the splendid side of the burials. The barbaric side was that the X-Group people were enthusiastic practitioners of human sacrifice. Along with the main burial, as many as a dozen other individuals were interred in the large tomb. These were apparently servants, who were supposed to go on serving their master in the next life. They had been killed by a blow on the head, as if by an executioner.

But the body of the girl was of quite a different character. It wasn't found in the interior of the tomb, but was discovered by accident as the archaeologists were digging through the mound itself. It appeared as though the body had been thrown on the mound while it was being built, and then covered over.

In the dry, almost germ-free Nubian soil, the body has remained remarkably well-preserved for hundreds of years. Indeed, it was in a better state of preservation than those found within the tomb itself. The brownish blood stains showed up in stark contrast to the pattern of the gaily colored dress which itself had lost little of its brightness over the centuries.

What had happened? Walter B. Emery, who led the expedition to Qustol which had opened the tombs of the X-Group people, said:

"One can let one's imagination run riot in seeking an explanation for this discovery. Was the girl originally destined for sacrifice with other women in the tomb and then escaped, only to be captured when the burial ceremony was over and the mound above it partly raised? Or was she sacrificed and placed in the mound as an offering? Or had she suffered death as a penalty for robbing a treasure chest which had been placed in the mound as an offering? For we found a rifled chest at no great distance from the body."

Emery doubted that the girl was an escaped sacrificial victim, because right by her body was a bundle of jewelry, and a satchel of valuables was found not far away. "If, as I suggested . . . the girl had escaped from the general sacrifice during the burial ceremonies in the tomb, it would appear unlikely that she would handicap her flight by being laden with the satchel and the bundle of jewelry."

To Emery the robbery explanation seemed the most plausible. The lock on the nearby chest had not been opened, but the hasps had been split with blows from a cold chisel. But if the girl had been captured and killed in the act of robbery wouldn't her captors have put the contents back in the chest? Surely the chest was part of the burial, and as such had a religious significance.

Says Emery, "Carrying one's imagination a little further, is it possible that the murdered girl was an accomplice of a group of thieves who killed her because they mistrusted her and thought she knew too much? Even this suggestion is rather weak, for after her elimination it is unlikely that such desperate men would have left the jewelry behind. Anyway here we have a murder mystery of 1500 years ago and there we must leave it."

The murder at Qustol was an isolated case. But another group of ancient murders may provide a clue to the downfall of an entire civilization.

On the Indus river in what is now Pakistan there are the remains of a civilization which nearly equals those of Egypt and Mesopotamia in antiquity and surpasses them in size. The center of this civilization is a place we now call Mohenjo-daro. The city that once existed there was a huge, orderly and strangely grim place. There is row upon row of plain, but well-constructed brick buildings. Very little art has been found at Mohenjo-daro and the buildings contain no ornamentation. The people of Mohenjo-daro had a written language, but we have not been able to decipher it. We know so little of the rise and fall of this civilization, that the city has a genuine mysterious, almost unhuman quality about it. The only trace of humanity is found in the remains of an ancient crime.

In the anonymity of the city ruins there are a half dozen groups of skeletons that give dramatic proof that the brick-lined streets of Mohenjo-daro were once the scene of human tragedy. These groupings occur in the highest strata of the city ruins. It is probable, though not firmly established, that they all come from the same period—in fact, that all the individuals in the groups met their deaths on the same day.

On one group are 14 skeletons of men and women and a child. The confused and contorted positions of the skeletons suggest that death came violently. Two of the skulls bear the traces of sharp-edged ax or sword cuts.

Another group of nine contains five children. The report on the excavation notes that all are "in strangely contorted attitudes, crowded together." The bodies may have been "thrown pellmell into a hurriedly made pit." As some elephant tusks were found in the pit the excavators guessed the group may have been a family of ivory workers "who tried to escape with their belongings at the time of the raid but were stopped and slaughtered by the raiders," then disposed of in a shallow grave.

The raid the excavators speak of is a presumed invasion by barbarians which brought down the civilization centered at Mohenjo-daro. In total of more than thirty skeletons have been found, and only nine, the presumed family of ivory workers, show any sign of having been buried at all. In the climate at Mohenjo-daro bodies would not simply be left lying about—decay begins too quickly. Therefore, after the killings the city must have been abandoned. Indeed, since a mere thirty skeletons in all were found, it is a fairly safe guess that the city was virtually uninhabited before the barbarians made their final assault to pick off the stragglers.

Death by accident or design is the problem which confronts archaeological detectives puzzling over the remains of a man found at Avebury, a massive megalithic monument in England. Avebury is a circle of huge stones, somewhat like its more famous neighbor Stonehenge, but much larger, though cruder and less well-preserved.

Avebury dates back around 2000 years, but the remains we are concerned with are dated at the fourteenth century. This skeleton of a man was found when excavators were raising one of the fallen Avebury stones. A pair of scissors found in the back pocket of the man have led excavators to refer to him as a barber.

Was the fourteenth century barber just standing there when one of the great stones happened to fall over on him? Hardly likely. The stones of Avebury were well set in the ground and they did not just topple over, and certainly they did not do so suddenly. There is another, and more probable explanation. During the middle ages ancient pagan monuments like Avebury were regarded as diabolical by the Christians and as gathering places for anti-Christian elements. Christians may well have thought it their sacred duty to destroy such monuments, and indeed a large part of Avebury and of Stonehenge itself were destroyed during the middle ages. In addition to religious reasons, there were good practical reasons for breaking up the stones of these monuments. They served as excellent sources of rock in an area where there was little natural rock. (The builders of Avebury had hauled their stones from a considerable distance.)

It is not hard to imagine a group of fourteenth century villagers digging and pulling in order to bring down what they had been told was a monument to Satan. In the excitement one of the huge upright stones is loosened too much, and before everyone has a chance to get out of the way it falls over crushing the hapless barber. Speculating a bit further, we may suspect that this death brought a temporary halt to the destruction of Avebury. Demons or not, the villagers may have decided the spirits of Avebury still had too much power to be offended.

Archaeologists have become quite used to burial customs, which to us, at least, are quite bizarre. But strange, and even ghastly as some of these customs may appear to us, they generally make some sort of sense in terms of the culture which did the burying. Nevertheless, there are still occasions where burials have been found in which the reasons remain genuinely mysterious, and even guesses seem inadequate.

For example, in England an elaborate burial mound was opened which contained a ship, and all of the artifacts normally associated with the burial of a warrior chieftain. It was similar to ship burials found elsewhere in Northern Europe, except for one thing—there was no body in the English mound and there never had been.

And in the Southwest of America, indian graves have been opened which contain nothing but skulls, not a body to be found. At another site there are graves that contain bodies but no skulls. The trouble is that the two sites are not connected with one another, and the skulls in one have nothing to do with the bodies in the other.

An even more puzzling discovery was described by Ann Axtell Morris, wife of the pioneer of indian archaeology in the Southwest, Earl Morris. Her description is of a pre-Columbian indian burial found in Tseahatso Cave, in Arizona.

"The circumstances were as follows: At the bottom of the cist (burial chamber) on a clean bed of grass, lay the two hands and fore-arms of an adult. The bones were held together by dried ligaments: the palms lay upwards. And this was every bit of the original human being there was to be found. The severed elbows touched the wall of the cist, and the two cists across the partition walls were empty, thus proving that the burial was complete as found. Moreover, there were burial furnishings, and here is where the almost ludicrous aspect of the matter comes in. For on these two poor lonely hands were bestowed two pairs of the most exquisitely woven sandals patterned in black and red that have ever come out of Southwestern soil. Not mittens but *sandals*! On top of these were three necklaces, two of which had abalone-shell pendants, while the third was a unique masterpiece. It was made of eighteen white shell rings, each about three inches in diameter and each lashed to a neck cord so as somewhat to overlap its fellow. As effective an ornament as could well be devised—but a necklace not a bracelet! There was a basketful of long crescentic beads with a large basket covering the whole, and finally—absurdity of absurdities—there was an enormous stone pipe. Shoes without feet, necklaces without a neck, and a pipe without a mouth—truly meta-physical triumphs over physical negation."

The body to which these hands had once been attached was never found. Nor has any similar burial ever been uncovered. Thus, this burial of hands does not seem to represent any general religious or symbolic act. It was a very special case—but why was it done in the first place?

Guesswork is all that we can fall back on, and here the best guess seems to be that the indians buried the hands of a departed comrade because hands were all they had.

In his book *The First American*, the popular archaeological writer C. W. Ceral speculated: "One explanation was that the man had been killed in a landslide; his body could not be freed; there were only his hands protruding above the ground from his outstretched arms. And so his fellows had cut these off and in his funeral honored the